LONDON LONDON

LONDON LONDON

Stephen Hargrave

Barrie & Jenkins
London

First published in 1989 by
Barrie & Jenkins Ltd
289 Westbourne Grove,
London W11 2QA

This book is a work of fiction.
Any resemblance to person or persons
living or dead is purely coincidental.

British Library Cataloguing in Publication Data

Hargrave, Stephen
London London
I. Title
823′.914

ISBN: 0–7126–2198–9

Typeset and printed by Butler & Tanner Ltd
Frome and London

for
Clare Pearson
and Nigel Mather

CHAPTER ONE

Oh hell, I thought. I may be young at heart but I'm thirty years old and I know, I know I mustn't get drunk. So why, on this day of days, this night of nights, the night of the Stock Exchange Boxing Dinner – why am I drinking so much?

But first let me introduce myself.

Call me London: not only because in my own person I sum up and display the hopes, the fears and the irreversible decay of our great capital city, but also because it was to these two syllables, Lon-don, or rather to these four, Lon-don Lon-don, that fate and the joy of a late and bibulous father yoked me one Friday afternoon in 1955 and would not let me go.

On the day of my delivery – prune-faced, grumpy, but safe – the Bull and Bladder in High Street, Wootton, five miles north of Buxton in God's own county of Derbyshire, a public house tenanted to my grandfather, Leopold London, stayed open from midday to midnight without a break and precipitated such scenes of drunkenness among the village's sheepswains, dry-stone wallers and policemen as had not been seen since VE Day, and have never been seen again. Only my grandfather's eye for a profit held him back from succumbing to the general euphoria.

His son, my father, Leonard London, was less restrained.

I was born, portentously, as the clocks struck opening time. My father was admitted shortly afterwards. Squinting and wailing, a boy-child, I was at once the red and wrinkled apple of his eye and the long-awaited saviour of the dynasty. The Bull and Bladder, the only house left in the county whose tenancy passed as of right from father to son, would remain in the hands of the Londons; and this after years of unspoken regret that my father, just turned fifty at my birth, would be the last of the line.

Leonard's first act of paternal devotion was to pick me up and tickle my chin. His second was to drop me, inflicting a certain flatness on the crown of my head which abides with me to this day. 'Ah well,' he said, or so my mother related, 'what is life but a School of Hard Knocks? I'll be off to tell his granddad. Well done, lass.' He was driven back to Wootton by Billy Ash, the baker. On the way they felt obliged to tell the news at one or two wayside taverns where Leo, my grandfather, was a well-known occasional visitor and his longing for a grandson a well-worn topic of after-hours conversation for more than a quarter of a century.

By the time they reached the Bull and Bladder the news had beaten them to it. Dominoes rattled, laughter bellowed, beer flowed and flowed.

'What'll tha call him, Len?' somebody asked.

'I were thinking Winston,' said my father, grasping the question at the second time of asking.

'Tha s'll bloody not,' said my grandfather. 'His name's Leopold, after his granddad. Anyway, tha'st drunk enough for now. Get down Buxton Registry and give the lad his name. Fit to drive again, Billy?'

'I'm not fit to shite, let alone drive,' said Billy Ash. 'Hey, young Bill!' He shook his own son by the shoulder. 'Get in the van and tek Len down Buxton Registry. He wants to give the lad a name.'

For what happened next we rely on the testimony, perhaps not entirely reliable, of the younger Billy Ash, whose steadying hand my father shrugged off as they made their way into the office.

'I want to register,' my father tried to say.

'Yes, sir,' said the clerk. 'Name?'

'London.'

'Christian name?'

'Leonard.'

'No,' said young Billy, 'that's your name.'

'Of course it's my name,' said my father. 'Don't I know my own name?'

'He wants *his* name.'

'His name? Doesn't he know his name? How do I know his name?'

'The deceased's name,' said the clerk.

'What deceased?'

'The one that's just died.'

'What d'you mean, died?' my father asked. 'The lad's only just been born.'

'This,' said the clerk, 'is Deaths. Births are across the corridor.'

Across the corridor, my father asked young Billy Ash to wait outside. What happened inside therefore went unrecorded; except on my birth certificate, with which they returned to the pub.

'What the bloody 'ell's this?' asked my grandfather, wresting the certificate from my father's grasp, and holding it proudly to the light. 'Where's the lad's Christian name?'

8

My father had surrendered the faculty of speech.

'Here it is, Leo,' said another. '... Oh bloody 'ell.'

Thus are dreams vitiated, even in their fulfilment, by too close contact with reality. Leopold London had a grandson – not Leopold London II, however, but me, London London.

Leopold died when I was eleven. Four thousand days had passed, on every one of which he had reminded my father of his folly that first Friday afternoon. On the day of his demise I was brought to the bedside. 'I know I'm on my way,' he said, 'so I've got some advice for thee, lad. Take note of this and tha'll be all right.'

'Yes, Granddad.'

'Never sit on hot pipes or cold ground,' he croaked. 'Now bugger off.'

An hour later I was summoned again.

'I've changed my mind,' my grandfather whispered. I readied myself to rush out and sit on the first hot pipe I could find.

'These are my last words to thee. Work hard at tha books. Wi' a name like thine tha'll need to.'

Since it was what I was used to, my name never struck me as in any way strange. At Buxton Grammar School, where my grandfather's dying admonition took me on a scholarship, I was quick to point out that Alcock, Dickin and Everard all had names of much greater comic potential than my own; but mine was the one they mocked. I responded by studying furiously. Leopold's well-intentioned advice broke the family connection with the Bull and Bladder. It carried me next to Oxford, that suburb of the town I was destined for, the city which bore my name.

Halfway through my time at university I was already wracked by the pain of decision. My parents were at retirement age. What should it be – my father's father's father's inheritance, or the glittering lights of the capital? How could I look the old man in the face and throw in my lot with the Southerners?

Decision was made easy. My parents took a day-trip to London: bottled beer, tongue sandwiches, songs in the round and all, in a thirty-one seater from Houghton's Hire in Buxton. The coach was driven by Billy Ash the younger: the elder was now baking for the angels. Traces of alcohol were found in his bloodstream, but he couldn't be blamed for what happened. The coach never reached its destination. Three miles south of Watford Gap it was struck by a light aircraft. The Bull and Bladder went to the Heffers, who had kept the Partridge for twenty years and always, I thought, deserved better.

I had matured at medium height, modest of shoulders, gritty of jaw, with slightly too large a head (though not in comparison with Michelangelo's David). I was to stay lean until the onset of middle age sometime in my twenties. From then on my jowls would start edging downwards and though my eyesight was to remain keen the growing squareness of my face would emphasise the closeness of my eyes. I would retain my native wit, the spirit that built the mills, and what I lacked in wit I would make up with spleen.

I went, as I was meant, to London; and there, seven years later, I was drinking too much at the Stock Exchange Boxing Dinner.

CHAPTER TWO

Sportwise, I'd had a bad year already.

Wimbledon, thank God, was by now a faded and largely unpleasant memory of champagne, strawberries and, worst of all, tennis. The best thing about it was the rain, which hammered down refreshingly for much of the time I was there. Don't misunderstand, though: I've nothing against tennis. On the contrary. But what does upset me is the thought of all the money these young louts are getting paid for playing the game nowadays. Did not our own Fred Perry win the Tournament for nothing fifty years ago? He did indeed – three times on the trot.

The Test series, likewise, that wintry summer of '85, came and went for the most part in the rainproof haven of the marquee and the pavilion. When players did appear it was mostly to sign autographs or be presented to the Queen. Thomas Lord's famous ground being only a quick taxi-ride down the Euston Road and the Oval a nip down the Northern Line, the clients we had invited to our box had only to look through the window to see it wasn't worth coming.

On the fourth day of the Second Test a miracle occurred. The scheduled cloud-cover failed to check in and the whole of the South was ablaze with brilliant sunshine. All over the City, from Blackfriars to Crutched Friars, our invitees blessed their luck and fingered their invitations. The Market, they decided, was about to enter the summer doldrums: yes, they could spare a few hours. They opened the post, filed it in the shredder, drank a cup of coffee and told their secretaries they'd be back tomorrow.

As evil chance would have it, this was the day the name London London came up on the duty roster to act as host in the Rogers & Prickett box. I made sure I had the right set of keys and set out at half past ten to give myself plenty of time. The others would follow on later.

Taking the Tube, I arrived at the Oval with twenty minutes to spare.

The streets round the ground were empty. Why no crowds? I wondered. I knew attendances weren't what they used to be, but this was ridiculous. You'd think they weren't having a Test Match here.

They weren't.

I hailed a cab.

'Lord's,' I instructed. 'As fast as you like.'

He'd have liked to go fast, guv, the driver explained half an hour later. If it wasn't for these bastards he *would* be going fast.

We had both forgotten that in a summer of many such events today was the day of the NALGO march to Downing Street to protest against the scrapping of the Greater London Council. We were lodged on the brow of Westminster Bridge.

'Look at 'em,' said the cabbie. 'Idle sods.' A column of marchers shuffled by, dressed for the Arctic in donkey-jackets and mufflers. 'They wouldn't be bloody demonstratin' if it was left to me, I can tell you. Back at their desks, that's where they'd be. Mind you, they'll do less damage today than when they do work – "work" so called, that is. Bloody bureaucrats. Give 'em a pen and they think they're Adolf Hitler. Shoot the lot of 'em, that's what I'd do. The sooner they get rid of this GLC the better, if you ask me. They'll be bloody sweating then, won't they, guv?'

My Aertex vest was sodden.

'They will,' I said.

'Should live in bloody Russia, this lot; see if that's more to their liking, eh, guv?'

'They should,' I answered dolefully.

It was half past twelve when I staggered up the steps to 'C' floor in the grandstand. I braced myself for Fat Percy, John-boy and a pack of grumbling clients beating madly on the door. Heroic excuses went through my head: a bombing, a mugging, an attempt on the life of the Sovereign, all averted by London London. First priority was staying employed, even if it was by Rogers & Prickett, stockbrokers, of Throgmorton Avenue, EC2.

The door was open. Through the box, on the balcony which overlooked the pitch, I saw Fat Percy knocking back a drink, surrounded by a group of adoring clients doing the same. Most had removed their jackets, and shirts ranged from the freshly-laundered blue striped, indicating that the wearer represented a distinguished merchant bank, to the half-ironed two-tone number sported by the envoy of a unit trust house or large insurance company. Trousers worn by the merchant bankers required to be held up by brightly-coloured felt braces; the rest used belts, if not elastic. Fat Percy himself had kept his jacket on. His glowing neck hung over a shiny collar, almost engulfing the tiny knot of a Middlesex Regiment tie.

'Ah London!' he said, delighted to see me. 'Come in, lad. A drink. Been having trouble? Well not to worry, old man. Happens to the best of us. Will this do?'

He waved a bottle of champagne, the one with the yellow label.

'Thanks, Perce. Very kind.'

'Here,' he said. 'Oh – silly me – you'll need a glass. Couldn't have you drinking out of the bottle.'

Detaching himself from the group, he put an avuncular arm round me and showed me into the luncheon room.

'Not that I'd give you a drink if I didn't have to,' he hissed. 'I thought you'd manage to fuck it up, so I brought the spare keys. Bloody good thing I did. Can't you do anything right? Too slow to catch a cold, that's your trouble. I've been having to look after these fuckers on my own.'

We went back through to the crowd.

'. . . Now, chaps,' Percy resumed brightly, 'I think you all know London, don't you?' Smiles, greetings, rolled-back eyes and a small ironic cheer signified that they did. 'Good. He's here to help us put a bit of this fizz away.'

'Do we need any help?' one of the group asked, laughing.

'Not with you here, Biffo!' Fat Percy retorted, laughing louder.

A sound of some sort came from the square. Fat Percy's face registered alarm.

'Christ, what's that?' he exclaimed. 'Another one out? I thought for a minute we'd scored a run!'

This time everyone laughed; myself, for shame, included.

Thus went the summer. Now it was autumn, and to bridge that dreary gap in the City's entertainments diary the firm took a table at the Boxing Dinner. No-one could say we knew much about stocks and shares, but Rogers & Prickett were second to none in keeping the client happy.

'I've got some good news for you,' Fat Percy said one cold November morning.

'Oh yes?'

'Oh yes. You're doing the list for the Boxing Dinner. Home team, guest team, seating plan. Twelve names in all. Five or six of us, yourself included, if you care to come, and six or seven guests. Don't forget to ask Our Leader: he's usually on for this sort of thing. Think your organisational skills are up to that?'

13

'I should think I could give it a try, Perce.'

'Good lad. Just what I wanted to hear. Only it's obvious stock-broking isn't taking up too much of your time at the moment, so I thought you might appreciate the challenge, being a bright boy and all.'

'Touching of you to consider me, Perce.'

'I'm glad you think so. This is a vote of confidence. Shows the esteem we all hold you in.'

His eyes narrowed, his lip curled, his face crumpled horribly: he was smiling.

I smiled too. At least I was going to the dinner. I'm not a man of great sporting enthusiasms, but boxing I'm relatively keen on. It takes me back to my youth. Ah, those sweaty Saturday nights at Buxton Boys' Boxing Club: the broken teeth, the bloody nose, the plangent slap of leather on cheekbone. I never practised the noble art myself, of course, but I did take great delight in watching my mates do so; and when in my mid-twenties I descried the arrival of businessman's belly I purchased a fifteen-kilo punchbag and a pair of mittens from the Charlie Magri sports shop in Bethnal Green Road and resolved to do a daily stint. I hadn't reckoned with the problem of suspending this great weight from a modern ceiling. There was nowhere to put the hook. I gave the bag one or two nasty beatings from a kneeling position but soon became disheartened and reverted to my former method of exercise, a nightly walk to the local and back.

Nevertheless, the prospect of watching a series of bruisers thumping each other senseless in the ring while I achieved the same effect out of it with a few large glasses of brandy to wash down my chicken Marengo and charlotte russe could hardly fail to fill me with eager anticipation.

Four of the five-man Rogers & Prickett contingent, namely Reggie Goddard, our huge and booming senior partner, Fat Percy, John-boy and your own correspondent, together with several of the clients, were already present at the pre-fight warm-up, a furious red-faced affair in the boardroom, as I poured a fourth sizeable gin and tonic for my own guest and fellow caustic Northerner, Stan Harbottle.

The general estimation of this squat mechanical was that acronym-wise his current place of employment, Terminal Invest-ment Trust, could only be bettered if in these days of getting on one's bike, he got on his and went it alone as the Stan Harbottle

Investment Trust; but I liked him. He was after all my best, not to say my only, client.

'Are we the token dissidents?' he asked, pushing up his blue-framed National Health specs.

Around us, jokes were being repeated, school fees discussed, Big Bang being looked forward to.

'It looks that way,' I said. 'Cheers.'

'*Solidarnosc*. Where's His Eminence?'

'Baxter? He'll be here. He told Jimmy Slim we were starting at seven, so he wouldn't have to talk to him.'

'Bringing Slim Jim, is he? What makes Baxter sweet on him?'

'Baxter's sweet on anyone who'll do the business.'

'Why do you keep looking over there?' Harbottle asked, waving his glass towards the door.

'Liquidity crisis. I was waiting to make sure the khasi was empty.'

'Is there only room for one? Not the bashful bladders, is it?'

I watched carefully until no one was out of the room, then went. I pushed the door of the Gents with confidence, brandishing a comb to show anybody inside that I was only here to reinstate my parting.

No one was there. I put the comb away and scuttled to the wall, running the tap and then whistling in a show of braggadocio. Relax, I thought; relax.

Five – four – three – two –

Hell! A movement in the air, the slightest increase in pressure, betrayed an impending intrusion. The muscles locked. Hopeless. The door opened. I shook my member mightily, wiggled it, fair waved it in the air with a proud relieved smile that said, Oh yes, when it comes to peeing I'm up there with the best of them. First division. One thing you can't say I can't do is pee.

A pair of low-cut mocassins drew up next to me.

'*Bonsoir*,' said the newly-arrived.

It was Baxter: beautiful blond Baxter; tall, slim, triangular Baxter – 'Buck' Baxter – mothers' darling, debs' delight, fêted habitué of Eaton Square parties and well-informed gossip-columns; fast liver, smiling seducer, black slope skier and Cresta runner; laird of an isle; Himalayan trekker; renowned rider of handsome horses and of horsey women. Baxter, they said, was the future of Rogers & Prickett. While I, two years his senior, was only an employee, Baxter was the youngest partner, and it was Baxter, not Reggie, John-boy or even Fat Percy, who made my life there what it was.

'Good evening,' said I, swallowing bile as Baxter produced an instant effortless gurgle.

'Slim Jim here yet?' he asked.

15

I sniffed twice, testing the air. 'Not that I've noticed.'

'Thank Christ for that. Your man here on the dot?'

'Matter of fact, he was.'

'Hoovering it up, I imagine.'

'I thought that was the idea,' I replied, standing over the hand basin combing my hair. My parting displayed its habitual errancy.

'Best behaviour tonight, eh?' Baxter exhorted. 'Good name of the firm, and all that. Straight bat, eh? . . . Reggie here?' He dressed his own hair perfectly with a single flick of the fingers and sneered into the mirror, which his eyes never left as he washed his hands and checked his cuticles.

'Yah,' I snapped. 'Home team all here, with you.' There had been a time when I wondered why no one in the City spoke in sentences.

'Good,' said Baxter, tugging at his pocket handkerchief to make it droop the more stylishly. 'Right, then. Once more to the beach. *Allons-y.*'

The main event of the evening took place in the Plumbers' Hall on the south side of London Bridge, headquarters of the Honourable Company of Plumbers. Real plumbers weren't allowed in, but boxing dinners were business.

In the great hall, under the Royal coat of arms and the Plumbers' standard and motto (*AQVA; AQVA: VBIQVE*), were thirty or more tables the same size as ours, and amid the tables a raised boxing ring and a bank of overhead lights. In the old days, I was told, when brokers went home at four, they came to the dinner in evening dress; but now it was business suits. A single splash of pink in the distance disclosed the presence of a woman.

The underlying principle of the seating plan was to arrange the company in descending order of congeniality away from myself. This made it difficult to decide who apart from Harbottle should sit next to me, but it did ensure that I maintained maximum possible distance from Baxter.

Elsewhere I tried to maintain my reputation as a stirrer. Lifelong friends were separated. Reggie Goddard's chief guest faced squarely away from the ring. Johnnie Johnson was only a left jab away from Dickie March-Hare, who some years before had taken first his job, then his wife (but it was all very amicable); and John-boy was well-placed to entertain his old school prefect, 'Basher' Bagshawe. Between John-boy and me sat Harbottle, wearing what he called his dining tie, a wide Sixties model, specially for the occasion.

We were well into the hors d'oeuvres before first blood was

16

drawn. A bread roll, thickly buttered and carrying an Havana cigar still in its aluminium sheath, caught John-boy a glancing blow to the side of the head, grazing him over the eyebrow. John-boy winced, then laughed as convincingly as the pain would allow and looked round the room for the culprit. Some tables away, Biffo Smith was acknowledging the plaudits of the crowd and showing how it was done. Half-standing, John-boy pretended to revenge himself with a wine bottle. Biffo shied away, pretending he thought John-boy was serious.

'Thought you might use that one later, John-boy!' he called, meaning the cigar. 'I shall,' John-boy responded, 'and I'll tell you exactly where I'll stick it!' We all laughed, and John-boy resumed his place, though not before Basher Bagshawe had managed to slip on to the seat of his chair a small cushion which emitted a loud farting noise as John-boy sank back on to it. Shortly after that John-boy surrendered a tenner in return for which Dickie March-Hare, deputy Lord Lieutenant of Berkshire, tweaked a waitress's bra-strap. Not to be outdone, Johnnie Johnson started to relate the story of how he himself had once done something similar; but the tale was spoiled when Dickie March-Hare produced a pair of ear-plugs and screwed them into his ears. Nor were these any old ear-plugs: they were the pair he'd been sent by Johnnie as a wedding present when he finally made an honest woman of the latter's ex-wife, who snored. Then a chimpanzee in shorts and boxing gloves appeared in the ring and everyone started laughing again. Fat Percy wanted to know why the Chairman of the Stock Exchange was gloved up; others identified the chimp as the senior partner of a rival firm of stockbrokers or the leader of the Greater London Council.

As soon as the cheese course was on the tables the MC climbed through the ropes with the two West Indian cruiserweights lined up for the first bout. Baxter asked what the odds were against the monkey.

'Which one?' said Fat Percy.

It was then, just as the serious drinking was about to begin and the stories of previous evenings of drinking began to dominate the conversation, that I started to think I might already have had too much; or maybe not yet too much, but too much not to want more.

'Feeling all right?' Harbottle asked.

'A marked upturn.'

'Don't confuse brains with a bull market,' he warned mysteriously.

Three fights later John-boy had lost two hundred pounds, while

17

Basher Bagshawe and Johnnie Johnson were counting their winnings.

'He doesn't look too upset about it,' Harbottle whispered into my ear.

'Oh really? See who he lost it to?'

'Favourite clients? By George, you're not suggesting there's a sinking fund, are you, old boy?'

'They called it bribery where I come from, old boy.'

'Didn't catch a bit of a slur in your speech then, did I?'

'Don't be ridiculous,' I replied, somehow finding this simple expression hard to get my tongue round. 'Pass the port, would you?'

'Shertainly, old boy.'

By the fifth fight of the eight the atmosphere was livening up. On our table Reggie naturally gave the lead with applause for the winner and a sporting hand for the loser while Baxter, with his sharp eye for the finer points, rewarded well-thrown blows by tapping on the tablecloth with the tips of his fingers. Slim Jim cemented his reputation by coughing a glass of port over the back of Fat Percy's suit. Perce's conflicting emotions played openly on his face. It took some while for him to register what had happened; then shock was replaced by murderous wrath, which changed to a hearty grin as Perce remembered that Slim was Baxter's, and therefore the firm's, best client.

I was chuckling to myself at the slowness of Perce's thought-processes when I saw Basher Bagshawe and John-boy sniggering in the direction of my midriff, where I found that half of my tie had been snipped off. I hadn't noticed this happening. My alertness wasn't what it ought to be.

'Don't want to be a spoilsport, but I should take a look at your shoelaces too,' Harbottle mumbled. Leaning down slyly, I found my chin resting in a plate of dolcelatte that hadn't been there before.

'I think you might find a fork useful,' said our senior partner.

'Sorry, Reggie – I was trying to pick something up.' The look on Reggie's face suggested he wasn't entirely happy with this explanation, or possibly with the way I'd phrased it, but it sounded all right to me.

'Manners maketh man,' he said. I gave him my most winsome smile and felt Harbottle's elbow in my ribs, I couldn't quite work out why. Nor could I have said why the hall was suddenly so hot.

'Is it getting warm in here?' I asked Harbottle, loosening my tie.

'What?'

I asked him again. He didn't seem to understand.

'Hot,' I said, as clearly as possible.

'Oh hot, yes, you do look a little flushed,' he replied. 'Too much port. Port. Too much port.'

Repeating himself, I thought. Bad sign.

'Shouldn't have drunk it, should you?' I jibed.

I leaned past him, retrieving a wine-glass which had fallen into John-boy's lap as I did so, and took the last bottle from a silver bucket of melting ice. Then I poured myself a nice refreshing tumbler of kümmel. After all that red wine the kümmel slipped down very sweetly indeed, and also very fast, as did the one that followed it, which Harbottle poured for me. Despite his drunken condition, or possibly because of it, he himself took only a thimbleful.

Shortly afterwards I was regretting not having turned to the kümmel earlier. It improved my sense of wellbeing no end. Self-possession returned and the vague suspicion that I might be making a fool of myself disappeared completely. After that I started cracking some very amusing jokes. The stony-faced response they elicited from everyone else on the table save Harbottle was a disappointment. I got the impression that Baxter in particular was failing to appreciate the humour of my observations. Harbottle, however, had to hide his face in his napkin, he was laughing so much.

Then Slim Jim choked on a wedge of cheese and sent a morsel flying across the table, where it clung to Harbottle's collar.

Scraping it up with a thumbnail, Harbottle viewed it closely and said, 'Couldn't favour me with a biscuit now, could you, Jimmy?'

Baxter leaned forward as if about to say, 'Look here,' but was prevented by the roar which followed the end of the final bout. The next item on the programme was a 'charity auction'. The whole purpose of the evening was, after all, to raise money for distressed gentlefolk.

Before that there was to be an interval when the girls could bring more coffee round and the men could wash their hands. John-boy and Basher went off to speak to old chums on the far side of the hall and the conversation at our table turned finally to the state of the Market, on which my own views were cut short in mid-sentence by Baxter's suggestion that I might benefit from a breath of the cold night air. I assured him I was feeling well and was on the point of telling him how much better I felt than most people here looked when he stood up and assumed a beatific smile. I realised this was not for my benefit and thinking it might be time for a second performance of God Save the Queen I too jumped to my feet, unfortunately forgetting that my shoe-laces were still tied together. Harbottle helped me up. He needn't have bothered, though, for all the help he proved. He was so cut he kept putting my chair in the wrong place.

By the time I was back in position Reggie and Baxter were deeply involved in a back-slapping session with a thick-set brute who might easily have arrived direct from the ring but whom Harbottle, whispering slowly into my ear, identified as the managing director of one of the City's leading investment houses; a most important client to every third-rate broking firm in town; a man too important to assent to an invitation from Rogers & Prickett but who, coming here from the East End via Billericay and now Weybridge, still liked to be on good terms with real old-fashioned gents, especially when like these two, they were now telling him what a fine upstanding fellow he was, despite all that Press talk to the contrary.

'Here,' Harbottle whispered. 'Tell him you never knew he was so keen on the limelight. Go on – tell him.'

'I can't do that,' I protested. 'They'll string me up. What do you think I am?'

I repeated the question more forcibly, attracting one or two unflattering answers.

'Ah, yes,' said Reggie. 'Let me introduce you to the rest of the gang. Ron Rackett – you all know Ron, don't you?'

'We read the papers,' Harbottle mumbled.

'Or know of me!' said Ron.

'See?' said Harbottle. 'He won't mind.'

No, I thought. Take no notice of him. He was winding me up. He was just trying to get back at me for the time I rang up pretending to be the Fraud Squad, not realising I was speaking to his boss and not to Harbottle himself.

No, I thought.

'Yes,' I said. 'We certainly do. Now just remind me. Wasn't it – wasn't it – ?'

I named the satirical magazine in which the allegations had first appeared.

'Eh?' he barked. 'Who is this?'

Reggie stalled. Harbottle hunched himself forward with his elbow on the table and a hand over his face.

'What's your game?' Rackett asked.

I tried to explain, but found it hard going. I reached for the kümmel, the room uncomfortably hot again, but the bottle was empty.

'I'm sure London, er – ' said Reggie. 'I think he's, er – '

'Is this one of yours? I'll break his fuckin' neck, the little bastard.'

'Well, Ronnie, let's not, er – '

'If you don't, I will,' said Baxter.

'Little – ' Either Rackett didn't finish or I didn't hear. He picked up Reggie's glass of port and threw it in my face. Goddard's astonished guest, a quiet Scot from one of the ecclesiastical assurance outfits, drew his chair back from the table. Harbottle did a 'look left' through his fingers, motioning towards where the ice-bucket stood, dripping with condensation, devoid of bottles but full of water.

'Look at him,' Rackett mocked. 'Doesn't know what to do with himself.'

I stared back coldly.

'Lost for words. Chicken.'

I sat my ground.

'Can't hold his drink, that's his problem.'

No, I thought: that's your problem, Ron. Leopold London's grandson won't stand for that.

Seize the moment, I thought. Take the future in your hands. I rose to my feet, stayed on them the second time, and seized the ice-bucket. I drew it back and swung. My aim was hard and low and deadly.

Picking my elbow out of the mint creams, I was surprised to find that although the bucket was now empty Rackett was dry and laughing very loudly. Then I saw Baxter, who was wet and red-faced and not laughing very much at all, heading round the table towards me. Seizing my lapels, he told me briefly what he thought of me and said this was the final straw. Trying hard to maintain my balance, I took a handful of Baxter's broadcloth and inadvertantly thrust the toecap of my brogue into his shinbone. He leapt away in pain, not letting go of me, and toppled backwards over the leg which Harbottle had left extended behind him. We fell in fond embrace to the floor. In the resulting scramble, as I tried to find my feet, my knee rested heavily on a part of Baxter's body where he made it plain he didn't want it to be. Then, magically, I found my own body being lifted clear of the scene as the occupants of adjacent tables, mistaking this friendly exchange for a brawl, pulled us apart and told us to calm down. Baxter tugged furiously at the arms that held him back and I pretended to do the same, not wishing to appear cowardly but feeling perhaps a shade less sanguine now that the kümmel had run out.

It must have looked convincing. By now all eyes were on us, and while some of the crowd, myself in particular, were all for seeing us shake hands and let bygones be bygones, others felt that a matter of honour should be honourably settled.

'Get 'em in the ring!' I heard.

'In the ring!'

'In the ring!'

'In the ring?' said Baxter.

No one was interested in my views on the matter. Pinioned by handlers, encouraged by my self-appointed second, Harbottle, who was now strangely sober, I was led away to the changing-rooms.

Five minutes later I was sitting on the stool in the red corner fully kitted-out in shorts, vest and gloves. The audience was cheering wildly as Baxter pummelled the air across the ring. If all this seems unlikely to you, just imagine how I felt about it.

'Now look, Rocky, it's all very simple,' said Harbottle, leaning over me nose-to-nose. 'Keep your hands up and your head down. When you get in close, butt him in the mouth. Shatter the bastard's teeth. Break his chin. But keep your hands up – like this. OK?'

'OK.'

'Head down, hands up – '

'Butt him in the teeth.'

'Great.' He leaned out of the ring.

'Don't go yet.'

'Hold on,' said Harbottle. 'Here.'

I took a large swig of brandy and soon felt much better. I also realised that when you looked at him, Baxter was a bit on the thin side. Rather gangly, really. In fact it wouldn't be much of an exaggeration to say he was nothing but a big streak of piss. So he couldn't be that hard to topple. I mean, he wasn't going to be a pushover. Far from it. It wasn't going to be easy. But it was perfectly possible. The more I thought about it, the more possible it seemed.

The bell rang.

'Head down, hands up – '

'Butt him in the face.'

I bounced jauntily out of my corner. The problem with this 'head down, hands up' business, I immediately discovered, was that it made it impossible to see where I was going. A hoot of derisive laughter and cat-calls arose from the crowd, presumably directed at Baxter, and then a voice close behind me said, 'Hey, laddie!'

I turned round and peeped. 'Over here!' said the referee. 'Box on!'

I brought my gloves down low enough to see over. On closer inspection Baxter looked faster, fitter and better-built than he had before. I jogged towards him, leading with my forehead.

Connecting it with his jaw proved harder than expected. He moved out of the way, smiling to hide his nerves. This happened again. The third time it happened Baxter attempted the first real blow of the contest, a chancey hook which skidded off my ribs and somehow nudged me off balance. To give him his due, Baxter was shrewd enough to keep his distance after this stroke of luck, and gave me another nervous smirk. I lowered my arms a little to guard the ribs.

The next thing I did was to stop a powerful left jab dead in its tracks with my eye. Show him he can't hurt you, I thought. Nevertheless I went back to Harbottle's advice and raised my guard again, which provoked Baxter to land a quick right hand to the liver (as if that, of all my organs, didn't have trouble enough already).

That little flurry must have tired him quite a bit, I thought. It had certainly tired me. Time to attack.

I moved in closer and threw some jabs, several of which stopped inches short of Baxter's face and gave me great encouragement. He, meanwhile, had stretched out his long left arm and was vibrating it close to my own face to prevent me from closing the gap. Ill-mannered laughter arose from the crowd at Baxter's refusal to fight.

'In close,' Harbottle screamed. 'Get inside!'

Inside, I thought; inside. Gloves up, head down, I burrowed forward and in exchange for an uppercut to the side of the head I shook him with a stinging combination to the body that left Baxter reeling and retreating and me face-down on the canvas with a mouthful of grit. I assured the ref it was only a slip but he made me take a count of eight while Baxter cringed in a corner.

The crowd was roaring. Resuming the attack, I darted forward and reached the centre of the ring only seconds after Baxter. I ducked, I dodged, I hooked, I jabbed, I cut. The only thing I couldn't quite do was hit him. Head down, I thought; gloves up. A left to the ear found its target; followed, in rapid succession, by a doubled-up jab, a right cross and a vicious straight arm to the solar plexus. In return I landed a punishing rabbit-punch and withdrew to the ropes. Baxter's glove got caught under my arm. In the ensuing clinch I could smell fear mingled with Paco Rabanne on his chest. Someone somewhere called 'Break', which I took to be advice on what I ought to do to Baxter's nose, and Baxter, I didn't know why, relaxed and tried to back off. I saw my chance and hurled an uppercut that knocked all the wind from his body.

He winced and sank to his knees. Following the rules, I went to the white corner and waited for the count to reach ten. Poor, crumpled Baxter was roundly booed.

After a while I noticed the count hadn't started. Then I was being shouted at:

'Now look, son. Do that again and you're out, OK? No low blows in my ring, or you're back in the dressing-room fast. And when I say break I mean BREAK!'

Baxter was soon on his feet again: this time, at long last, in more aggressive mood. Wheeling away, sapping his strength, teasing him, I hit him with another crunching right to the forearm, after which a fluke left cross clipped me on the chin and I was granted a further eight seconds' respite. He wants it rough, I thought, he can have it rough.

Inveigling him into my corner, I absorbed a further battery of attempted lefts and rights while I focussed on working my forehead into his face.

'You little bastard,' he grunted, clearly rattled.

Then there was more shouting from the voice I'd heard before, and hands were on us trying to separate us. As Baxter moved back I knew that my moment had come. Screwing my eyes tight shut, for I don't like to see a man hurt, I launched into full attack and blindly landed a left, a right, a cross, a hook, an uppercut and finally a killing haymaker. The crowd went silent, then groaned as I heard him hit the canvas with a sickening thud, taking his scrambled senses with him.

This time I didn't follow the rules. I didn't go to the neutral corner. I stayed where I was, raised my arms in triumph, hovered savagely over my flayed opponent. I opened my eyes and gloated.

That's odd, I thought. He wasn't wearing that white shirt before; or that bow tie.

Oh dear, I thought. Oh dear oh dear oh dear.

I looked up to see the red flash at the end of Baxter's right arm come looping towards my jaw.

CHAPTER THREE

On the basis of the foregoing discussion there is little doubt in the mind of the current writer that the task of employee motivation in the next decade will be made at the same time both more straightforward and, paradoxically, more complex by the introduction of this new management tool in areas as diverse as personnel performance evaluation and market penetration analysis. The manager's ultimate ambition will of course continue to be a sustained increase in penetration through improved 'on the job' involvement.

Slumped in one of those low-slung continental chairs, the chrome pipe and leather kind designed to make you fall over when you try standing up, I raised my eyes from the latest issue of *Management Monthly* and stared straight ahead for what seemed like a very long time but not quite long enough.

Ultimate ambition; sustained penetration; on the job involvement ... And when, as now, she raised both arms above her head to adjust her hair-band as reflected in the glass of an all-black Rothko print – oh dear! I could think of a number of ways in which one particular management tool might be introduced, preferably during a very long lunch hour, possibly upstairs at the Great Eastern Hotel. Employee motivation wasn't the word.

Straight ahead of me, almost in touching distance, sat lovely, cooing, twenty-four-year-old Lucy Trender.

When we first heard that in addition to his secretary the senior partner had appointed a 'personal assistant', it was taken as a sign that the old boy must be generating more work than anyone had hitherto suspected; and with Doris nearing an age when arthritis would surely claim her one remaining skill it was natural that extra help should be required.

When it was discovered who the new girl was, and whose daughter she was (viz. none other than Sir Alfred Trender's), eyebrows were raised to suggest that it wasn't so much what as who she knew. She arrived a fortnight overdue after fine late snow at Zermatt. Eyebrows were raised again, but this time all the better to see her as she ran her perfect statistics through the office. The sociology of the English language followed where'er she walked. 'I say – ' said the gilt-edged department ' – not bad.' The equity salesmen were less restrained: 'I think we'll have to call that a Buy.' And the boys on the dealing desk were disinclined to argue: 'You don't get very much of that for a pound, squire.'

'He won't keep you a minute, London.'

She knew my Christian name. I was astounded. What's more, she had spoken without moving her lips, apparently without noticing I was in the room. I'd guessed from the start there was something special about this one; something that had nothing to do with the looks, the money, or the rumoured large pad in Chelsea. It was something in the way she eyed me without ever actually looking; in the way she showed not the slightest interest, yet seemed to know me utterly. And the voice – the voice; till then it had sounded tinny, high-pitched, almost vacuous; but now, directed at me for the first time (and that after only six months) it had a strange familiar resonance; a depth, a texture, a shaky sensual richness that somehow suggested experience. . .

The voice was Doris's.

'He won't keep you a minute,' she repeated.

'Oh – D – thanks, D.'

'Cup of tea while you wait?'

'I'd be sick.'

'I should think you're feeling sick already, with a face like that.'

'Thanks, D.'

'Oh, I didn't mean – I mean that eye of yours.'

'Eye? What eye?'

I'd a fair idea which eye she meant: my left eye, whose resemblance to the inside of an over-ripe fig had not escaped my attention in the course of the morning shave. (Fat Percy had thought of a much less delicate comparison.)

'I'll give you what eye,' said Doris. 'Let me get you that cuppa. It's all right, he'll be a minute yet. Sugar?'

'No thanks.'

'Sweet enough, aren't you?'

I looked to Lucy Trender for confirmation, but Lucy was flipping through a magazine full of photographs of people famous for being photographed in magazines, and didn't raise her head.

Doris went off to the drinks machine in her flowered dress and stiff hairdo. She changed, but only slowly, and generally for the worse. She'd switched her glasses recently, dropping the old pair with the flyaway brows for a modern design from one of the same-day shops that were opening up all over town just then, with big lenses and see-thru' frames, which confirmed my view of the unscrupulous rogues they employed as salespersons in these places. She moved with waning confidence. The thugs on the money desk called her Grandma or Big D, but the older hands remembered her as beautiful. That was when she was knocking round with a pushy young bluebutton called Reggie Goddard. She still dressed all right, they said – took care of her appearance – didn't have such a bad face, really. But there's not much you can do when your back end falls on hard times, is there?

I was sitting in the airy ante-room to Reggie Goddard's office, the nervous buffer-zone through which all penitents and supplicants had to pass. Until recently this had been Doris's sole domain, and she the keeper of Reggie's ear. Now there were two desks where there had been one, and Doris must have noticed that although young Lucy's function in the firm had not yet been fully defined the office was more than twice as busy as before. For those few who wanted to communicate with the senior partner, the phone or internal mail had been thought to suffice up to now; but growing numbers were starting to think it might be better to see the old man personally, while others, not disposed to face him, began to deliver their notes and memos by hand, via Doris, or perhaps via Lucy, rather than trust to the porter. Doris's occasional absence from the office spurred a frenzy of epistolary activity, particularly among younger members of the firm. (For myself, I relied on the time-honoured stratagem of resentful passivity – ignoring her, getting on with life, hiding behind cupboards, etc. This approach had failed so often of late it must be due for a comeback, I reasoned.)

The telephone buzzed. Lucy looked up slowly, saw no Doris, flicked through a few more pages, glanced at me quickly and uncomprehendingly (but in a way burningly) and answered it.

'Yah? . . . Sooozy!' Her knitted brow unravelled. She beamed and leant back in her chair, telephone receiver in her right hand, nape of her neck in the left, breasts thrusting up through a thin red pullover. 'How *are* you? Oh really? Suzy!'

My eyes focused fiercely on the margins of the 2M. 'Gentle and low' was not the first phrase I'd have used to describe her voice; and she'd have found it difficult to say 'I want to be alone' in quite the right tone. But then, perhaps she never did.

'Oh no! I don't believe it! Fantastic!'

Good news or bad? There seemed to be some doubt. But I did glean one essential fact: they hadn't met since last week and both of them thought it scandalous.

'Well what about Harry's? Will you be there?'

The outer door opened and one of the young bloods from gilts poked his nose in. Lucy didn't look up. She was sweeping her hair back. Quite right too, I thought. The young scapegrace retreated, taking his memo with him.

'Oh no! ... Well, won't you be at Julian's? Why not? ... Yah. No. Yah. But who is he? ... Norwich? Oh God, no. Not for *her*.'

This was followed by a catalogue of exotica: Zara, Kiki, Pandora; Antelope, White Horse, Cod. All animal life was there. What a world she must move in. There was no slowing-down when Doris came back, either. The catechism rolled on regardless: Zena, Tina, Thomasina ...

'There you go,' said Doris. 'Just keep your cool and you'll be all right.' The tea was in a cup and saucer. She must have decanted it from the plastic beaker dispensed by the machine.

'Thanks, D.'

'Yah, yah, we'll do it, soon as poss. Bye, then. Bye.'

The room went quiet. The tea was very hot, scalding my lips. Kissing Lucy Trender must be something like this, I thought.

'Oh Doris?' she said, smiling instantly: hair of corn; teeth as white and regular as bathroom tiles; eyes – oh my – talk about the blue lagoon – I swam in them: backstroke, breaststroke, every stroke imaginable.

'Yes, dear?'

'I was wondering whether I could have the early lunch today. Only there's someone I'm supposed to see.'

Since time before my knowledge, Doris had lunched at half past twelve.

'Of course, dear.'

'Oh great. Thanks. Great help.' She picked up the phone again and dialled.

Five minutes later the only part of me that was keeping its cool was my crotch, over which when the Senior Partner's door had swung suddenly open I had poured half a cup of tea as I struggled to my feet. Boilingly, blisteringly, sterilisingly hot as it had then been (adding, I suspected, a touch of dementia to my intended deferential smile), it had certainly cooled off since.

It was a glittering winter's day. Reggie stood behind his desk with his back to me, enjoying the easterly view over the Aldgate and out to the Isle of Dogs, Greenwich and beyond.

'A faint heart never won a fair lady,' he said. 'That's what I always say ...' He turned and lowered his massive frame into the chair. '... and over there is the most exciting piece of real estate in the world. Right on our back doorstep.'

Reggie was facing me across a broad swathe of polished green leather. Although the block was put up in the seventies Reggie's office was pannelled, the struts of the pannelling painted white and the infill the palest green. The carpet was duck-egg and the furniture Hepplewhite, clean and spare; and all these things were tax-offsettable.

'Don't talk to me about New York,' he said, though I hadn't thought of doing so till then. 'Or Tokyo. It's here – Docklands. Some people have made a lot of money out of it already. Some are still going to. And some are going to lose it. Don't you agree?' he boomed.

'Oh I do, sir, yes.'

He nodded for a long time, as if thinking.

'Good,' he said at length. 'At last a reversal of the great move west, don't you think?'

Of course not, I thought. It's a publicity stunt, this Docklands nonsense; it's all to do with politics, or something equally nasty. It's nothing to do with the great move anywhere. And if it were, how would you know?

'Oh quite so,' I said.

'Good.' He nodded again. '... Now tell me, London: would you call yourself an ambitious man?'

'Moderately,' seemed the safest reply.

'A good answer,' said Reggie. '*Moderately*. Yes, a very good answer. The middle way is best. There's too much greed around these days, altogether too much. These people, university graduates or whatever they call themselves, they come into business and they're not happy unless they're a millionaire by the time they're thirty. Oh yes. The City isn't what it used to be. Not the same thing at all. But tell me – what exactly *are* your ambitions?'

That was an easy one. Health, wealth and happiness would no doubt feature somewhere on the list, arguably in that order, but surely the only thing really worth going for is revenge. But where to start?

'A difficult question,' I said. 'I don't suppose they're really much different from anyone else's. Career, pleasant place to live, family. That sort of – '

'Home, career, family. Good. That's the kind of thing I like to hear. The kind of thing I wanted to hear. That's what we're in business for, after all.'

29

I nodded brightly.

'Where is it you live, again?' he asked, implying that he had unaccountably forgotten.

'Oh – in Town,' I said, trying to make it sound like Onslow Square or Hyde Park Gardens.

'I see. But you're not married?'

'Not at the moment.'

'I had an idea you were.'

'I was.'

'To some sort of madwoman, did one of my sources tell me? Or was that just gossip?'

'Fair comment, I'd say,' though she of whom we spoke scarcely deserved such leniency. If my ex-wife had merely been mad my life might be so much sweeter; and if 'madwoman' was the worst thing Reggie's source had to say about Margaret he couldn't have been much of a source, let alone a gossip. More of a saint, in fact.

'Not to worry. They mostly are. Mad. Treat her badly?'

'I thought I was rather considerate.'

'You shouldn't have been. A woman, a dog and a walnut tree, the more you beat 'em the better they be. Went ex, did you?'

'Last year.'

'Fair distribution of assets, I trust.'

'She thought so.'

'One of those ones, eh? I blame the courts. Don't let it get you down. Bugger 'em, that's what I say ... I was married once before, of course.'

I knew. It was Reggie's favourite story.

'Oh really?'

'Oh yes ... yes indeed ... Shot her. Right between the eyes. An accident, of course. Terrible mess, though. Women and guns don't mix – a fact worth remembering. Rather missed her for a while. Nice little thing, she was. But there's always another one round the corner. Like London buses, aren't they?'

Try waiting for a number 15, I thought.

'Good,' he continued. 'That's that. Now –' the giant hands folded, the deep voice dropped yet deeper – 'how are you, London?'

'Not awfully well this morning.'

'How's the eye?'

'Could be worse. Feels worse than it looks. I mean – '

'Looks worse than it feels. I hope so, for your sake. Mmm ... Mmm ... I don't think – I can't swear to this, but I don't *think* I've ever seen a worse display from a member of the Stock Exchange than I saw from you last night.'

30

'Oh.'

'I mean, quite apart from the matter of the poor referee. I don't *think* so.'

'No, sir.'

'Certainly not from a member of this firm.'

'Obviously I'm terribly sorry it happened.'

'So am I. So am I. To call the whole performance childish would scarcely begin to express my feelings.'

He shook his great head sadly.

'As I say, all I can do is apologise.'

'Apologise ... Apologise ...'

'I'm afraid it was a case of too much drink.'

'I'm afraid it was. But that's when a real soldier comes to the fore, is it not? Discipline, lad – where was your discipline?'

I shook my own head forlornly.

'Your feet, lad!'

I glanced down at my shoes, buffed them slyly on my calves.

'Where were your feet?' he demanded to know.

A fresh accusation seemed about to be levelled. But no.

'Dance,' Reggie said. 'Dance!'

'What – now, sir?'

'Eh?'

'Did you want me to dance now?'

'Dance? Here? Don't be a fool, man. It's too late now.'

I glanced at the clock. Reggie caught me looking.

'Last night, man! I'm telling you you should have been using your feet! And your right – where was your right? I've never seen boxing like it in my life!'

'I'm terribly sorry,' I said. 'I thought I was – I thought it was my, er, general demeanour – '

'General Demeanour, who's he? No, lad. Don't know what you're talking about. Touch of high spirits never harmed anyone. Didn't do the referee a lot of good, but I gather he'll be all right. God no. I'm talking about your boxing ... Technique, lad, technique! Quite frankly I thought you were brave to volunteer. Must have taken a lot of courage, Buck the bigger man and all.'

'Thank you.'

'Right ... Right ... That's it, then.'

'Will that be all?'

'Indeed.'

Gagging on gratitude, I made for the door.

'Wait a minute,' Reggie added as my hand touched the doorknob. 'Silly me. There was something else.'

31

As I resumed my seat Reggie rose from his. He turned eastwards, sighed deeply, nodded for some time and sat down again.

'To err,' he said, 'is human.'

A long pause obliged me, I thought, to say: 'It is indeed.'

'And that explains why I almost forgot the main point of our meeting,' he added. 'Mmm ... There was indeed something else. The question of your professional competence.'

'Oh?' I said, attempting to sound at the same time highly surprised and deeply dismayed.

'There are those in the partnership who seem, shall we say, unconvinced. You do have your supporters, of course, but not, unfortunately, among the professional staff. The, er, janitorial operatives appear to be the main focus of your, er, power base.'

'Ah.'

'And the telephonists.'

'I see.'

'In fact I have to tell you that the cost-benefit boys have been casting their beady eye over your performance in the last few months. Awful bunch of people, mind you. Accountants mostly. Didn't have them in my day. Things are different now, though. Big Bang next year. It's going to be tough; or that's what everyone seems to think.'

Which is why you think it, I thought; why you only think anything ever. And yet it was hard at times not to feel sorry for Reggie – bloated, pompous, idle old fool that he was. The City was changing; the Yanks were coming, with their high-pressure selling and their round-the-clock arbitrage. Soon there wouldn't be room for people like Reggie. I knew how he must feel.

'And these cost-benefit wallahs seem to have come to the view that the cost of your services to the firm is considerably outweighing the benefits ... Does this surprise you?'

'It disappoints me.'

'It disappoints me, too,' Reggie countered. 'So much so that I feel I have little alternative but to fire you.'

'I see.'

'With immediate effect.'

'Ah.'

'Instanter.'

'Oh.'

'What do you think of that, then?' This was just the sort of question other people used rhetorically but Reggie would expect you to answer. I could, of course, have answered it, and very succinctly too, though not without abandoning the decorum Reggie always expected of his chaps. I could have jumped in the air and shouted hooray. I could have pulled down my trousers and shown him my bottom. I could have thrown myself at his oversized feet and begged for mercy. Rogers & Prickett was widely known as the last throw of the desperate broker. What was there left for me now? The long walk, the early bath, the sad ride home on the bus.

'I'm sorry to hear it,' I said.

'Ah, but you needn't be,' said Reggie. 'You needn't be at all. Notice I said "little" alternative – not "no" alternative.'

'Oh, I did, I did.'

'And I don't believe in a world of no alternatives. There's more than one way to skin a cat. That's what I always say.'

I couldn't help agreeing; and thus it was that I became involved in a Very Important Matter.

CHAPTER FOUR

My own little corner of London was not, in truth, Onslow Square or Hyde Park Gardens, or anywhere else covered by the concept of 'Town'. It wasn't even up and coming. One day, no doubt, it will be discovered; the halal butchers will be bought out by estate agents, and the gutters now full of Coke cans and chip papers will be littered with BMWs and Renault 20s; but in my time the neighbourhood's socially-mobile were all in the downward stream.

I had lived since my divorce in a bed-sitting room at that windy, noisy end of Ladbroke Grove known as North Kensington. I don't know who thought up the name, but he certainly must have been a dry one. Kensington? I preferred to think of it as Notting Hill International, and after a few drinks with Kenny Morgan at the Green Man one night I'd almost made the appropriate adjustment to the sign outside the nearby Tube station – spray-cans were widely available – and would have, if not for the approach of a solitary police officer putting me off my stroke. It wasn't fear that did it. It was the shock. They didn't often walk the streets alone in these parts.

Nor, for instance, did the milkmen. In fact they didn't walk the streets at all. They'd stopped delivering long ago. The milk was usually stolen, they said, and when it wasn't stolen it wasn't paid for. When it was paid for the takings were stolen.

Other services were also collapsing. There were launderettes, but long queues formed at the few machines that still worked. There were newsagents, but most of the papers sold, other than cigarette papers, were foreign or tabloid or both. There were supermarkets, but most of the foodstuffs I was brought up on seemed to be thought outmoded. As regards personal safety, there were generally though not invariably no problems provided you remained indoors; otherwise you had to know where you were going. That was all right by me: I was never going anywhere, when our story begins, which it soon will do, other than down to the Warwick Arms. Early evenings were quiet except on riot days, and for those who had homes to go to there was a happy hour between closing time and midnight before any trouble started. Later than that you might find the boys getting thirsty and demonstrative. As a rule I therefore made my way home shortly after the close, a practice which by happy coincidence also allowed me maximum drinking-time.

If the walk home was on occasion perilous, it was no more so than minding your own business was in some of the local boozers. Many a quiet pie-and-a-pint was enlivened by the airborne passage of a stool or a couple of glasses across the public bar, often to be followed by the departure of one or two clients in similar manner. The Warwick was generally free of this sort of thing. I had once been chased from the bar, but once in three hundred and sixty-five consecutive appearances wasn't bad.

It had been a Scotsman and his lass. 'You're eyeing ma woman,' he had objected, and came round the bar in pursuit. Had I been eyeing her? I don't remember. She was as lovely as Paisley in the rain, but I was having a lengthy spell of involuntary celibacy at the time and it was possible my gaze had strayed. I broke the Buxton Grammar School old boys' record time for swallowing a pint of Bass and fled. After a brief chase I was backed against a wall and threatened with having my brains blown oot. There was no sign of a firearm under young Malcolm's T-shirt, so I concentrated on protecting my groin. An entente was soon reached whereby for the price of a pint the accusation would be withdrawn. I'm not a violent man.

My room, in College Gardens, lurked on a dark half-landing between the second and third floors. The spring-loaded light-switch in the entrance hall was fixed on so energy-conscious a setting that every time I came home I faced a terrible decision: press hard and dash upstairs at breakneck speed, or ignore it altogether and hope the Iranian student in the room under mine hadn't left her roller-skates on the stairs again. After three hours at the Warwick, disaster was likely either way.

The room itself was dominated by a large bed and its mustard-coloured counterpane. Other features included a cold, rotten smell and a two-bar electric fire unable to dispel it. The walls were painted dark orange. When I first arrived they had been decked with posters bearing slogans in an unknown script. The carpet was brown. It was like being inside an earthwork. Lights, heater and burner required to be fed on coins, and the meters, I had discovered, were voracious but not omnivorous. I often tempted them with rings, washers and knife-blades, but only fifty-pence pieces turned them on.

Although use of the electrical appliances was hazardous, there was at least no chance of being gassed to death, an elegant sash-

35

window providing ample ventilation even when bolted, wedged and hammered down. Through it, another amenity of the area being ease of communications, I could see the whites of the drivers' eyes as they sped westwards on Saturday mornings towards their weekend retreats in the Cotswolds. A previous occupant had had a go at double glazing, but the sellotape at the edges had cracked and the polythene had lolled away from the window, where I was content to leave it.

Tonight, however, this was hidden by the drawn curtains.

'It's no good, London,' said Margaret. At moments like this she always reverted to her youth as a Method Acting student, first staring hard at some object on the table, then rolling her eyes far enough back to be seen at the rear of the stalls.

'No good? What's wrong?'

'You know very well what's wrong. Everything.'

'Everything? That's terrible. And you know, I was sure I hadn't overdone the onions this time.'

'Oh London, will you grow up, stop this pathetic joking, which I hope you don't think is funny because I certainly don't, and listen to me?'

'Can I take that question in three parts?'

The candle between us flickered on its pink stick as Margaret sighed. Our shadows wavered, kissed, parted.

Had it been optional, even slightly optional, listening to Margaret would not in itself have been difficult. Her voice was melodious enough. Like the cobblestones in Dubrovnik, where we spent our honeymoon, any rough edges it might once have had had been worn perfectly smooth by continuous use. Hearing it now was disturbing: it reminded me that be it ever so unpleasant there's no place like home.

The problem was that Margaret's voice never was an optional extra. It was a given. It was like the tannoy at Liverpool Street Station – few men understood it, but for no man would it stop. Meaning, as for the tannoy, was secondary; and yes, I had been slow to grasp this fact. It was all the fault of my teachers, those dullards who had told me that conversation was part of being civilised, a meeting-place for the kindly-disposed, a forum and not an arena. Oxford had changed most of that; London had kept up the good work; but the clincher was marrying Margaret. I tried for a while to refine some of her grosser prejudices – but that was rejecting her, when I should have been embracing. I questioned her facts when they were wrong – but that was undermining, when I should have been supporting. And when differences were irreconcilable I even referred to higher authority – on one occasion the telephone directory, on another the A to Z. Margaret had no words for that kind of treachery.

'Anyway,' I lied, 'I was listening.'

'If you had been listening you'd have heard me say that marriage is just another way for men like you ...'

It wasn't easy to get the right blend of chilli and cayenne. Some people didn't discriminate. They seemed to think the one was merely a stronger version of the other. They were wrong, though. Then you had to get the beans right. Even with a peasant dish like chilli con soya, which was all you could cook in a dump like this, it was worth taking trouble with the details. Not that Margaret would have noticed. You could have served dog food for all she cared. Dog shit, for that matter. She'd have wolfed it down; or she would have before she went vegan. Good food was wasted on her. But tonight was more a matter of self-respect. I didn't want her to think I was living on fish and chips, just because I didn't have a woman looking after me. Anyway, I'd had my fill of fish and chips lately. I was sick of fish and chips. And in the event, self-respect was high indeed this evening: beans just right, soya tender and hot, a pinch of meat extract for spite and a strong pervasive flavour of garlic. Unusually for a radical feminist, Margaret didn't like garlic.

In the last two years of our marriage I'd hit on this simple solution to the problem of how to engage my wife in meaningful conversation: don't. Think about something nice instead.

Several gallons of vitriol later I said, 'Well, my dear, this isn't new ground, is it? But it's nice to walk the old paths now and then, provided you've got your gumboots on. Enjoy the meal?'

'It was fine.'

'Good. Now why don't you have some pudding instead of shouting at me?'

'I don't want any pudding.'

'Not watching your weight, are you? The sisters wouldn't like that.'

'I'm not watching my weight. What have you got?'

I ran through the menu: tinned peaches, tinned oranges, tinned pear-halves. I'd got so used to Margaret's canned cuisine I preferred it to the real thing now. Breakfast this morning had been a tin of new potatoes. (Of the two label-less cans in the cupboard I'd have sworn it was the smaller, fatter one that contained the grapefruit seggies, which I ate from time to time for sentimental reasons. I'd

37

have sworn in vain. I swallowed the potatoes unheated. They had mint in them. One mouthful and I was back in my childhood.)

'Or there's a tin of Polish plums,' I said.

'London, I haven't, I really *haven't* come here to argue with you. In fact, I really don't know why I've bothered to come round at all.'

This question had also occurred to me. Of our periodic reunion dinners since the great escape half had ended with Margaret storming out, the winds of recrimination howling about my ears, and half, which is to say three, had ended with sex; this delayed the most severe blasts until on one occasion the morning and on the other two the middle of the night. I'd been sound asleep the last time until roused by tear-jerking jabs in the ribs and piercing cries of, 'You bastard! You bastard! You're keeping me awake!' Good old Margaret. If ever you were tempted, even for a moment, to think she might be sane, you could always rely on her to remind you she wasn't.

Margaret's shrieks on that occasion also stirred from her slumbers my Polish landlady, Madame Romanowska.

I was well accustomed to fear of what the neighbours might think. Giving the neighbours no cause to think anything whatsoever was one of the major occupations of women back in Wootton: women who would put their best shoes on to fetch the milk from the doorstep; who would insist on lights being left off until curtains were drawn, even on the grimmest Sunday afternoon, in case anyone should see in. See what? I always wondered. Star Soccer? Auntie Edna's knitting?

Compared with the Romanowskis, Wootton women were exhibitionists. No doubt it stemmed from the traumatic history of the race, and no doubt the Inland Revenue was as yet untroubled by submissions from the Romanowski household (they had only been here since 1945); even so their terror of being seen, let alone heard, let alone in the middle of the night by their neighbours, was not so much an evasive strategem as a categorical imperative. Alone among its peers, which throbbed round the clock to the latest beat, number sixty-six observed a silence as of Warsaw after the curfew. So when I tried to creep back in under cover of darkness after following Margaret down the street demanding she return my first edition of *A Handful of Dust*, the old lady hit the light-switch, reared up horribly from behind the staircase and gave me my second berating of the still only three hours-old day. She couched it thus:

'Wotcha call this, then, wotcha call this? What you mean, this your wife? You tell me you don't got no wife. Now you tell me you got wife. You got wife or you don't got no wife? And you got wife or you don't got no wife is no problem, no problem for me, but no trouble here, no trouble. No shout in middle of the night or out, out you go. My husband sick. My sister sick. I sick. We all sick in this bloody country. We don't want no shout in middle of night. We want sleep.'

The light cut out and there was silence. I heard her turn towards the parlour where she slept on a battered chaise-longue and thought this was the end of it. Then I heard her turn again, her quilted dressing-gown rustling, and say: 'And we don't want no whores. I tell you when you get here, no whores. We got nice house.'

Then I remembered why Margaret had bothered to come round at all.

'I thought you were here to talk about the lad,' I said.

'I really do deplore it when you have to hide behind my son,' she said. Margaret was a great deplorer.

'My son too – or so you said.'

Her son and mine: the three year-old product of a drink too many and a Pill too few. (It was my fault. I'd been stung on the toe by a wasp that morning and my cries of anguish disturbed her routine.) Almost the beneficiary of natural childbirth (called off when Margaret asked for gas and air at the breaking of the waters), the huge screaming boy was eventually delivered by Caesarian section and thus avoided, as Margaret proudly pointed out, the trauma of birth-by-technology. He continued to scream for several weeks afterwards. On the Friday lunchtime at the end of the first fortnight, shattered by lack of sleep (Margaret needed hers: I'd only got my job to think about), I popped into Coates Brothers for a quick Bloody Mary and emerged some hours later with vengeance on my mind. I had myself taxied to the register office and it was there, amid looks of disgust from the female clerks, that Benjamin Arthur Woodhouse London officially joined the happy band, his initials a permanent reminder of his first few weeks on earth.

'How's he coping with the malnutrition?' I enquired. Now there was obviously no chance of sex I felt punchier. Ben, surprisingly enough, had decided to go vegetarian at about the same time as Margaret. ('You eat dead sheeps,' he had told me. 'It's wevolting.')

'Ben's very well, thank you,' Margaret replied. 'There's plenty of protein in beans. But I'll naturally pass on your concern, though I could think of better ways for you to express it.'

39

'Oh, yes? Well, I think I know what that means. How much do you want?'

'Is that all you can think about, money?'

'Thinking about it's the nearest I get to it these days.'

'It's nothing to do with money.'

'My God – it must be serious.'

'It's about his name.'

'Aha – his name!' For the next few minutes I hammered in the manner of a certain television comedian, something I always found irritating when other people did it, but which I thought I did rather well. 'No – no – let me guess – I know – got it! You want to change it.'

'Yes.'

'To – no, no, let me guess: got it! Nelson Mandela!'

'Ha ha.'

'No? Oh dear, oh dear. Think, think.'

'I want it changed to my mother's name.'

'Your mother's name – why of course! But – oh dear – but he's already got your mother's name.'

'If you mean Woodhouse, that's my father's name.'

'Oh, I see. How very dull of me. You mean her maiden name. Wilson, was it? Wilson. Okie-dokie, Wilson it is. Benjamin Arthur Wilson London. Perfect in every way.'

'I don't mean her maiden name. I mean her given name.'

'Oh, her given name! What the less enlightened of us still go on referring to in our quaint old-fashioned way as her Christian name. Winifred. Why of course. Why on earth didn't I think of that at once? Winifred. Winifred London. Winnie London. Every little boy's dream name. Little Winnie London. The key to happy schooldays. The door to social opportunity. My goodness, what a gift to the child. He'll sail through life with a name like that. Why didn't you tell me when you arrived? What a lovely evening it could have been.'

'Is that all?' said Margaret. 'Or am I to be treated to some more of this entertainment?'

'You've lost your marbles, Margaret Woodhouse – Wilson – whatever you call yourself.'

'Maggie Winifred.'

'Oh Jesus.'

'Well, I can't say,' she said, 'that I expected you to discuss this in a civilised manner.'

'A civilised manner? Too bloody right. Or any other manner.'

'So I can hardly say I'm disappointed by your reaction. May I have a drink, please?'

'Port? Brandy? Blood?'

'Have you got whisky?'

'Oh, it's whisky now, is it? Is that where my money's going? Any particular one? As madam can see, there's plenty of space in our cellars for a wide selection.' I opened my arms, palms outstretched, to demonstrate. The room looked better by candlelight, though not as good as by no light at all. 'Above the sink, our twelve-year-olds. Over by the gas meter our fifteen-year-olds, newly drawn from the cask. And just under the draining-board, for the real connoisseur –' I put on what I thought was the appropriate accent – 'a fine range of peaty malts from the Western Isles.'

'Whatever you've got. And coffee.'

'Certainly. Oh, sorry, we're out of Nicaraguan this evening.'

'Instant's fine.'

'Have you heard they don't have to roast their beans over there any more? Apparently the Americans are doing it for them.'

'Gosh, London, that's a terribly funny thing to say. Ever thought of writing comedy?'

I poured two large Johnnie Walkers and made Nescafé, continuing to react to my son's proposed name-change in a way calculated hardly to disappoint his mother. I was going to put the milk into a little jug from Portobello market, but I thought, Why bother? and poured straight from the box.

'No,' I said. 'No no no.'

'I came prepared,' said Margaret. 'Where did you put my bag?'

It was not the smart, shiny kind, but the more acceptable canvas, with a shoulder-strap; the sort people were ashamed of having where I came from. Out of it she produced a long pale blue envelope.

'So, I was right first time. How much?'

'Another twenty-five per cent.'

I dipped a corner of the envelope into the candle-flame.

'They keep copies,' she said with the characteristic stage sigh that had always sent me rushing for the nearest carpet to bite on. 'They'll just send you another one, and that'll be another tenner on the bill.'

'Not this time. I'm contesting. Anyway, there's no point asking for more. I haven't got the dough.'

'Find it.'

'As you can see, my extravagant lifestyle gobbles up most of my income.'

'The details are in the letter. Alternatively, if you're prepared to be reasonable – '

'No. No no no no no.'

'Sexist bastard.'

'Right – out. Now. And don't – !' I brought my hand down hard on her glass. Whisky wasn't cheap, even Johnnie Walker. The glass was, though. It broke and cut the side of my hand.

'I'm wounded. I'm wounded!'

'Bleed, then. I have to bleed every month, don't I?'

I ran my hand under the tap while Margaret picked up her bag and made for the door. The sound of rattling and swearing came from the hallway. Margaret was struggling with the front door. The Poles were very security-conscious. (And wouldn't you be, after all those invasions?) I made my way down in the dark – with caution at first, knowing my landlady didn't like noise, but latterly with spine-tingling speed as my left foot located a roller-skate. 'Nice trip?' Margaret asked.

Limping, agonised, I did the trick with the locks. At the gate she turned and glared. Streetlight became her, giving her short black hair a coppery glow. Her features were sharp and perfect and her grey-green eyes shone like a she-cat's. She looked serene.

'And another thing,' she hissed. 'Don't think I didn't notice the fucking garlic!'

'You didn't taste the rennet, though, did you?'

'London, you are pathetic. Just get back to the fourth form where you belong.'

Ah, go and get mugged, I thought. Get raped by a black woman. And as for your lawyer –

Turning indoors, I'd just finished suggesting what she could do with her lawyer when I found myself face-to-face, at closer quarters than ever before, with Madame Romanowksa.

The subsequent interview took place inside. I'd already made an exhibition of myself to the street, Madame Romanowska felt, heightening the drama by using only the present tense. Did I want the police round? (No, please, not the cops, I thought. Rape, sedition and GBH were the stuff of a quiet night's work on this precinct. But shouting in the street they really didn't take to.)

This woman, I explained – no, not woman, wife – not wife, ex-wife, woman I once married to but no more, no more married, finish; she not come again, not again, only trouble, trouble when she come.

'Why you not find nice girl?'

'Nice? She is delightful. I mean, when we meet, she is very nice.

42

Always smile, smile, smile. But then trouble. Problems. So we got divorced – no married no more.'

'So why she come? I don't like.'

'Me too. I also don't like. No more. She come no more.'

'You right, she come no more. You also, you come no more. Too old. I sick. My husband sick. My sister sick. You too much problems. Out. Tomorrow, out.'

'Tomorrow's Sunday. Sunday tomorrow.'

'Good. No work. Find place to live, place with young people.'

'Young people? I too old. They run away when they see me coming. Young people, see me, run.' I ran on the spot.

'Tomorrow. Maybe better tonight. You go tonight?'

'Tonight? Impossible.'

'Okay. I let you stay. Am I a pig? No. Okay, tonight you stay. Tomorrow – go!'

I didn't have much to pack: two suits, seven shirts, seven pairs of socks and underpants; a blazer, a few ties, a limited collection of leisurewear; Roger the leopard; some photographs. I was never one for self-indulgence. The nearest thing I had to a luxury was a jade-handled shaving-brush from Hong Kong. Putting it away, I thought fondly of the rows I used to have with Margaret because she wouldn't let me use it. She deplored cruelty to badgers. I told her they didn't actually kill the little dears. Of course they didn't. They held them gently down and snipped off a few choice bristles, that's all. Why would they bite the tail that fed them? I asked: but she still wouldn't let me use it.

I went downstairs with my suitcase and knocked on the parlour door. There was yet hope, I told myself. Even a hateful old paranoid like Madame Romanowska had a heart. She must have: the Poles were world-famous for heart. Surely in the dark watches of the night a tiny voice had whispered: Let him stay.

'Good morning,' she said. 'So today you go.'

'Yes?'

'Yes. Goodbye. I hope you find good place.'

'Thank you,' I said.

'Goodbye,' she said again at the door.

'*Naztravye*,' I replied. I was half way down the steps before I remembered that *Naztravye* was the Russian for cheers, not the Polish for goodbye. The door was already shut behind me. I walked a few yards, put the suitcase down, sat on a low wall, lit a cigarette and wondered where to go next.

43

And a voice came down from heaven and said: 'Hey you!'

I looked round to see a man in a vest leaning from a first-floor window. Curly grey-haired, bespectacled, a white man but unseasonally suntanned and shaped like a bottle of chianti: fat, but with a long neck.

'Good morning,' I said. 'Not so nice today.' It was cold, dark, ready to rain.

'Get outa here!'

'You're a friendly fellow.'

'Get off-a ma wall, OK? What's in the suitcase?' The man disappeared.

I finished my cigarette and was thinking of moving on when there was a sound on the pavement next to me as of an ice-cream coming to grief at great speed.

I looked down: a shattered ice-cream lay at my feet.

'Hey you!'

I looked round again.

'Get off-a ma wall. This time vanilla. Too light. Next time I don't miss. Next time tutti-frutti.'

'Make it a ninety-nine. Double flake, no nuts. And put it in a cone, will you? We don't eat off the floor in this country.'

A minute passed without further incident. I was thinking of moving again.

'Hey! Mister! You got nowhere to go? You wanna place to live?'

'Not with you.'

The man appeared at the front door and ran down the steps clutching a vast creamy cone, pink with a chocolate flake.

'Here. A masterpiece. Ricardo Modigliani, pleased to meet you. Peach and bardolino. You try. Very good.'

He was right. It was very good.

'You like?'

'Not bad.'

'Not bad? It's-a fantastic! You take-a the room?'

'Let's have a look. Bring my case, will you?'

I was starting as I meant to carry on with this one. That had been the problem with the Poles. I hadn't shown them who was boss. The room felt disturbingly familiar. Through the window the traffic sped westward.

'Just like the room up the road.'

'You living up-a the road?' Modigliani panted, patting his heart, crossing himself.

'Left today. Madame Romanowska.'

'You in trouble?'

'No.'

'She's-a crazy, that mad old Polak. She throws out a nice-a young-a man like you. Crazy.'

'I know. I was crazy to stay.'

'So. You like it?'

The walls were dark green, the carpet brown, the whole room dominated by the bed and its dusty bedspread. Pinned to the wall, Jesus held his tunic open to show off his enlarged sacred heart. Polythene double-glazing flopped away from the window-frame.

'How much?'

Modigliani surveyed the room with pride.

'Very cheap,' he said.

'Yes – how much?'

'Forty.'

'I'm not that crazy. Twenty.'

'Twenty? You think I'm-a crazy too?'

'Twenty.'

'Thirty.'

'Twenty-eight.'

'Thirty. Free hot water.'

'How often?'

'Whaddaya mean, how often? This is a nice-a place. Five days a week.'

'I'll take it,' I said.

The light expired as I unpacked. I found a coin and revived it. It's about time something went right, I thought.

CHAPTER FIVE

It was no surprise to me that when I was next summoned to see the senior partner several weeks later I still hadn't found out what the Very Important Matter was that he had referred to in our previous interview. Goddard moved in a mysterious way, his wonders to perform; and his unflagging application of this principle to friends, colleagues and partners had taken Rogers & Prickett under his guidance from what it was twenty years ago, a mediocre firm struggling to keep pace with the sixties, to what it was today, a mediocre firm struggling to keep pace with the eighties.

According to later tradition he had preferred even as a fledgling bluebutton to keep himself to himself. His allegiances remained unstated, it was said, and his integrity unimpeached. It wasn't until Reggie stepped over a dying man's body that the victim realised he had been knifed. Thus by a combination of good faith and bad judgment (other people's) with high scruples and low cunning (his own), Reggie was drawn irresistibly forward. Reflecting on this, as I sometimes did during my trimestral work-out at Fatso's Gym in Leadenhall Street, I realised that Reggie's best weapon in the early days must have been his size. There was something buffoonish about such a giant. No one had known that inside the big man there was a little man wanting to be big.

'Do sit down,' he said. 'Make yourself comfortable.'

The military precision in the way the papers were arranged on his desk brought to mind another snippet I'd picked up about the great one's career. This one concerned his wartime experiences. The information had, mind, been obtained from John-boy, who claimed to have obtained it many years ago from an unwontedly drunken Reggie, and it was unlikely *a priori* to show him in the best light; but its improbability gave it the ring of truth.

Young Reggie was only just old enough for the officer corps, it went, and was naturally dismayed when the War showed every sign of ending before he had time to prove his worth. Happily, he was assigned a rookie platoon and made it to Germany for the later stages of the advance on Berlin. When the rest of the western forces gave up the unequal struggle and left Berlin to the Russians, Reggie

continued to advance until, in an episode unrecorded by the
official historians, his hungry young men were all killed by a Red
Army mortar shell whilst entertaining a group of hungry girls
from the German Women's Army Corps in a barn just outside
Magdeburg. Lieutenant Goddard, hastily taking his bearings,
stole a bicycle and was given a hero's welcome by the Canadian
infantry division he encountered two days later. He ended the War
as a captain.

'Thank you, sir.'

'Mmm. Do call me Reggie. Market?'

'Not a lot happening. Easier if anything.'

'Yes. We need some news. Now tell me ... Mmm ... ' He
straightened his back, spread his wide hands over the leather top
of his desk, and paused for a good long nod. 'Tell me, how's it
going?'

As an up-to-date version of 'How are you?' the question seemed
out of place coming from Reggie, but not impossible. He was known
to use expressions less than twenty years old, though not as a rule
less than ten.

'It's going all right,' I ventured.

'Mmm ... ' said Reggie. 'Mmm ... *What* is going all right?'

'Life?' I tried.

'Mmm ...' said Reggie. 'As I thought. Well that may be what
you mean by "it", but when I say "it", I mean "it", man. "It." The
project. The very important matter. The one I told you about last
time you were here.'

'Ah – yes, you did, sir – Reggie.'

'Well – how's it going, then?'

'Er – I'm afraid you didn't actually mention what the project
was, Reggie.'

'Oh, didn't I? And didn't you ask?'

'You wouldn't tell me.'

'Are you sure? ... How very odd. Dear me. There's no fool like
an old fool, that's what I always say.'

He rose, turned his back on me and looked east through his big
windows.

'East London,' he said at last, sitting down again. There was no
denying that. 'Know it?' he asked.

I did know it. In the golden days before Margaret, I had lived in
an East End tower block for eighteen months with a young doctor
whose choice between a career and the man she loved eventually
removed her to an institute for the terminally ill in Santa Monica,
California. For several months afterwards I received passionate but

47

increasingly guarded letters. Then she became Mrs Gross, or Klein, or whatever it was, number three. Her final letter failed to make clear whether he was the third Mr or she the third Mrs. When the authorities discovered the girl had gone they evicted me and our tastefully-appointed tenth-floor flat with its sanded floorboards and white walls was allotted to a problem family. Happy hours we had known. The flat was boarded up now.

'Parts of it,' I said.

'The company,' Reggie sighed, nodding like an executive toy, meshing his massive hands. 'Not the place. I'd hardly expect you to spend your weekends there. The company. East London Industries, plc.'

'Oh, yes, you mean the old, er – ' I tried to look as if I knew.

'Limehouse Estates.'

'Limehouse Estates. I thought they'd changed their name.'

'Right,' said Reggie. 'Good man. Of course, I remember them from the days when they were called the Cairo Jute Company. A good little outfit, Cairo Jute. Then along came whatshisname and wallop – sorry, chaps, off you go. A hundred years of history down the drain. They all remember the Suez Canal, but they forget the Cairo Jute Company. I didn't forget, though. I had shares in them. I reckoned someone would get rid of this Colonel chappie, old Nasser – I reckoned somebody'd bump him off. Well, somebody should have, shouldn't they?

'So when the shares went right down to a bob, down from two pounds I think they were at one stage, I bought 'em. Buckets of 'em. Up to my ears in them, I was. Contrary thinking, you see. The Market does one thing, you do the other. Often works. You can make a lot of money like that. Only in this case I lost a lot. No compensation, y'see. Not a penny. Sold 'em at a farthing a share. Lost a packet. Should have known they'd never play the white man. Halfway to being niggers after all, aren't they? But no use being wise after the event. That's the Market for you – you win some, you lose some. Swings and roundabouts ... But if I read you aright you're not exactly intimate with the company.'

'Not intimate, no.'

'Mmm ... I think you should be. Get the file and have a look. A good look. All the files, all the information, everything you can find. History, trading, prospects – the lot. Don't leave a stone unturned. The others can see to your clients for a few days. From the look of the commission figures it doesn't appear they regard your services as indispensable. All clear?'

'Absolutely.'

'Good. Now this is important. You can do yourself a lot of good on this project, lad. You can also do yourself a great deal of harm. I know which of those two I want it to be, and I hope you do too. And above all, it's highly confidential. All will become clear, but for the time being if anyone asks, mum's the word. Refer 'em to me. Good. Snap to!'

'Conference room,' said Baxter.

'What?' I hadn't had time to take my jacket off, let alone unwrap the sticky bun I'd bought for my elevenses.

'Conference room. *Tout de suite*. Now.'

Baxter marched me out and locked the double doors behind us.

'I presume you've been discussing Eli,' he said.

'Who?'

'ELI. East London fucking Industries, you dozy bastard.'

'You're in a jolly mood, Bax.'

'I said, I presume you've been talking about ELI.'

'Can't say.'

'What?'

'Can't say, Bax. Our Leader's orders. Any questions, refer to him.'

'Now look, you little prick, don't get clever with me, I know what it's all about. As a matter of fact, I know a lot better than you do what it's all about.'

'Good. You won't have to ask me, then, will you, Bax?'

'Now look –'

'Ask Reggie.'

'All right, all right, you want to be smart, be smart. But I'll tell you one thing – '

'You didn't want me involved in this project, whatever it is, in the first place.'

'Correct.'

'That didn't take much guessing, Bax.'

'Are you trying to annoy me, London?'

'I'm not trying, Bax, no, but I'm pleased to see I'm doing it anyway.'

'Are you going to stop calling me *Bax*? You know I don't like it.'

'Sorry, old chap.'

'And one other thing I want to make clear. This project is no joke. Okay? It's important – really important; important for me, important for Reggie, important for the future of the firm; important for your future too, of which there won't be one if you put a foot out of line. Got it?'

'I think that's sufficiently clear for now, yes.'

'Good ... You know, London, what bothers me about you, what really bothers me about you – '

'Oh good. I was dying to ask. I know you think I'm a shit, Bax – I mean Buck – which might give you a fair idea of what I think of you.'

'It's not that you're a shit. At least, not only that you're a shit. Nor is it that you don't pull your weight. There are others round that desk who don't pull their weight, and I don't have to tell you who they are. Unprofessional. Too fat. Had it too good for too long. They don't care enough, and neither do you, and that's an attitude I don't like, because I believe if a job's worth doing it's worth doing well.

'Work hard and play hard, that's my philosophy, and if there were a few more round here who thought as I do we wouldn't be in the mess we're in. We'd be in the big league, with the Yank banks chasing round to buy us out. Instead of which, we're third division. When I think of the firms I could be working for – Christ! People think it's easy when your grandfather worked in the firm. They don't realise it brings responsibility too. *I* can't just chase the biggest mess of pottage. I've got to stay, get the firm back on its feet.'

'You should launch an appeal, Bax. You know I'd be the first to give.'

'There you go again. Proof of what I was about to say. You see, what really bothers me about you, London, is not the fact that you've made every cock-up in the cock-up manual since you came here, as well as one or two that aren't in the book; or the fact that you're the bone-idlest soldier it's ever been my privilege to encounter. No. It's the fact that you're a piss-taker, and piss-taking's one thing I can't hack. If you don't want to do something, you can at least let the next man get on with it. Them's my sentiments. So it's got to change, and change now. I want to see you working, all right? ... Got it?'

'Can I go and eat my bun now?'

'You can do what you like with it. But I'm warning you – no fuck-ups, or you're out. Clear? Out!'

From the little I knew about the company, I found it hard to imagine why Reggie had singled out East London Industries, plc, as the object of his attention. Four clear days, three trips to Companies

50

House, two to the Cripplegate Library and one to the Reading Room of the British Museum did little to solve the conundrum.

The unencouraging facts were clear enough, though. When old Elijah Flower, clothing manufacturer of Halifax, West Riding, found in March 1888 that his supplies of jute were again being interrupted en route from Bengal by disputes among the quarrelsome merchants of Port Said he decided it was finally time to get over there and sort them out himself. He had long thought it a nonsense that goods shipped from a British colony to a British destination should be bonded and factored by Mohammedans, but owing to some imagined conflict with the Egyptian cotton industry this was the current practice, as I confirmed by reference to Smollett's *History of the East India Company*.

With prophetic insight, Elijah realised that the establishment of a British-owned jute merchanting enterprise on the Canal would circumvent these continual dislocations and also deprive the Said middlemen of their quite unwarranted turn. To this end he bought his passage on *M.S. Triumphant*, where he was berthed next to a young Scot, James Wilkie, to whom he confided the details of his mission.

Wilkie was on his way to India to make his fortune but wanted first, at small extra cost, to see the Pyramids. The two men travelled to Cairo together. Elijah had heard that whoever drank the waters of the Nile would be sure to return one day, and having formed a favourable first impression of the country he eagerly did so, against young Wilkie's advice. Four days later he died of amoebic dysentery in his room at Shepheard's Hotel. Wilkie arranged for the body to be shipped back to Yorkshire in a barrel of brandy – an unfitting end for one who had been all his life Temperance.

Wilkie continued his journey, not stopping at Bombay as he had intended but continuing all the way to Calcutta and thence to the offices of the late Elijah Flower's chief suppliers in Chittagong. There, brandishing Elijah's seal and notepaper, he directed that all future shipments were to go via Jas. Wilkie & Co., forwarding agents of Port Said and Cairo. This arrangement was subsequently confirmed by Elijah's heirs.

The Flowers withered, but Wilkie flourished. He expanded. He factored for other shippers. He became rich. He built the Jute Wharf at the Imperial India Dock in London E. Profits grew annually, and in 1900 his chief accountant calculated with a prescience which in later years might have earned him a job as a securities analyst that by 1915 he would be the richest man in the world. Wilkie considered this unlikely, but the public and its brokers thought otherwise: in 1902 ninety per cent of the shares in the holding company, Cairo & Oriental Jute, were issued at a high price on the London Stock Exchange. The Great War proved ruinous. James Wilkie retired to a mansion on the banks of Loch Lomond. His only son, Ronald, wished he could have lived in the nineties and wrote short novels so exquisite that he was obliged to pay for their publication. He died of pneumonia after attending his father's funeral in May, 1926.

For the next thirty years the company made slow progress under the guidance of a series of professional managers, usually retired India Civil Servants or former employees of the great trading houses in the East. The facilities at Jute Wharf were mechanised, extended, upgraded and finally flattened in the Blitz. After the War the land on which the Wharf had stood and the surrounding acreage were packaged into a property division and sold to the London County Council for housebuilding, though the houses were never built.

With the proceeds of the sale Cairo Jute, as it was now called, purchased a thriving cotton-plantation in the Nile Delta and a number of high-grade jute estates in Bengal, known by then as East Pakistan. In a demonstration of loyalty to King Farouk all these new acquisitions were assigned to the ownership of the Egyptian trading arm of the group rather than directly to the holding company in London, and such was the goodwill generated by this gesture that when Jas. Wilkie & Co., forwarding agents of Port Said and Cairo were nationalised in 1957 the estates were also confiscated. Reggie Goddard and other shareholders complained bitterly and fired their directors, but nothing could be done.

Cairo Jute was bereft. Its shares languished. The company was mentioned as a potential candidate for a takeover bid, but predators soon discovered that its only assets were the leasehold on an office above a wet fish shop in the Commercial Road and a lawsuit against the Republic of Egypt. A small balance of cash was enough to pay the accountant's fee and the travelling expenses of the three directors.

In 1967 David Epstein, property developer of Hampstead Garden Suburb, relieved them of the burden this journey imposed by purchasing their shares and appointing himself chairman of the company, the name of which he changed to Limehouse Estates. No-one could see the reason for this move. I managed to trace one of David Epstein's former business associates, the only one not in hiding, who commented: 'No comment, mate. David's mouth was as tight as his fist, and you can guess what that was as tight as. You could ask his brother.'

52

'Where's he?'

'Pentonville. But he wouldn't tell you even if he knew. Which he don't.'

At the age of thirty-seven David Epstein dropped dead of a heart attack at Bloom's Restaurant in Whitechapel High Street. 'A tragedy, a tragedy,' I was told. 'Some said it was the lockshen pudding. But I'll say one thing for David – '

'Yes?'

'He was a businessman to the end. Went like a real pro. I was wiv him. It wasn't just that we hadn't paid the bill, though of course we hadn't, and never did. But it was more than that. He went like a property man ought to go. We was just discussing how to get rid of a family from this promising little situation in Stepney Green – you know, mother and four, that sort of thing, not easy – and bang! Over he goes, just like that. As a matter of fact he was trying to say something about the old Jute Wharf when he passed on. Must have been going back, you see. They say you do. But I couldn't make it out. And the number of times I heard his old mum tell him not to speak with his mouth full.'

Epstein's stake changed hands several times over the years. The fashions that brought the entrepreneurs in – skateboards, dartboards, home computers – also got them carried away. In 1983 Swraj 'Call me Tony' Patel, clothing manufacturer of Tottenham, became chairman and Limehouse Estates became East London Industries; ELI for short. For the thirty per cent of the company he now owned, Patel had paid £360,000 in cash but not, as was rumoured, in used banknotes. For this sum he acquired just under three million shares at twelve pence a share. In the Market these shares now stood at ten, valuing the whole company at exactly a million pounds. Its assets were a string of sweatshops in Poplar, Bow and Mile End which had he been allowed access would have had Her Majesty's Inspector of Factories reaching for his cut-throat razor and Patel for his styptic pencil; or so I surmised. The company's earnings were negligible.

When I rang Patel he became concerned that I should form a fair impression of what his company was doing and where it was going; or at least a different impression from the one I'd already formed. They were all the same, these small company operators. You only had to mention you were a stockbroker and their eyes would light up at the thought of what you might do for their share price. Although this did not involve seeing the factories it did entail lunch at the Savoy.

The first thing he did when he arrived, his minder discreetly cracking his knuckles a few yards behind, was to take a long look at my clothes. I returned the compliment but refrained from commenting on the disparity. He was wearing several times my net worth. Whereas my suit and even my shoes shone in places, Tony Patel shone all over.

I might have explained that some of us liked to display what we had and some of us didn't: but it would have been hard to express without giving offence. It was also true that some of us didn't like to show what we had because we had nothing to show. In any case, no one who chose to dress as he did would have understood why anyone who chose to dress as I did, did: even if I had chosen. He rubbed my lapel between finger and thumb and smiled, affording me a quick glimpse of something akin to what Howard Carter must have seen when he first looked into the tomb of Tutankhamen.

'I made it,' he said. 'Not personally, of course, and not terribly recently, but yes, I made this suit. It's wearing quite well, don't you think?'

'I'm pleased with it,' I said. I'd been pleased with it for a long time.

'Built to last,' he said.

We ate in the Riverside Room, overlooking the Embankment, surrounded by the usual crew of dealmakers and PR men. For starters I ordered half a dozen Pagglesham Number Ones.

'Not a dozen?' Patel asked. 'I'm sure you could manage a dozen.' With a show of reluctance I agreed.

'No starter for me. Must watch my weight,' he said. The make-him-feel-greedy trick had been tried on me before: when he handed me the wine list I ordered a Meursault Blagny to show I wasn't going to be intimidated. Disappointingly he looked at the label and indicated that he wanted some too. I gulped the first glass quickly, hoping we might make it to the second bottle. It was wonderful. After a magnum of something similar Margaret and I had once slow-waltzed round the living-room of our newly-acquired house in Clancarty Road, SW6, to the tune of 'I know that my Redeemer liveth'.

'Well chosen,' said Patel. 'Delicious. And even more delicious when one reflects that the tax-man is footing a large part of the bill.'

It came as no surprise that for the purposes of Patel versus HM Commissioners for Inland Revenue I, London London of Wootton, Derbyshire and Ladbroke Grove W11, was deemed to be an over-seas resident and therefore tax-allowable. As the only taxpayer present I felt it my duty to extract compensation in kind. From now on I was eating for England.

'Ah – your oysters. Something I've never tried.'

'Have you not? Take one.'

'Thank you, no. My father warned me off them when I was a boy. But these are very big ones.'

'Uhnnng – enormous,' I replied.

'Tell me – what exactly do they taste like?'

Professional discretion prevented me from telling him exactly.

'Brine,' I said. 'Sea water.'

'The world is your oyster,' he replied, a sentiment I couldn't claim to share. My own image, had I been contemplating the cosmos in terms of seafood, would have been of life as a giant clam which had me trapped full fathom five with the oxygen running out.

'Your oyster,' he repeated. 'I have always liked that expression.'

I could tell this was the lead-in to his party-piece, namely the lecture on where his company was going and how I could help it get there, but with my mouth in flagrant delight there was nothing I could do to prevent it.

So it proved: 'As a matter of fact, quite by chance,' he continued, 'this is my motto in business. The world's our oyster. A fact which most of our compatriots in the business world seem to overlook, don't you think?'

'Mmm – ah – mmmgh,' I said, nodding vigorously.

What they all forgot, it transpired, was that in Britain we still had the finest brains and the finest workforce in the world, *bar none*. What was more, we had a workforce hungry for work. In Kenya, where Patel grew up, it had been different. All *they* were interested in was drinking, fighting, and you-know-whatting. So in a way the Patels' expulsion, their reward for too much enterprise, was a blessing in disguise. And their arrival in England had come at a particularly fortunate time – a time when Mrs T was rolling up all the old carpet and throwing it away, when people were starting to realise that the world didn't owe them a living, when hard work earned its reward. After all, these were the 1980s.

I tried to interject a question about how this analysis (his philosophy, he called it) was being applied to the fortunes of East London Industries. I presumed what he meant was that he employed pregnant women and immigrants on the run (not in itself an obstacle to share-price appreciation), but I didn't say so and nor did he. While I chomped my way through a Newlyn sole poached in cream and armagnac, garnished with Beluga, he picked at a plain grilled trout and offered his thoughts on the decline of the West.

At some point in this disquisition I noticed a change in his manner. He was relaxing; or perhaps I was. The less wine there was in the bottle the less he sounded like a Brick Lane wide-boy and the more like a cross between David Niven and Pandit Nehru. Now I came to think of it, he was a handsome man, strong-faced, hair slightly greying. He'd have looked splendid in one of Nehru's frock-coats. Certainly it would have done him more justice than the glistening mohair he was wearing now. The suit also went badly with the 'old boy' tone he adopted when telling me that all his workers wanted was something to do and a bit of pocket-money at the end of the week. The essential thing was not to mix the races. That only led to trouble, and no one would thank you for it; only the bloody stupid politicians who didn't know there arse from their elbow. Ideas, ideas, he said. Such dangerous things.

'They are,' I said. The only idea I had at that moment was the notion that in ten years' time, if the company did well, he'd be hob-nobbing in Chelsea, 'Tony' to his friends, and pretending to have gone to Harrow; and nobody would care if he had or he hadn't, provided he footed the bill.

'Furthermore,' he was saying when I next tuned in, 'I can hardly deny that I would like to see our shares at a more realistic level.' He meant higher. 'Then we can issue some paper and begin our expansion. You do see what we're trying to do?'

I was losing concentration. I'd already lost it enough to order profiteroles for pudding and a half of Château Climens to go with them. (I almost went the whole hog and asked for Yquem. Gluttony is a charge that cuts no ice with me. I've been kicked around enough. I deserve to be pampered. But the charge of vulgarity I couldn't stand. The profiteroles were anomalous.) After pushing that lot back I thought a little brandy might assist my digestion and Patel broke off from analysing the problems of democracy to order me a very large Hine. Whether by the time it arrived I'd have noticed the difference between it and a glass of motor oil, I can't say. The low winter sun, I saw, was sparkling on the river.

The solar system being what it is, the same sun sat slap in the middle of the eastern sky the next morning expressly to shine over Reggie Goddard's shoulder and into my throbbing eyes.

'Oh yes, it's obvious enough what he's up to,' I said with some authority. 'Jack up the share price, knock out a bit of stock at the new improved level in exchange for unprofitable assets, sweat the assets for a year or two, get known in the Market as the next big winner and sell out at the top of the cycle.'

In the form of a wracking vibration through my head each of these words, strung together with such easy eloquence, making it all sound so simple, cost me another reminder of yesterday.

'Clever man,' Reggie said.

I shrugged my shoulders modestly.

'Patel,' he clarified.

'Oh – yes indeed.'

'Clever enough to get from nowhere to where he is, anyway. But how clever? That's the question. How clever?'

'Surely the real question is whether there's going to be anything in it for the shareholders. As soon as the cash starts flowing he'll be out with the milking machine.'

'You may be right, you may be wrong,' Reggie asserted. He rose, turned, faced the rising sun; sat, nodded, exhaled. 'You'd sell, then.'

'Wouldn't touch them.'

'Good. Yes indeed. Good work. Just tell me, though: what did you think of the assets?'

'A small amount of cash and a few low-grade workshops.'

'Not saleable?'

'Not for a lot.'

'You had a good look?'

'Yesterday afternoon,' I said. In a sense this was true, though not in the sense that it had actually happened. I *had* insisted on seeing the factories. Patel had reluctantly agreed to let me do so. Had I not been held back by an unprecedented attack of agoraphobia in the back of Patel's limousine (symptoms: panic, perspiration, nausea), I undoubtedly would have seen them. In the event, however, I had been obliged to retreat to College Gardens, there to spend the afternoon in a deep and dreamless sleep.

'Falling to pieces,' I elaborated. 'Shouldn't think they're worth more than fourpence a share.'

'And no potential?'

'No sign yet. And as I say, the moment they go up he'll be issuing more, so there's no hurry.'

'Good ... Good ... Now I'll tell you what I want you to do next.'

'Thank you,' I said, pathetically delighted that at last my professional acumen was being valued at its worth.

'You'd sell, eh?' he asked.

'I'd sell,' I confirmed.

'Right. The price is ten, you say?'

'Ten, yes.'

'Right. Well, what I want you to do is to go back to your desk and buy as many ELI as you can get at ten.'

'Buy?'

'Buy. Then as many as you can get at eleven. Then at twelve. As many as you can get. No half measures. Fortune favours the brave. Then let me know how you're getting on. Clear? Good,' said Reggie. 'Chop chop!'

At twenty to eleven I rang down to Ken in the Market and the buying began.

CHAPTER SIX

'Oh, it's you,' said Margaret in a tone suggesting she'd rather it were the man from the finance company come to repossess the cooker.

'Good morning,' said I.

'You're early.'

'Is he ready?'

'He's having his breakfast.'

'Shall I wait in the car?'

This was the tenth time I'd visited Radcliffe Hall, home of the Rainbow Co-operative, in Coulthard Street, E2, and I'd never yet been asked in.

'Oh, the *car*. Where did you get that?'

'Kenny Morgan lent me it.'

'Oh, him.'

'He's away. Scarborough. On a British Rail Golden Weekend. The heating's gone, though, so don't be long.'

The only consolation I'd had as I sat through a pre-Christmas traffic jam in the Euston Road, teeth chattering and hands turning blue, was the thought that at that very moment Ken would be having to take Jean and her mother for a bracing pre-lunch constitutional.

'Ben will freeze,' Margaret said.

'Wrap him up. We're not going far. Anyway, you're no doubt giving him a good solid English breakfast. That should keep him warm.'

'I can't stand here talking,' Margaret said. 'It's bitter.'

'Okay. Hurry him on, then, can you?'

'Well, you'd better come in.'

'Oh – may I?'

'Come in.'

The house, elegant but dilapidated, was in a street of such houses which had somehow escaped the enthusiasms of the town planners. Fifty yards down the road the tower-blocks began. Thinking of them as I stepped over the threshold (Motto: 'Begin to hope, all you who enter herein' in medieval Italian over the door-frame), I couldn't help thinking of my doctor friend and the good gone days

59

we'd had, high above the Isle of Dogs not very far from here.

The passageway through to the kitchen was full of a rich vanilla smell which I took to be stale incense. The walls were covered with the usual posters (fight cuts, fight Trident, fight Thatcher: these peace-lovers always like a good fight) and caricatures of Ronald Reagan dressed up as a monkey. Indian music from somewhere upstairs competed with rock. Children shouted and wailed. It was much as I'd imagined.

The kitchen, stretching to the back of the house, was bright green and there were more posters with slogans urging repentance on any high-livers, fur coat-wearers and Conservative voters who happened to visit the place. At the table, public park style with benches attached either side, a pale redhead was breast-feeding a baby with bright red hair and a chubby brown face.

'This is Jen,' said Margaret. 'This is London.'

I was glad I'd worn my jeans.

'London?' I thought she was about to make one of those side-splitting remarks about my name which have had me howling with laughter for the past quarter of a century, but all she said was, 'That's nice. This is Cal.' She had an Irish accent and marvellous eyes. Next to her sat Ben in a baby boiler-suit with a big '*Atomkraft? Nein danke*' sticker on his back, spooning up a bowl of something off-white.

'Here's Daddy,' Margaret said. Ben put his spoon down and I picked him up and hugged him. His hair was darkening. He looked more like Margaret every time I saw him: hard and lean. It must have been something in the lentils.

'How's my boy, then? How's my boy?' Ben struggled to get free.

'Do you think you should clean your teeth?' Margaret asked him.

'No.'

'Why not?'

'Why should I?'

'If you don't your teeth will drop out.'

'They will anyway. They're my first teeth. Ha!'

'I know that, but if you don't clean them –'

'Ben,' I said, 'scrub 'em.' Off he went.

'Short-term result,' said Margaret, but I wasn't in the mood for socialization theory.

'Any chance of a cup of coffee?' I asked. There was a pot gurgling on the stove by the back window.

'Help yourself.'

The room was full of good smells – coffee, mother's milk, bread baking. There was talk, laughter, movement. Children – forget the

60

squawking, I could cope with that – children were being raised. The place felt like a *home*, damn it. I could have imagined – oh yes, I could have imagined.

The window gave on to the garden, where a deep pit had been dug.

'What's this?' I quipped. 'The well of loneliness?'

'We're building a fallout shelter.'

'That can't be cheap.'

'We've got a grant.'

While I was drinking the coffee a small child pushed open the door and said, 'Poo-poo.'

'Poo-poo?' said Margaret. 'Have you done poo-poo? Good.'

'Good,' the child said. I couldn't tell its sex. It had cropped blond hair. Then Ben came in, laughing.

'Gabriel shitted on the carpet,' he said, clapping his hands. 'Ha!'

'On the carpet?' Margaret said to Gabriel. 'Good. Shall we go and find it? Everyone has to learn, don't they, Ben? Just as you had to.'

The object of concern wasn't hard to locate. It sat proudly in the middle of the hallway. 'Good,' Margaret repeated, scooping it up. As this operation was carried out another girl appeared from upstairs, also dressed in an overall, her short hair cut viciously into points. This one's child was dark-haired and golden, baked to prefection, with pretty Chinese eyes. For women without men, they seemed to be producing a remarkable number of babies.

I strapped Ben into the back seat and drove us down to the Island. I could just see his face in the mirror, framed by a yellow knitted bonnet, peeping over the neckline of his poncho. He was very quiet, frowning at a book Margaret had given him.

'You can read, then, can you?'

'Yes.'

'Good lad. What's the book?'

'Carmen.'

'Carmen? My God, that's heady stuff, Ben. Is it in English or French?'

'Don't know.'

'I think it's probably in English,' I said. You could never be sure, though. Margaret was a wonderful teacher. I wouldn't have put it past her to teach him to read French before English.

'I'm very clever,' Ben added. 'Jen says I'm very clever.'

'Watch it. Mozart was writing symphonies when he was your

61

age.' Ben ignored this lie. Perhaps he knew better.

The Approach, like many other pubs on the Isle of Dogs, was the only pre-War building in half a square mile or more. Like a church in the City, it was leant over on all sides. Billy Hyam was lucky, though, because one of the blocks had been turned over to students, who managed to reserve a portion of their modest stipends to spend in the public bar.

The students were never there on Saturday mornings, presumably needing to lie in after a hard night's rutting. The bar was left to the old stagers like Brian and Kath, and the one who always wore a suit; then there was Frank with his dogs, John with his eels, and Grace with her artificial foot.

'Oh, Christ,' said Frank, 'look who's 'ere. Go on, Shane, bite his leg off. No offence, Gracie. Go on, boy. We don't want no bleedin' once-a-monthers in this pub.'

Shane didn't budge. He was halfway through a dish of Guinness.

'Mind your language,' Gracie said, 'he's brought the boy. What a darling!'

Ben hid behind my legs.

''allo, son,' said Frank. 'What's that you're wearing, a spud bag?'

'Leave off,' said Grace. 'He's a lovely lad. Aren't you, son?'

'He wants the Gents',' I said.

'No I don't.'

'Oh yes you do.'

'*You* do.'

'I do, that's right. Is Bill about?'

'Changing the barrel,' said Brian from the bar. Between us the sun was catching on cigarette smoke. 'Nice to see you.'

'Nice to see you, Brian. I'll have a quick half when he comes. I'll just take the lad to the Gents'.'

'Right,' I said once we were in there. 'Let's get this lot off and put you some nice clothes on.'

'What for?'

'Because look, I've brought you your jeans and boots. Something different for you.'

'But I like my poncho, Daddy.'

'Do you? Well, you like these others things, too, don't you? And I've brought them here specially for you.'

While he was thinking I whipped off the poncho and unzipped the boiler-suit. We quickly buttoned him into jeans, jersey and anorak, but his boots were suddenly too tight. The plastic wellingtons he was wearing were cute but cold.

'Shall we go and buy you some more boots? Eh? Would you like some warm boots?'

'I like my wellies.'

'You can have wellies *and* boots.'

Ben's change of style went down well with the crowd. I sat him on the bar next to the pumps and drank my half.

'Anything for the lad?' said Billy Hyam. 'On the house, this one.'

'Mine's a pint,' said Frank.

'You know what you'll get. What would you like, son?'

Ben put his face to my shoulder. Billy, small and grey, dour, a man who could laugh without smiling, shuffled to the optics and came back with a small glass of Advocaat.

'Here you are, son.'

'Come on, Ben. Pep up. Uncle Bill's got you a drink.'

'Uncle?' said Frank. 'Great uncle, more like.'

Ben clutched the glass and hid his face again.

'Thanks, Bill. He's not used to having all these men around him. Your health.'

'Still with his mother, is he?'

'He is, but it looks as if we may be able to appeal it again. I don't know. I expect it's money down the drain.'

'They're a band of rogues, these lawyers. A band of rogues.'

'Come on, Ben. Try it. You'll like it. Here – ' I dipped my finger in his glass and pushed it to his mouth   'try it like this.' He tried it. 'Nice?'

'Yas,' said Ben. He raised his glass and tipped back the yellow goo.

'Make it a double next time,' I said.

'On the 'ouse?' said Frank. 'You'll be lucky!'

'You're barred, Frank,' said Billy.

It wasn't like having a home, but it was better than College Gardens.

Oxford Street was like Wembley Way on Cup Final day. The crowd heaved, the buses parped, the man with the sandwich board, the 'Less Protein, Less Passion' man, was pushed and buffeted, his slogan swaying overhead. I had to carry Ben round the shoe shops for fear of losing him.

'This is a good one, Ben. Let's try here,' I said. 'I tell you what: we'll get you something here and if you don't like them I'll buy you another pair for Christmas. Good?'

'Good.' Like his mother, Ben believed in providing for contingencies, especially at my expense. His aesthetic criteria, however, were severe. So far we'd been to four or five shops and the only thing to have caught his eye was a pair of blue ankle-length wellies identical to those he was wearing. This, added to the customary friendliness, efficiency and courtesy of the British shopgirl, was tempering my wonted bonhomie.

'Good,' said Ben. 'Two pairs.'

My mother taught me all I know about shoes. I looked on smugly as a poor family bought their child a pair of slickly-cut Space Walkers, life expectancy two months. No wonder they were poor.

'I want those,' said Ben.

'Sssh.'

'That's what I want. Those.'

'We have to wait our turn.'

We waited our turn, then waited while the family's other child had hysterics, then while the assistant had a giggle with her friend, then I asked for a pair of leather boots.

'For this one?' the girl said. She had a bright purple stain on her neck and a rich, confident voice. 'We haven't got leather in his size.'

'I want the others,' Ben said. 'Daddy, I want the others.'

'I don't like the others, Ben.'

'Daddy, I want them. Daddy!'

'He wants the Space Walkers, but they don't last five minutes, do they?'

'Dunno,' she said, chewing. She was about sixteen. 'They're not too bad. The kids all want them.'

'I know,' I lied. 'Haven't you anything stronger?'

'They don't go so much for the strong ones these days.'

'Daddy!'

'Ben, don't do this to me.'

The girl giggled again. My collar was getting tighter.

'There's always the Rocky boots,' she said.

'Oh God, no, I daren't.'

'Daddy, please!'

'You can't have the Space Walkers, Ben. Don't you know they're sexist? Mummy would hate them.'

'Mummy hates you.'

'Ben! I think we'd better try somewhere else, thanks.'

'You could put them on, see how they look,' the girl suggested, not very helpfully.

'No, I think we'd better, er –'

Ben's previous remark had already silenced all other conversations. He looked at me with such malice as he could muster and said, 'You're no good in bed.'

'What did you say?'

'Mummy says, you're no good in – '

I clamped my hand on his mouth.

We dropped the car at Lancaster Gate. Ben sprang out and jumped up and down, pounding the pavement with his Space Walkers. As I was closing the back door I noticed his book lying on the seat. It was the story of Carmen, a little girl from Trinidad who wanted to play cricket.

We took a ball into the park and kicked it around for a while. Ben's chief aim seemed to be to reduce his boots to tatters in as short a time as possible. He'd had enough of football, I decided, at about the same time as I started getting short of breath, and we went for a walk by the duck-pond.

'Here's some bread, Ben. See if they want it.'

He ran to the edge of the water and threw a whole slice.

'Look, Daddy. They're fighting! More.'

He threw the next slice nearer, and when they came up to take it he kicked mud at them.

'Ha!' He clapped his hands.

'Going to be a trouble-maker when you grow up, Ben? Eh? I think you've all the makings of the school bully.'

'Doctor,' he said.

'A doctor? Is that what Mummy says?'

'Yas.'

'Good lad. That's a nice steady job for a son of toil.'

The park was cold and glittering, empty for the time of year. A few people were taking riding lessons, a few jogging, a few taking brisk strolls.

'Shall we see the horses, Ben?'

We went over to the gallops. Most of the customers were being led round slowly, looking bored and foolish. We walked down the side of the track. In the distance I spotted a horse rear and run.

'Look, Ben. Here comes a fast one.'

It was a big chestnut with a white breast and white tape round its front feet. As it got closer I saw that the rider was a woman; a girl; a blonde, most of her hair tucked under the hard hat but some of it escaping. She was shouting at the horse. Her mouth was open, her eyes grim; her features mobile, perfect, familiar. Hair of flax, eyes of sapphire, teeth of pearl: it was Lucy Trender, I realised as she thundered past without a glance.

Then there was another roar. I looked round to see a second horse, a man astride it, the man the image of confidence, relaxed, in pursuit but biding his time, knowing he would catch her when he wanted.

Shit. It was Baxter.

CHAPTER SEVEN

Sprawled in his chair with his feet on the desk and looking like one who had recently stepped off the set of 'The Great Gatsby', Baxter popped a scarcely necessary parma violet into his mouth and said, 'Good morning, London. Nice of you to come in.'

'Good morning,' I replied, though it was Monday.

'*Ça va?*'

'So-so. You?'

'*Très bien*. But if I were you I'd have his balls.'

'Oh yes?' I said, wincing at the prospect of one of Baxter's breezy early-morning jests. 'Whose balls are those?'

'The bugger that drives the Tube's. Always seems to get you here late.'

'Oh, him – yes – he seems to have it in for me.'

'Perhaps you should try the earlier one. I'm told he's much more reliable.'

'Perhaps you could ask your chauffeur to give me a lift.'

'Can't afford a chauffeur,' Baxter replied. 'Not with what we pay you.'

I ignored this remark. Baxter had a talent, even when he wasn't trying, for making me feel worse than before. In one so coarse his ability to tap the springs of regret was uncanny.

Hanging my jacket on the back of the chair, I unwrapped a buttered bun and provoked a further observation from Baxter, this one linking my eating habits with my recent showing in the boxing ring. A gentleman, it seemed, was expected to have taken breakfast before leaving for work. Baxter himself could have a mid-morning dish of kedgeree, oh yes, but that kind of rakish indifference to convention was quite another thing.

To show how keen I was I switched my Topic machine on and stared at a few prices. Since the Market was not yet open, none of them had changed since Friday night. Round the desk, where all twelve places were now occupied, some of the boys were discussing the weekend's golf while others shared their expertise with clients in Rome and Geneva.

'What?' said one. 'Thinking of selling some Chemical? Good idea. I think you should.'

'What's that?' said another. 'Thinking of buying some Chemical? Right. I wouldn't put you off.'

At the top of the table Fat Percy's attempt to merge his receiver with the underside of his chin suggested he was advising a prized client to do himself a favour and have a few of these. Later in the morning he'd be counselling the big institutions to do the same, and when they piled in and moved the price up there would be a nice turn in it for the fat man and his chum. To Percy's left, John-boy was exploring an alternative method of getting rich quick, scrutinizing this afternoon's investments in the *Sporting Life*. They couldn't say we didn't offer comprehensive coverage.

I was on the point of putting myself abreast of world events with a quick flick through the *Daily Express* when Baxter clapped his hands.

'Parade! Parade! All present and correct? Right, you 'orrible lot, get fell in. Parade!'

Fat Percy made a noise like a bugle. The desk rose as one. Calls were terminated, sleeves adjusted to show exactly an inch of shirt-cuff. Rogers & Prickett men always wore jackets to a meeting, no matter how informal. Despite being in the forefront of the financial services revolution the firm retained its links with the past. As our advertising said, we liked to think we had the best.

Of the old.

And of the new.

Parade, Reggie Goddard constantly affirmed, was a powerhouse for the rest of the day's activities. It was the arena in which ideas could flow and the forum in which barriers could be broken down. Where Reggie had acquired his mastery of metaphor I couldn't say; but I did know that the only flow generated by Parade was a steady stream of applications for jobs elsewhere. As for breaking down barriers within the firm, the success of Parade in achieving that laudable goal was demonstrated by the fact that the boys from the gilts desk sat at one end of the long table, the equity salesmen at the other and the analysts generally somewhere between. The atmosphere, moreover, was imbued with all the warmth, friend-liness and relaxed good humour of the Nuremburg Trials, each group sniping the others with reminders of recent atrocities.

Further to lower the barriers that divided them, each group maintained its own strict dress codes. In their own estimation

Baxter's team, the equity salesmen, in near-Italian slip-on shoes and racy pink shirts, were the best dressed of the lot. (I was the exception that proved the rule.) But the gilts desk, in shiny collars and minutely-knotted ties, would have disputed this claim. These two groups jointly looked down on the third, the bearded and bespectacled analysts, who bought their suits off the peg and their shirts God alone knew where (a secret He kindly let me in on). The job of the analysts, as Baxter was kind enough to remind them from time to time, was to come up with ideas which the salesmen would then push to the clients, earning commission for the firm if they dealt and tempting punters with the lure of big profits and free lunches. The advice could be to buy or sell; long term, or short term; solid or speculative or straightforward invention. As long as it turned the clients from fear to greed it was a winner as far as we were concerned.

'Right,' said Baxter. 'Market?'

All eyes searched to see who was here from the dealers. When they weren't here the dealers were condemned for life to wander the floor of the Stock Exchange, checking prices, passing on jokes about the latest natural disaster and buying or selling stocks at the behest of the desk.

'Easier all round. Opening ten points down,' said Kenny Morgan. Ken, forty years old, married with three (the bitch and the batch, he called them), pink of face, long of limb, short of hair, was my only ally at Rogers & Prickett. Until recently I'd had two, but the other, Lenny Morgan, Kenny's older brother, had twisted his back during a Friday afternoon caper on the floor and was now at home in traction.

'Easier,' said Baxter. 'Brilliant.' He didn't mean it. He meant the opposite. Falling markets made for miserable and therefore inactive clients. 'Any features?'

'Oils holding steady,' said Ken.

'Why's that, then? Sheikh!'

'Over here,' said a small and frightened voice. The Sheikh was the Rogers & Prickett oils analyst. He hadn't been with us very long. They had trouble finding a replacement when the old oils man left. No one wanted to admit they'd sunk so low. Then this poor sod poked his head over the parapet, clutching a degree in geology and wanting to be something in the City. Since he was on the happy side of twenty-five my sympathy, though great, was limited.

'Why are the oils holding up, Sheikh?'

'I think the Saudis are rumoured to be raising the price of crude.'

'Are they?' said Fat Percy.

'Er – yes.'

'Yes what?'

'Yes, Percy.'

'I mean are they fucking raising it or are they just fucking rumoured to be raising it?'

'Or are they just fucking?' said John-boy.

'They're – they're just rumoured to be.'

'So are they raising it?'

'I shouldn't think so, no.'

'Very useful,' said Baxter. 'Anything else from our highly-paid research department? Any other little money-spinners? Come on, girls, don't be shy.'

Responding to Baxter's challenge, the engineering analyst chipped in with three minutes on computer-aided design, two and a half of them successfully devoted to hastening my ulcer, and then the stores analyst stepped forward to say he thought the public would be doing a lot of shopping this Christmas. We had advised our clients to sell all their shares in retailers at the start of the year. They were obviously overpriced. The revolution in the high street had unfortunately continued. All the nice old shops carried on disappearing, and shares in the big stores doubled. Now we were calling them a 'Buy'. (The electronics shares which we had persuaded many of the same clients to buy in immoderate amounts with the money raised from cashing in their retailers had, by contrast, fallen abysmally: now we were boldly changing our view to 'Sell'.) The analyst spoke for a long time and felt that everything depended on the government. This gave Baxter a chance to interrupt.

'Right,' he said. 'Perhaps the economics department would like to cast some light on this benighted gathering.'

'Yes, well,' said the economist, pushing his glasses up his nose. Twenty-seven years old, the economist had narrowly failed to be selected as Liberal candidate in the Finchley constituency, on the strength of which he was widely regarded as a Marxist. 'At eleven-thirty we're expecting the latest money supply figures.'

Four minutes and fifty-one, fifty-two, fifty-three seconds later by the digital clock on the wall I was reflecting that this mesmerising bore did have one redeeming feature: apart from the constant references to motorways (M1, M2, M3: who cared where he was going as long as he was going?), everything he said was incomprehensible. Just at that moment the door opened and in came Reggie.

'Morning, chaps,' he said. The chaps responded in kind.

Baxter leapt up to offer his chair.

'No thanks, Buck. I've only dropped in for a second. Am I interrupting?'

'Not at all,' said Baxter. 'We were just discussing the money supply figures.'

Reggie's brow darkened. The economy was another subject on which he tended to share the last opinion he had heard.

'Mmm,' he said. 'Actually it was last week's commission figures I was thinking about. They didn't seem terribly good. Is there some reason for that?'

'Market very weak,' said Baxter.

'Market dull as ditch water,' said Fat Percy.

'Flat as piss,' said John-boy.

'Fair enough, fair enough. Can't make a silk purse out of a sow's ear, can we? Nothing much we can do about that, is there? Keep up the good work. Any stories today?'

'Not a lot,' said Baxter.

'Bit of a buzz on the oil price,' said Fat Percy. 'Could do some biz on the back of that.'

'Good,' said Reggie. 'Good to see we're on the ball. I want this meeting to be a powerhouse – a powerhouse.' He nodded a few times and left.

'So now we know,' said John-boy. 'Wherever would we be without him?'

'Anything else?' Baxter asked. 'Right. Let's go.'

I waited for Kenny Morgan by the door.

'How's it going?' he asked.

'Pretty badly so far.'

'Snap. There's a word for people like Fat Percy, though.'

'I know, but I'm too polite to use it.'

'And he's not the only one. Oh dear me!' Ken was suddenly gawping over my shoulder. I turned to see that Lucy Trender had arrived in the office, leaving the swing doors bouncing behind her. As she walked along she was taking off her coat to reveal a short dress in yellow and green check, belted tightly at the waist.

'That shouldn't be allowed,' said Ken. 'Not on a Monday morning. Wicked, that is. Talk about a firm market.'

'Imagine the performance.'

'I do, mate, every time I see it.'

'And it's got the asset backing. But there's bad news on that stock, sport.'

'What bad news? Not fully subscribed, is it?'

'I'll tell you down the Tuns. Half twelve?'

'Better make it one.'

'I'll be there.'

I stopped off briefly at the coffee machine in the hope of another glimpse of Lucy's golden thighs, but she wasn't there. Back at the desk, hoping to prove it was a man's job really, the boys were in a panic: buttons were pressed, keys punched, prices flashed up on screens; telephones grabbed, telephonists barked at, dealers paged, traced and argued with; cigarettes lit, heads scratched, fingers tapped.

Baxter, cooler than the rest, was gently wheedling and cajoling. Most of his clients were chums from school or the Regiment, and to those whose misfortune it was not to have belonged to either of those establishments his attitude was, he often boasted, professional. 'That's something you learn in the Army,' he liked to add. 'In these days of fair shares for all there's no knowing who'll be giving the orders, especially at Brigade level, and there's no point either in hanging round asking where the CO got his accent. If he says jump, you jump. Same with these buggers, our dearly beloved clients. Blacks, commies, queers – I'll deal for anybody. And I'll call 'em "Sir". That's business. That's what it's all about.'

I spoke to Ken on the radio to ask how we were getting on in ELI. Since Friday morning we had bought three hundred thousand shares on rising prices. The shares were now twelve pence. After telling Ken to go on buying I turned my attention to the few third-rate clients whose very occasional dealings with Rogers & Prickett had earned them a place on my list of contacts. Most of them, when I got through, developed sudden attacks of urgent business elsewhere. Finally I tried #1 on my autodial. 'Oils,' I wrote on my pad. 'No rise – sell into rally.'

'*Terminalgoodmorning*,' a woman's voice sang.

'Mr Harbottle, please.'

After a pause, during which she had doubtless raised my prime client from his morning snooze, she said: 'Who's speaking, please?'

I told her.

After a further pause, during which Harbottle would have groaned in despair and asked her to think of something, she said: 'I'm afraid he's tied up at the moment, sir. Can I take a message?'

You too, brute, I thought. 'Just say I rang, please.' I didn't greatly mind being trodden on. After all, I was only a stockbroker. But when it came from Harbottle, a fellow jumped-up Northern intellectual who'd rather be in a beach-hut somewhere translating the Odyssey, I resented it. I knew I was the last shit in the investment

72

business but I didn't like being treated as such by the penultimate.

'You know what they say about money,' Kenny Morgan said, raising an eyebrow and leaning towards me over the table some time after one o'clock that day.

'Do I?'

'Money goes to money. That's what they say.'

'Unto him that hath shall more be given.'

'What's that, the Stock Exchange Gazette? It is depressing, though. Same again?'

Over the first pint I'd told Ken about the riding lesson, and over the second we had reached outline agreement on what we thought of it. We were sitting in the corner at one of the Square Mile's less fashionable houses, the Three Tuns. It was one of the few the dralon covers and brass lamps hadn't yet got to. Also, jeans were allowed, which they weren't in the smarter places, so that it was thronged every lunchtime by workmen from the building sites sucking up plates of sausage and mash (not a gramme of smoked mackerel pâté in sight, thank God), which had the further advantage of ensuring that Baxter and his cronies were never to be encountered there.

Ken came back with two more pints.

'Thanks, Ken. Here's to the past. Here's to the day I went into the City. Why am I a broker, Ken?'

'Cheers. I don't know, mate. Why are you?'

'Because the ex would have to work if I went down a coal mine. Mind you, so would I. But I wouldn't have to see Baxter every day.'

'*Nil carborundum*. Who'd want to be Baxter, anyway? Apart from me and you, that is. I don't suppose you've asked him if he had a good ride?'

'Wouldn't give him the satisfaction.'

We discussed what we would give Baxter if we had the chance, then I bought another round. Ken wanted to know what all the fuss was about in East London Industries – ''cos I thought you went to see old Meat Madras and said you wouldn't touch 'em with a bhaji.'

'I wouldn't. And how many have we bought?'

'Half a bar.'

'Five hundred thousand. Five per cent of the company. And what are they now?'

'Thirteen p.'

'Brilliant, eh? No stock, strong demand, and Bob's your uncle, up thirty per cent in two days. Matter of fact, I got a call from Chicken Bhuna this morning. Wanted to know if we were the ones doing the buying.'

'Tell him?'

'Why not?'

'I should think he's well pleased with you.'

'Oh God, yes. Asked me when I was on for the next tranche of luncheon. I said we should leave it a few weeks, till things settle. He's sending me a case of whisky instead.'

'Have they booked 'em yet?'

They hadn't: the shares had not been allocated. They were sitting in a suspense account waiting to have an owner assigned.

'So Reggie's breaking the rules,' Ken observed.

'Must be.'

'And you've no idea who the client might be?'

'Oh, I think I'm developing a very good idea of who the client might be.'

'Oh yes? I wonder if that's the same idea as I'm developing? Someone with the initials R.G., perhaps?'

'Chinaman to a clockwork orange,' I said. Or should it have been a clockwork orange to a Chinaman? Or a clockwork Chinaman to an orange? There were times when my attempts at East End vernacular led to confusion. 'But what does Reggie Goddard want with five per cent of ELI?' I pondered.

'Couldn't tell you, mate. But it sounds like we should be having a dabble for ourselves.'

'They're embargoed.'

'That wouldn't stop us buying a few round the corner, would it?'

'We'll need to find out a bit more first. We need to make sure it's not one of Reggie's hunches.'

'Let it be so. Oh – you've reminded me – wouldn't be interested in a microwave, would you? Cheap, like.'

'How many have you got?'

'Not me. Mole. Fourteen dozen, I believe.'

'Direct from the factory?'

'Very direct.'

'Not this time.'

'Oh. Oh, but I tell you what else: fancy an evening out Friday? Jean's off on a ladies' night. Some fashion show, it's supposed to be. More like a minibus to Romford for the wrestling, if you ask me, but it gets her out of the way. One or two in the Green Man, then down the West End, I thought.'

'You've dealt ... One for the road?'

'Churlish not to, old fellow.'

We made our way back after the fourth pint, nodding to a few stragglers on the way. I asked Ken how his brother was.

'Len? Hard to say. One doc says this, another says something else. First it's a slipped disc, then it's lumbar trouble. Still on his back, anyway.'

'I'll come down and see him one of the days.'

'I'll tell him. Keep it up.'

'I would if I could.'

As I crept in Lenny Morgan's health was again under discussion. Fat Percy, glowing, a king-size Romeo and Juliet projecting from his mouth, was calling Len an idle bastard. One or two others were agreeing.

'Not as idle as this fucker,' said John-boy. I was about to respond in acid vein when I noticed he was wearing an earpiece and must be tuned in to the 3.15. Wack Boy trundled in fourth. Baxter, meanwhile, was maintaining dental hygiene with his great-grand-father's ivory toothpick. According to Baxter this relic, set in gold, had passed into the clan's possession following the battle of Rorke's Drift.

'London!' he said. 'Good to see you, boy! Nice lunch?'

'Not bad for the price. The Tuns. Shepherd's pie, broad beans, treacle pud – two-fifty the lot. You've got to call it value.'

'Bump into a lot of clients there, do you?'

'The more discerning.'

'Yours are all discerning, from what I can make out. They seem pretty fussy about who they do business with.'

He pushed the toothpick between a canine and a molar. Had it still been attached to that whence it was hewn I could have suggested somewhere else he might care to insert it; but as it was I pointed out that I'd been working on the ELI business for the last week, hadn't I?

'Oh, of course. I knew there must be some logical explanation. What about the week before?'

'The week before I was compiling a list of all the things I like about you, Bax. A very time-consuming activity.' Without the four pints I wouldn't have spoken like that: but what's drink for if not to make a difference?

'Oh,' Baxter said as I sat down, 'there's a message on your desk. See it? Reggie was looking for you. Had to tell him we didn't know where you were. Your diary didn't give much of a lead.'

'Thanks, Bax.'

'Pleased to be of service.'

The note was in Reggie's own hand. 'Open red account name of Inter-Commerz Anstalt', it read. The address was in Zurich. A red account was one whose dealings were kept secret from the rest of the firm. This meant that they were not recorded with the salesman's name on the Mousetrap, a sheet of the previous day's business that went round the office each morning. As a rule I avoided looking at this document, not least because of the infrequency with which my own name appeared on it and the ubiquitousness of the name 'Baxter'. I'd been looking forward to seeing a few hundred thousand ELI chalked up against my name. 'Book all ELI to this account, then see me', the note continued. 'Destroy this. RG.' I slipped it into my top drawer, ostentatiously tearing up an economics briefing-note for Baxter's benefit, and filled in the appropriate form.

I put my jacket on and was about to obey Reggie's penultimate instruction when John-boy winked in a way which could only mean one thing.

'Eyes right, chaps,' he said. Every head turned as Lucy Trender swung past the desk.

'Thirty-four-six,' someone suggested.

'Buy,' said another.

'Do they do options in that one?' asked a third.

'What do you think, Perce?' said John-boy. 'High beta? Out-performs in a rising market?'

I watched Baxter closely. He glanced up, then punched the auto-dial and concentrated on the phone. Lucy didn't look his way at all, but beneath her eyes I spotted the clinching evidence of a certain late-night puffiness.

When she was gone I went in to see our leader. Doris had had her hair done again. The curls had gone and what was left had been straightened out, ageing her by a decade.

'Blimey, Doris. I thought they'd got a teenager in for the day.'

'Do you like it?'

'It's terrific. Going to a disco?'

'I would if they had them for my age, I tell you. I was a fair dancer, you know.'

'How would I know? I wasn't born then.'

'Cheeky monkey! I'll slap your legs for you.'

'Ooh – when?'

'I'll give you when. Anyway, bad luck, she's not here.'

'She?' I said, hinting at outrage that I should be classed among the Lucy-watchers.

'She. Lady Muck.'

'I was here to see the Führer, actually. Aren't you getting on with her?'

'The way she treats me?'

'She probably needs a bit more time to settle in.'

'I'll tell you what she needs,' said Doris. Having a good idea of the way Doris's mind ran on matters of chastisement, I suspected the thought she was about to put into my head was one I'd rather were not there. 'She needs to be taken over somebody's knee – '

'Oh don't, D.'

'Eh? Taken over somebody's knee and given a good spanking.'

'Do you think that could be arranged, D?'

The connecting door opened and Reggie leaned out.

'Ah, good, you're here . . . Come in . . . Sit down . . . You've done the booking, have you?' He closed the door behind us.

'I have, yes.'

'And you've opened the account?'

'Yes.'

'Red?'

'Red, yes, Reggie.'

'So: you've opened a red account *and* you've done the booking.'

'That's right,' I said. Why did everyone round here talk to me like a fool? I knew there must be an answer to this question.

'Good,' said Reggie. 'Very good. Splendid. Price?'

'Fourteen,' I guessed.

'Fourteen. You checked it just now, did you?'

'Yes,' I said, my auto-lie leaping into action. Then my job-preservation mechanism came into play: 'Or in fact that was before lunch,' I added, 'but I did ask to be kept in touch with any change.'

'Let's be sure, shall we?' he said. 'A stitch in time saves nine.' He leaned out again and spoke to Doris.

'Now,' he continued. 'How many have we got so far?'

'We've taken another fifty, twenty-five at a half –'

'Forget the prices. How many are we up to?'

'Four hundred and eighty thousand.'

'And what's the position now?'

'We've bought every share in the Market. If we try buying any more we'll just be forcing the price up against ourselves.'

The telephone rang. Reggie said 'Good' to it and put it down.

'Fourteen before lunch, were they? Well, they're sixteen and a half now. Good. Now tell me: have you ever met Sir Alfred Trender?'

'I haven't, no.'

77

'I presume you know who he is?'

Reggie's charm was multivariate – stealth, opacity and vindictiveness were among its more prominent features – but he was rarely facetious. Asking anyone in the City if he knew who Alfie Trender was, was like asking a bookie if he'd ever heard the name 'Lester Piggott'.

'Oh yes, of course.'

'Of course. Good. A very good man, Sir Alfred, don't you agree?'

Now I may not be the most subtil beast in the garden but even after four pints of Bass I can spot a man-trap. There must, I imagined, be some definition of the word 'good' that could apply to Alfie Trender; and 'Good man' was no doubt what was said down at the golf club every time he ordered champagne all round. So who was I to gainsay? Added to which, rumour had it that Sir Alf and our leader had made a sizeable amount of money together over the years, not always in the most odourless of circumstances. I proceeded with caution.

'As I say, I've never met him personally. He's certainly very successful.'

'Lucy's father, of course.'

'Yes.'

'Charming girl, eh?'

'Very.'

'*Very* charming. Has her mother's looks, thank God, not Alfie's. I remember the day she was born. Come on a bit since then. Out of little acorns. But that's beside the point. You've never met him, then. I think you should.'

'I'd very much like to,' seemed appropriate at this point.

'Today.'

'Oh, really?'

'You're presumably aware that ExpoTrend is on at the moment?'

'Indeed.'

'And today is City day, as you know.'

'Yes,' I said, attempting as neutral a tone as possible in case of follow-up questions.

'Good. Very good. You're obviously keeping in touch. I like to see it. Today could be a big opportunity for you, London.'

CHAPTER EIGHT

At half past five exactly on that dark afternoon the lights went down in the Grand Ballroom of the York Hotel in Kensington Gore, SW7. A spotlight hit the lectern centre-stage and a great hush descended on four hundred of Alfie Trender's best friends – stockbrokers, electronics analysts, fund managers, accountants, bankers and public relations men.

'Wait for it,' said Stan Harbottle, seated next to me. We were almost at the back of the hall, largely because Harbottle had wanted one last quickie after the take-your-places bell. I had travelled over on my own and arrived feeling dazed and ready for sleep, but hoping a few glasses of Taittinger might perk me up before the show. Harbottle was easily spottable in the crowd pressing the bar for a freebie by virtue of his Prince of Wales check suit. His great uncle was a bookie, he once told me, and no bastard with a velvet collar was telling *him* what to wear.

'My God,' he said when he saw me. 'They've been combing the highways and hedges this year.'

He thought he had me there, with his A-level in religious studies; but no.

'Many are called but few are chosen,' I countered. I hadn't done ten years of Sunday school for nothing. 'Bit early for you to be drinking, Stan.'

He smiled grimly. 'It's always six o'clock somewhere in the British Empire. Chin-chin.'

'Cheers. Funny, isn't it? Every time the figures get worse the booze gets better.'

'I wonder why that is?'

A voice, disembodied, boomed through invisible loudspeakers: 'Now, ladies and gentlemen, it is a very great pleasure to welcome to this year's Trendix International exposition, ExpoTrend '85 – '

'Mr Frank Sinatra,' Harbottle suggested.

'– the Chairman and Chief Executive of Trendix International, Sir Alfred Trender.'

'Cue applause – now,' said Harbottle. A tide of clapping swept through the hall, propelled without doubt by the ten or so per cent of those present who were currently employed by Trendix International, augmented by the fifty per cent kept in business by Trendix and taken up with less enthusiasm by the remainder, namely the shareholders. Mounting the dais with a glass of clear liquid in one hand, Trender waved the other and grinned. I couldn't see him very well at this distance but even so I could see he had done his very best to dress up smart for the City. In his brightly-striped shirt, shiny collar and MCC tie he looked like a bit-player in a Lloyds recruitment film.

'Thank you very much, ladies and gentlemen, thank you. Thanks. Thanks. Okay, now, first of all I want to say how pleased I am to be with you this evenin' and to see such a wonderful gathering of our friends, old and new, at this historic occasion – the twentieth staging of the Trendix annual jamboree, ExpoTrend. And my goodness, 'ow things have changed in these past twenty years.'

Credit where credit's due: Trender's PR boys might have vetted his wardrobe but they hadn't managed to make him talk right. Sir Alf stayed faithful to his native South London.

'The world is a different place than twenty years ago,' he announced. Alfie was proud of writing his own speeches. 'The pace of change is fast. It gets faster all the time. All over the world new products, new technology and new competitors are at work twenty-four hours a day to steal a march on us and undermine our position in the marketplace.'

'Seventeen-eighteen in minutes,' said Harbottle. 'Any takers at seventeen-eighteen?'

'Size?' I asked.

'A fiver.'

'I'll buy five,' I said.

'Liberal Liberal buys five pounds at eighteen. Right. Seventeen and a half-nineteen now in five. Any more for any more?'

'Ssh,' said a voice from the row in front.

'Objection from the stewards. The book is closed.' The speech was now three minutes gone. I'd got him this time. It was common knowledge that Alfie never spoke for less than half an hour, and I'd be taking a fiver off Harbottle for every minute over eighteen.

Alfie was soon reminding us that there was no substitute for hard work. In the world of today there were no prizes for losing, we heard – no prizes even for coming second, as those who had followed the fortunes of the England cricketers over the years could testify. The hall chuckled dismally.

'And with this in mind,' he continued, 'it must be said that in the current year Trendix is not a happy scene. We're nearly three-quarters the way through the year, and I'll be quite honest with you, the results so far are disappointing.'

'Christ, it *is* an historic occasion,' said Harbottle, as someone behind us rushed out for a telephone, 'that's the first time he's told the truth in twenty years.'

'In fact it's probably true to say that the results for the current year may well turn out to be lower than last year's. In fact, significantly lower. Now I don't want anybody panicking and saying Trendix is going to make a loss. We're not. We're going to make a profit. A good profit. Under the circumstances an excellent profit. But not as good as last year's. No one here today regrets this more than I do, because no one knows as well as I do what a magnificent effort the entire team has put in to try and match the performance of last year, and even more the performance of the year before. And indeed the year before that.

'Okay, so what's happened? And more to the point, what are we going to do about it? I know you'll want the full details. As our friends and supporters you deserve the full details. Therefore because of this we've decided to change the formula this year. I'm pleased to say you won't have to listen to my dulcet tones for as long as you usually do – ha ha – because what I'm going to do is to ask each of the divisional heads in turn to go through their own areas. Then at the end, if there *are* any general questions I'll take them myself. Okay? Now I know you're busy people, so let's get on with it, shall we? Thank you.'

'Thank *you*,' said Harbottle. 'That's five, let's call it six minutes – eighteen minus six is twelve at five pounds – sixty notes exactly. Nice to do business.'

I checked my pockets. I had thirty.

'Owe you thirty?'

'I think we can stretch it till tomorrow.'

'Bastard.'

'Don't blame me, sport.'

'Not you – him.'

I'd never met the Chairman and Chief Executive of Trendix International, plc, but I knew already what I thought of him.

Alfie Trender was a shit.

There were those in the City who liked Alfie. They liked his style – his earnestness, his directness, his shrewdness – all too often masked by a bluff and jovial manner. Alfie was always ready with a joke and always prepared to laugh at other people's, no matter how old

81

they were, provided they laughed at his. He was always ready to extend the hand of friendship to anyone who might influence the share price of his company, and as the right hand was withdrawn the left would be there to back it up with the offer of something special. So they also liked his generosity, his bonhomie, the fact that for Alfie, people came first. (They also went first.) They liked his down-to-earthness, his sincerity, his contempt for the old boy network. With Sir Alf, it wasn't who you knew, it was what you knew, and for this reason Alfie's money had sent his children, Hugh and Lucy, not to Oxford or Cambridge but to the University of Life: Hugh, more specifically, to the Coldstream Guards and Lucy to Cheltenham Ladies' College and thence to a finishing school in Geneva.

In business it was Alfie's canny eye that set him apart: somehow Alfie could see an opportunity where others could see only problems. The word 'can't', not to be confused with a term of abuse he was often heard to apply to his detractors, did not feature in his limited vocabulary. Alfie could see success where others only saw failure; even, at times, in hindsight. He could, furthermore, smell a rat. He had nose. He had feel. He was a glutton for the taste of success, the sound of the cash-register. He was in every sense a businessman.

Between getting my orders from Reggie, splashing my face with cold water, cleaning my shoes, gargling with toothpaste and departing from the office, I'd found a few moments for a quick glance at Trender's entry in *Who's Who* and the Extel card on Trendix.

Born in 1933 in Balham, South London, the son of George Trender, builder, and Doreen Trender, housewife, Alfie demonstrated at an early age the foresight and good sense which were to project him in the fulness of time to the commanding heights of the system. Realising that he was approaching the age of conscription, young Alf became apprenticed to a firm of electrical engineers, D. Bainbridge & Sons of Battersea. By thus joining a reserved occupation he avoided the honour of being called up to defend democracy in Korea. Released from his bond in 1954, A.Trender, electrical repairs specialist, originally operated from home but soon acquired small premises in Brixton. At first it went well. Then he encountered a problem: spares. For long periods they couldn't be had, and no spare meant no repair.

A hand reached out from across the sea. In France, too, they were having problems with ageing British washing-machines. Lacking the British sang-froid in the matter of waiting, they started to make their own. Some of these parts reached Alfie's workshop. They were cheap and good. For several months the repairs business didn't seem such a bad game to be in. Then Alfie started wondering what might happen if he took one of each of these spares and fitted them together. One day he sat up all night and did it. The result was a cheap new washing machine, and Alfie was on his way.

In three years he was a manufacturer in his own right, building machines with automatic settings and electric-powered mangles. He advertised on television. He won an award for enterprise. His payroll grew – ten, twenty, a hundred men called him governor. Washing machines had never had it so good. Alfie could have taken it easy, rested on his twin-tub, but for him it wasn't enough. Kettles, cookers and refrigerators began to appear with the T for Trender logo affixed.

In his personal life, too, Alfie was always looking for the next step up. In 1955 he had married the girl next door, Ada Taylor, who looked good (for a while) but said little and produced no heir. Many a man would have let a lapse like that dog him forever, but not Alfie. In 1960 Trender Electrics became a public company, Alfie became a paper millionaire and Ada became a single woman again. Tough and rich and going further, the kind of man novels were being written about, Alfie had no trouble in persuading the lovely Jill Scott, his secretary, to give him a touch of class. The first Mrs Trender spent her honeymoon at Margate; the second went to a pretty, undiscovered Spanish fishing village called Torremolinos. Alfie always got in ahead of the crowd.

After ten years in washing-machines and toasters Alfie got restless again. Children had not satisfied his creative urge. In the mid-sixties, for a diversion, he bought a badly-run radio manufacturer's in Ealing. He fired the workers and sold off the land for building, a nice below-the-liner for the next set of figures, but as an afterthought, since there was a market for such things, began to turn out transistor radios of his own. One day he heard that the military were crying out for something more reliable than the old walkie-talkie. Now a strong patriot, Alfie saw this as his great chance to make up for his absence from Korea. Eighteen months later, expanding and acquiring, he was supplying NATO not only with radios (made by the new subsidiary, Trendio), but also with radar equipment (Trendar) and a missile guidance system (Trendguide). By the end of the decade Trendix International, as A.Trender, electrical repairs specialist was now known, was out of radio and into munitions, making not only guidance systems but also the bombs and missiles to be guided by them. All this loyal service was, naturally, performed at a price.

The seventies, great years for armed conflict, were even better for Trendix. The shares rose steeply. Alfie bought a larger house, with horses and grooms. The consumer division of Trendix was sold off, front-loaders and all, to a rival firm which subsequently went bankrupt. Many thousands of housewives were left with broken-down machines and no one to repair them but that, as Alfie pointed out, was not his problem. The shares rose again. ExpoTrend, once a display-case of coffee percolators and eye-level grills, now paraded night-sights, rockets and cluster-bombs. With each new war Trendix raised its dividend. Alfie was in the pink. A captain of industry, generals and governments asked his advice; TV reporters camped at his gate. Then came near disaster.

According to a report in the *Sunday Times* a large consignment of steel drums marked 'Danger – crop protection chemicals' had recently been purchased by an African government at a price many times the going rate. These drums, the newspaper alleged, contained that most unconventional pesticide – napalm. Impossible, said Alfie, but after the follow-up report he acknowledged there was no smoke without fire. A culprit was found and despatched, not without what was rumoured to be generous compensation, and the flames died down. In future, Alfie said in private, or so it was whispered, all such shipments were to be marked 'Napalm'.

Profits that year, and for several subsequent years, reached new heights. In 1978 the Labour government assisted the company's export drive by arranging for a troupe of officials from the Ministry of Defence to accompany Alfie on a sales tour of the Middle East. The oil price was rising; the sheikhs were worried about insurgents: the results were sensational. The board of Trendix voted a large donation to the Conservative Party and on New Year's Day, 1980, Alfie became Sir Alfred.

Harbottle nudged me.

'Oh yes, yes. Eh?'

'Wakie-wakie. Superman's back.'

'Right, then,' said Trender. 'First question, please.'

Harbottle jumped to his feet. Someone passed him a radio-microphone.

'Stanley Harbottle, Terminal Investment Trust,' he said.

'Ah yes,' Sir Alfred responded from the stage. 'Very good friends and supporters of ours – have been for a long time. Very pleased to see you here tonight.'

'Sir Alfred, you said last year that you were looking for major expansion in the Middle East this year. Now we're told this will have to wait till next year, when you say your customers' revenues from oil will be picking up again. But the price of oil is still falling. Spot crude is down again today, I believe. Can you explain the grounds for your confidence?'

'Yes. Products. Ours are the best. It's as simple as that. Area denial systems, armour disposal systems – you name 'em, ours are the best in the business. They need 'em, it's as simple as that.'

'But isn't it the case, Sir Alfred, if I may say so – '

Be my guest, Alfie gestured.

'– that some of your best customers are having trouble supporting their own economies, let alone importing expensive military hardware?'

Showing us his palms then replacing them on the lectern, Trender smiled.

'*Expensive*,' he said. 'Well, *expensive* is a matter for the customer to decide. You want a nice suit, you pay the price. The client thinks it's good value, he buys it. But quite frankly, I don't think we can really discuss our customers in the public arena. They're very sensitive people, and rightly so.'

This was certainly true. Most of them, rumour had it, were government officials the size of whose Liechtenstein bank accounts bore an uncanny relation to the size of the orders their governments had recently placed with Trendix International. In the halcyon days of 1980, with spot crude at $40, one state took delivery of ten thousand rocket-launchers for an army of three thousand men.

Now came the plants: various hirelings, easily distinguished by their eloquent and simpering phraseology, asked questions about the future of the company. The further into the future one looked, it emerged, the rosier a future it was.

Harbottle stood up again.

'Right,' said Alfie. 'Since there are no further questions, perhaps we can adjourn for informal discussion. Remember we're all here to help you and give you as much information as possible. There's one other thing I'd like to say before we do that, though. I own twenty million shares in Trendix. That's a lot of shares. No one knows better than I do how the company is doing and what the outlook for us is – and I haven't sold a single share in three years.'

'How many has he bought?' said Harbottle, sitting down.

'A drink to start, gentlemen?' asked the waiter.

Reggie and Baxter ordered gin and tonic.

'London?'

It was nine o'clock and we were in a private dining-room at the York Hotel. Twenty floors below us the classy Kensington night-clubs were preparing to open their doors to the Arabs, arrivistes and pop-stars who frequented them (or so I'd read in the *Daily Mail*). Slightly less far below us, on the third floor, TrendEx was still raging.

'Perrier for me,' I said, rhyming it carefully with 'terrier'. During the informal discussion following Sir Alfred's performance I had negotiated my way through a significant volume of Taittinger and a yet more impressive quantity of food: drumsticks, cheese-sticks, Twiglets, canapés, sausages plain, sausages dipped, chicken and mushroom vol-au-vents and a mouth-puckering tonnage of peanuts. I never drink on an empty stomach. As the evening wore on I sensed a change in my colouring from the normal healthy yellow to green.

'What's wrong with you?' said Alfie Trender. 'Have a drink.'

'Have a drink, old chap,' said Reggie.

'Have one with me,' Alfie commanded. 'Two vodka-lemonades, chief. Large ones. All large ones.'

'Thank you, sir.'

'Is it warm in 'ere, or is it just me?' Alfie asked.

'I hadn't noticed,' said Reggie, looking to Baxter for con-firmation.

'I don't think so, Sir Alfred,' Baxter added.

I was more worried by what was going on inside me than out. The Trender vodka-lemonade switched my stomach straight to tumble-dry.

'Better take my jacket off, then.' Before starting on his smoked salmon he twitched his shirt-sleeves like a mechanic about to tinker with an engine.

'Anyway,' he continued, licking a sliver of pink off his chin, 'what did you think?'

'Mmm,' said Reggie, nodding. 'Not a bad show, Alfie, all things considered.'

'Not bad?' A morsel of brown bread looped through the air and landed on my cuff. 'Who d'you think I am, Laurence Olivier?'

'I think you may have left a few questions unanswered.'

'A few? A few? Fuck me – more than a few! If this oil price don't go up soon we're all down the gurgler. These Ayrabs haven't got the money to buy a bag of marbles, let alone an area denial system.

They couldn't pay their way out of jail.'

'And do you think the price of crude should be going up soon?' I ventured, feeling it was my turn to speak.

'Dunno, mate. What do you think?'

'There seem to be some grounds for optimism,' I said, the nearest available response to saying nothing.

'Such as?' said Baxter.

Alfie came to my rescue. 'Optimism? Who's that when he's at 'ome? If I can find him I'll sell him a barrel. Oil's going down, mate, and there's no two ways about it. There's too much of the bloody stuff, and nobody wants it.'

'Oh, I see. I'd thought from what you said in your speech –'

'My *speech*. Oh yeah – I'd forgot that.' He winked horribly at Reggie, who looked down quickly at his empty plate.

'Forgive me my ignorance, Sir Alfred,' Baxter said. In matters of social propriety his alertness, damn his eyes, was exemplary. 'But what exactly *is* an area denial system?'

'I know what you mean, mate. These fuckin' names! They get on my fuckin' wick. System this, system that. But if you don't call it a system, the bar stewards won't buy it. Area denial system: simple. A box of land-mines. Put your foot on one, and wallop!'

'Blown to bits.'

'Don't be daft. What's the use of killin' people? They cause more trouble half-alive than dead. No, what these little bastards do is blow your foot off.'

'Of course,' said Baxter.

'Mmm,' said Reggie. 'But he who fights and runs away will live to fight another day.'

'Not with no feet he won't, cunt. State of the art, this. But that's nothin'. We've got one – ah!'

The main course was arriving. I hoped it would be something light, to suit the late hour. The waiter staggered in under a wide salver of pork chops.

'Tuck in, lads,' Alfie encouraged. 'It's all gotta go. If there's one thing I can't stand, it's waste. We'd have killed for this when we was lads, wouldn't we, Reg?'

Reggie nodded, his eyes misted the while with thoughts of his own deprived childhood in Henley. I managed to stop the waiter before he gave me a third tranche.

'Fantastic,' said Alfie, taking a fourth. Then he described the KY-69, the latest generation of Trendix cluster bomb.

'And when you come over to clean up the mess,' he concluded, 'these little bastards see you coming and blow your bloody legs off!'

He slapped the table, bent forward laughing, and on his return to vertical drained a glass of claret.

'See a lot of young Lucy, do you, Alfie, living down in Sussex?'

Reggie's question did nothing to calm my digestive unease. After the first chop I was wondering what to do with the second. Baxter put down his knife and watched Alfie closely.

'Now and then, y'know. How's she getting on?'

'Very well, I think. Good little worker, the lass. Popular in the office, of course.'

'Well she would be, wouldn't she? Got my looks,' Alfie grinned, his pug nose almost disappearing, his tiny eyes testing. I responded with the old half-suppressed smile, but Baxter allowed himself a quick respectful chuckle.

'A great hit,' he said.

'Eh? Great tits? Oh – a great hit. I should think so.'

'She certainly seems to enjoy it,' Reggie observed.

'She does,' added Baxter, taking up his tools again, carving a mouthful of meat, dabbing at his lips with his napkin. 'Lovely girl, Sir Alfred. Very keen rider, of course.' I thrust my mental chop-knife into his heart.

Sleet slapped against the window and drew everyone's attention, which provided the chance I was looking for to dispose of the second *côte de porc*. I slipped it deftly into my napkin and wrapped it, laying the package on my lap. When heads turned back to the table I motioned with my left hand as if to raise a point of order and chewed my tongue with enthusiasm.

'Anyway,' said Alfie, 'forget my daughter. Too much like 'er mother for my liking. What I'm interested in is how we're getting on with these ELI, Reg.'

'Mmm – yes – indeed – well young London here's your man on that one. How many have we managed to buy, London?'

'Just short of half a million by the close tonight. I thought we'd better not push it past that level because then we'd have five per cent of the company.'

'So what?' Alfie asked.

'So then we'd have to make an announcement.'

'Oh we would, would we?'

'Well – yes, according to the Yellow Book.'

'The what?'

'Stock Exchange rules,' said Reggie.

'Well, what about the ten per cent we've already got?'

Reggie and Baxter looked uneasy.

'You realise, London, that anything we discuss here is in the strictest possible confidence?'

'Indeed,' I said, and I couldn't help smiling. With one word I had achieved the secret ambition of every frustrated intellectual. Why did Ben Jonson die in a bar-room brawl? Why did Dickens while away the hours at the Old Bailey? Why did Sinatra get mixed up with the Mob? After all these years of bourgeois conformism, I'd finally made it. I was a criminal.

I played the part well. Twisting my mouth into a wry smile I leant back and took a slug of vino. Then I felt ill and had to sit up straight.

'Fifteen per cent in all,' said Alfie. 'Good going. Price?'

'Seventeen p at the close,' said Baxter.

'Great. And what are we going to sell at? Sixty pence, was it? Seventy? Come on, boys, don't be shy. An honest turn's an honest turn.'

'I feel,' said Goddard, but his feeling was never shared, because the waiter came in to collect the plates.

'Very good, chief. *Very* good,' Alfie told him. 'My compliments to the chef. There's nothing like a nice bit of pig.'

'There was one thing,' I said after the waiter left.

'Yeah?'

'May I ask –?'

'Fire away, chief.'

'Well, since I seem to be involved in this venture, may I ask who exactly we're buying this stock for?'

'I don't think –' Reggie tried to interrupt, but Alfie's hand bade silence.

'Of course you can ask. An' I'll tell you. M.Y.O.F.B.'

'Oh.'

'Know who that is?'

'No, Sir Alfred.'

'Mind Your Own Fuckin' Business, that's who that is. Get it?'

'Of course, Sir Alfred.'

'Right ... Ah, here's pud. Now I never seen you eat much of the first course, so I want you to put some of this back, which I've also chose personally. Bread and butter pudding and custard. Fantastic.'

'Looks delicious,' said Baxter. Baxter knew the rules. Perhaps he could have told me whether being sick or passing out was the more correct form. I tried to decline custard, but Sir Alfred insisted.

'Fuckin' eat it,' he urged.

I tried to swallow but it wouldn't go down. Indeed its rapid return to my mouth seemed to be encouraging the rest of the meal to do the same. The room pitched and tossed. I tugged at my napkin and raised it to my face, forcing back the bile. When I opened my eyes everyone was looking in my direction – not at me, but at the pork chop sitting on my hillock of pudding.

'Some air,' I said, and rushed for the door.

We left the hotel by a side door, where Alfie's noiseless limousine (registration AT 1T, often misread) was waiting to take its owner and Reggie to the green baize tables of Challenger's.

'Remember,' Alfie reminded me as he clambered in, 'nothing's been said. Right?'

'Right.'

'Nothing's been said. Repeat.'

'Nothing's been said.'

'Correct. You're our man.'

'Yes, Sir Alfred.'

'You're – our – man.'

'I'm our man. I'm your man.'

'Correct. Now let's go and *make some money*.'

'Rather Reggie than me,' I said to Baxter as the car slid away.

'You think so? It'll do him good to lose a few shekels. Not greedy enough, that's Reggie's problem. You've got to be greedy these days or you don't get anywhere. That's the trouble with the world: not enough greed about. And you shouldn't knock Sir Alf, either. Bit of a rough diamond, but he's all right. Got the right ideas. Just can't pronounce them. And he's certainly made money – a lot of it. Serious numbers.'

We were making our way to the front of the hotel. I couldn't reply – I had a stitch. Baxter was sauntering so fast I was having to jog to keep up.

'Quick!' he said. 'There's a fast black. Taxi! . . . Don't mind if I take the first, do you? Only I'm on a bit of a hot one tonight.'

'Do,' I panted. 'I hope it keeps.'

'Oh, it will,' he said. 'But I don't want it to get *too* hot, do I?' He got into the cab and pulled down the window. 'Incidentally –' From the hip-pocket of his overcoat he handed me a little parcel of linen. 'Get it right next time, old chap. *Bonne chance!*'

He pushed the window back up and the car drove off. Baxter's chops were steaming slightly as I unwrapped them in the cold air. I took a bite out of one while I waited for the next taxi. We were in the Bayswater Road before I remembered I'd lost all my money to Harbottle.

90

CHAPTER NINE

'*Mon dieu*,' said Baxter.

I was early: not in the Baxterean sense of arriving to whistle in the dawn after twenty-five lengths of the Grosvenor House swimming pool and a quick jog through the *Times* crossword, but at any rate on time. The walk home last night had cleared my head and steadied what was left of my innards.

'Good morning,' I replied.

'Get back all right?'

'Oh, yes.' Oh, yes indeed, if you call a two-mile hike through the driving rain all right. 'You?'

'Well, not exactly home, but it was certainly all right.'

At this, the day's first intravenous injection of bile, I laughed connivingly. Us bastards had to stick together. But why was it always the bastards with the nice homes to go to who ended up not going home? Not that I was jealous of Baxter, I reminded myself as I peeled a Christmas tangerine.

'I don't know how you could face it after that food.'

'Oh, just practice, I suppose,' said Baxter with a self-effacing smile.

'There's no substitute for that.'

As soon as the office got noisy I rang Ben's broker, my old friend Brian Puffer at Stag & Co., and bought a hundred thousand shares in East London Industries. Having them in Ben's name rather than my own was an elementary precaution, especially as he used his mother's maiden name for investment purposes. Nor would we ever have to pay for the shares: we'd sell them before the end of the two-week account. I told Ken what I'd done, then rang Harbottle to tell him.

'Well, they're not going down, are they?' he concluded after I'd outlined last night's proceedings. 'Should I have a few?'

'I wouldn't put you off.'

'Now come on, less of that. Should I have some or not?'

'Yes.'

'How many have you got?'

'Me personally? Not a share.'

91

'Oh, I see. But young Master Benjamin's got a few tucked up with his teddy bear, has he?'

'A few.'

Just then Baxter came round the desk as he often did and peered over my shoulder. 'So I think the oils should be sold,' I told Harbottle. 'There's nothing to go for. The price is going down.'

'What?'

'Shell, BP – any of the majors. I'd sell the lot.'

'What are you talking about?'

'You may well ask. Oh yes, the Americans too.'

'Ah – there's somebody listening.'

'Uh-huh.'

'His Eminence?'

'That's right.'

'So I'll just go and buy myself a few ELI.'

'I think that would be the right thing to do.'

'And you're sure they're going up?'

'You won't regret it.'

'You'll fucking regret it if they go down,' said Harbottle.

By mid-afternoon I was his favourite stockbroker. Between ten o'clock and three ELI had risen from eighteen to twenty-one.

'And this is only the start,' I bragged.

'It had better be. Oh, and put this on your sheet: Terminal Investment Trust buys a quarter of a million Shell at market. *Solidarnosc.*'

This was my biggest order for months, and precipitated a brief upturn on my popularity-graph. Broking could be so easy. Nor was letting my best client in on a choice piece of inside information the least subtle way of winning an order. I was once at lunch with Fat Percy and a Welsh fund manager in his late thirties who looked as though his wife only fed him on the Lord's Day. He ordered steak, and had to wipe the drool off his beard when it arrived. Before he had time to make the first incision Fat Percy slapped the palm of his hand on to the steak and said: 'Business first.'

Late in the day Patel rang, his voice atremble with avarice, to ask the latest price.

'Twenty-two, sir.'

'Twenty-two? My God, crazy! I mean, crazy that they should have gone up so fast.'

'Crazy that they should have been so low before, you mean.'

92

'Of course. But don't you think I should sell a few now, Mr London?'

'Sell? Now? If I didn't know you were such a shrewd businessman I'd say don't be ridiculous, Mr Patel. They're worth more than this, aren't they? A man of your calibre must surely value himself at more than twenty-two pence a share.'

'Oh, indeed, indeed. I was only concerned that there should be an orderly market. We don't want them going up too fast, do we?'

'Don't we?'

'Perhaps if I sold just a few hundred thousand?'

'If you insist, Mr Patel. Your wish is my command. But if you did sell we would of course have to declare the fact that the chairman of the company was selling, and I'm sure you realise what impact that would have on the value of the rest of your holding.' More to the point was the impact it might have on the value of Ben's holding: *my* holding. 'Tell me honestly, Mr Patel. Are these shares worth more than twenty-two or are they not?'

'Of course they are worth more than twenty-two,' he said.

'In that case, hold them. I'll tell you when to sell.'

Dog days, I thought, wiping the sweat off my hands. This wouldn't have happened thirty years ago. In the fifties I'd have been writing a play about how ghastly they all were. What happened? Why did it all have to change?

'Christ,' said Kenny Morgan. He tipped his head a quarter of an inch to show me where to look. I often tried to imitate this gesture, but lacked the years of experience on the trading floor of the Market.

'Where? Oh dear.' The Friday evening outing was at its starting-point, the public bar of the Green Man, and Big Brenda had just walked in. Still to fancy the stalwart waitress of the City Hearth gentlemen's luncheon rooms was the mark of a certain seniority in the City, like remembering ration books or Labour governments. For bankers and brokers of a certain age she conjured up the freedom and sudden easy money of the sixties.

'Just look at it.'

'You wouldn't, would you?'

'I would have once. Anyway, we're in the pound seats with these ELI, are we?'

'It seems so. What was it we picked up today? Another two hundred thousand? So now we've bought seventeen per cent of the company in all. I can't see them going down.'

'Me neither. And all booked to the yodellers?' Ken asked.

'All booked to Zurich.'

'If the Council finds out we'll all be taking a long walk on a short pier.'

'The Council won't find out. We're the only ones who know.'

'It would be nice to let it slip, though.'

'It would be very nice. It's having your balls chewed off by Alfie Trender's minder that wouldn't be so nice.'

'I'm with you there. Drink up.'

'Where are we going?'

I had a nasty feeling that Rick's in Covent Garden might be where we were going: and so it was.

Ken smiled proudly.

'What about this, then?'

'Not bad,' I said as gloom rose within me. The ceiling was low, the crush tremendous. We shoved our way barwards. There was something to be said for having to forge a passage between so many breasts and buttocks.

'Sorry. Sorry,' I said, groping freely.

'What shall I start with?' Ken wondered. 'Shall I have an In Between the Sheets first or go straight for the Pink Pussy?'

'Here's lookin' at you,' he said when the barman finally delivered.

'Cheers. What do we do now?'

'The idea is we knock this back, have another, knock that back, then start looking.'

Two drinks later the plan was going smoothly. I was on my third dry Martini, Ken had switched to a Slip It In and we were looking.

'Aye-aye,' said Ken, bruising my ribs with his elbow. 'There's two over there might be all right. They'll go for the older man. Forward!'

I followed him through the ruck, deeply afraid.

'Ken,' I said. 'Ken! What do we say?'

'Easy. Go up to 'em, give 'em a nice smile and say, "I'm hungry, can I bite your neck?" Works every time. Then flash the gold card and they'll be crawling all over your back. Here they are. Watch.'

I watched. What I saw was a sudden movement of bodies carry Ken away on a wave of flesh, leaving me beached in front of the girls. At first sight I'd have put them on either side of twenty; but they aged in the last few yards, giving me cause for hope.

'I'm hungry,' I said to the one in pink. 'Can I bite your leg? I mean neck?'

'Haven't got the teeth to bite anything at your age, have you, Granddad?' said the one in green.

'Here, try this,' said the pink. My mouth must have dropped

94

open. Soon there was a cocktail cherry in it on the end of a little umbrella. The girls made a noise like parrots.

'Sod off, Grandpa,' said the green. 'Pick on someone your own age.'

Ken was waiting for me at the bar.

'Any luck?'

'Bad luck.'

'Sorry about that. Shall we move on? The next place might be more up your street.'

We took a cab to Sloane Square. The driver was doing a degree with the Open University and gave us a quick run-through of the architectural history of London. He'd just reached the New Brutalism when he pulled up sharply, projecting us into the glass screen.

'Sorry about that, gents,' he said. 'I'll knock a quid off.'

We flopped out at Algy's in Spencer Gardens. It hadn't changed. The men were still blond and disagreeably tall. Many of them wore a fashionable make of waterproof, and green gumboots to keep out the cowshit that littered the streets so liberally in this part of Chelsea. The girls were clean and fair and talked very fast without moving their lips.

'Bottle of, er –'

'Suits me.'

'Can't be the odd ones out, can we?' Ken thought.

We drank the bottle and looked round. Ken told me one about Jesus on the cross and I told him one about Elvis Presley and the Pope. Next to us the young ones were saying what a bore Christmas was going to be.

'Another bottle?' Ken asked some time later. 'Or should we try somewhere else?'

I said I wasn't confident.

'Think positive,' he urged. 'There's always the pair from the old folks' home over there.'

'That's probably what they're saying.'

'Sorry, sport. I could have taken you to a lovely chip shop in Southend. Incidentally, you wouldn't be interested in a few mini cassette-recorders, would you? Very cheap.'

'I'll think about it. Where's the next hot spot?'

As at Algy's, so at the Duke of Clarence in Portobello Road. The faces didn't change. It was still black ones in the front bar, Irish in the back. We took the less conspicuous option. It was past ten o'clock, and with College Gardens just a quarter of a mile of no-man's land away I felt a surge of satisfaction that the only performance the evening could now require of me was to drink three pints of beer and keep my head low all the way home.

'There's plenty over there for both of us,' Ken said, raising his glass, tipping his head an eighth of an inch to the right. A lady giant sat by the taps, occupying two stools and threatening a third, a three-hundred pounder who shook the bar as she tapped her hand in time with the music.

'How would you like that crouching over you?'

'Thanks, Ken. Another?'

I stood next to the woman to order more drinks.

'Ah don't understand how you Ainglishmen can drink this bitter beer,' she said.

'Oh, it's quite easy really,' I replied. 'We sort of open our mouths and pour it in. We're very old-fashioned.'

'Ah suppose that must be the way.'

'They teach us at school,' I said. The barman was having trouble with the pump. ' ... You're, er, from the United States, are you?'

'No, sir,' she said.

'Oh –'

'Ah'm from Texas.'

'I should have guessed,' I countered. 'Everything's bigger in Texas.'

'You Ainglishmen!' she chortled. 'Ah do like your *drah* sense of humour!'

'Very kind of you to say so ... Your first time in England?'

'Yes, sir.'

'Oh, good. Well I hope you like it,' I said as the barman handed me the change.

'Ah sure do,' she said. 'An' you know what else? Ah also like fuckin': in lots an' lots of different ways.'

Her hand thumped her knee and another trumpeted chortle followed me as I hurried away.

The agenda for the next day, the last Saturday before Christmas, looked promising: coaxing my deranged senses into action might take a while, but after that there was a trip round the West End with Ben to pick up a few war toys for the Season of Goodwill and in the evening a quiet pint at the Warwick. My mouth, meanwhile, felt like I'd been sucking a mothball all night. It wasn't the dehydration that woke me up early, though, or the incipient frostbite, it was Placido Domingo belting out a dawn chorus of '*Nessun Dorma*' on my landlord's stereo set two floors below.

Forgive me if Ricardo Modigliani has to be an ice-cream manufacturer in search of the perfect formula; forgive me if he has to
be a man of passionate temperament who stamps around the
house and curses the Almighty, waving his hands in the air and
speaking fractured bel canto English; and now, to cap it, forgive me his devotion to the opera. These things were not of my
choosing, nor of his. They were chosen by his parents who taught
him, after a fashion, to sing, took him to the playhouse, introduced him to the alchemy of ice-cream and failed to insist, after
the War, that their boy return to Naples – with the result that
I shall always associate the smell of ice-cream with the sound of
Caruso, Gigli and Pavarotti; and the sound of *Othello*, *Pagliacci* and
Turandot with grease on the banister and burning sugar in the
air.

My Italian wasn't up to full comprehension of '*Una furtiva
lagrima*' but I soon discovered that by listening to the song several
dozen times a week it was easy to commit it to memory. Modigliani
was also providing me with a course of more practical instruction:
lying in my bed late at night, stomach soothed by a few quarts of
beer and nerves by the distant strains of '*Celeste Aida*', I would be
roused by the slamming of a door as another major step in the
history of confectionery had to be retraced. After this, Modigliani
would pace up and down the hallway, at each about-turn abusing
his Maker or one of His associates. God, if I understood aright,
was a dog, and sometimes a pig – as was Mary, though she might
also be a bitch, a cow, a whore. The animals multiplied: 'Cats!' he
would hiss. Then the door would slam again as he went back down
to the lab.

I struggled to the sink and bathed my tongue in Alka Seltzer.
The fissures eased together; feeling returned; slowly, reluctantly, the
taste-buds were teased into life. Time for a smoke, I thought.

'No smoking in bed', said a metal plate screwed into the wall – but
where else was there at this time of the morning, with condensation
running down the window-pane and a rime of hoar frost gathering
on my socks? In a room as damp as this there was no chance of
anything catching fire. I made a tent with my knees and lit up,
reaching out from time to time to flick away the ash. For this, as a
schoolboy ('Brains', 'Swot', 'Creep' to my colleagues, top of my
year, winner of the White award and seven consecutive book-
tokens), I had fitted myself with earplugs to shut out the siren-call
of the TV set and study all evening at a time when my peers were
playing snooker in the Spread Eagle and fumbling with girls' zips
behind it; for this I had run the gauntlet of my doubters and

progressed triumphantly to Oxford, there to spend three admittedly drunken and where possible priapic years being buffeted and insulted in the scramble for personal progress; for this I had graduated with distinction, collected another book token; I had worked, been fired, worked again; I had married, gone into the City, made a child, lost my looks – for this.

I doused a second cigarette in the dregs of a cup of coffee and smiled: I've always been an easy-going chap. Gathering a blanket round me I lit the gas-fire and went to the bathroom to cough. Then I turned on the radio, tuned to the World Service. 'This is London,' it said. Too bloody right, I thought, and just when I didn't need reminding. Why couldn't they have called me Paris Paris? Or Sydney Sydney or Florens Florence or Baden Baden?

There was a knock on the door, and a shout:

'Hey Mister!'

'*Ja, mein Kommandant!*'

'Mister! Open the door!'

He stood on the landing, beaming. 'Here. Try. A masterpiece.'

'Jesus – you know what time it is?'

'Sure I know. You think it's too early to try a masterpiece? I'm up all-a night making it, the new recipe, and now you can't-a be bothered to taste it. And for thirty bloody pound a week you share my house. *Dio cane!*'

'We'll get the Rent Office round if you like, *Meister.*'

'Okay, okay, very funny. Now come on, you try this. I make it specially for you. Morning Glory. Zabaglione alla Marsala. You try.'

It was delicious. I let out an exaggerated, 'Mmmm!'

'Hey – you see – not bad, eh?'

'Disgusting. But I tell you what, *Duce –*'

'An' look – you know I don't-a like this *Duce* business.'

'I tell you what, Ricardo. You know what people fancy first thing in the morning, don't you? Or second, at any rate?'

'What?'

'A cigarette.'

'Oh, yeah, I know. That's-a why you smoke in bed all the time, don't think I don't know that as well.'

'There's your answer, then. That's how you'll win the competition. Forget the zabaglione. No one can even pronounce the word. Tobacco – that's the thing. All the flavour of a real cigarette, and you live to be a hundred.'

'You're crazy.'

'Imagine the adverts: "Lick the habit". They'd love it, *Duce.*'

'Crazy. Crazy. What brand, then, eh? What brand? Tell me that, clever man.'

'Any brand. Every brand. A whole range. Marlboro Melba. Silk Cut with Camel topping. It's a cert.'

'You're crazy,' he said again, and retreated down the stairs, peeling the paper off the walls with '*Che faro*'.

It had been like this ever since I moved in. On the evening of that first Sunday I'd found him swearing on the stairs. Over two bottles of Barolo we had compared and contrasted our life-stories. Over a third he had told me he liked me.

'Very kind, maestro,' I'd replied. '*Prost.*'

'You're a cheeky bugger, you. That's-a why I like you. An' I tell you something else. I'm gonna be rich.'

'Uh-huh? Why've you waited all this time?'

'A big ice-cream company, they offer a prize for the best new ice-cream. Ten thousan', then the percentage. Every time somebody lick it, they tell the bank manager. All you do is count the money. And – *and* – I'm gonna win.'

'Balls.'

'Not-a balls. Walls. Big company – big, successful. Big percentage. Make me a millionaire.'

'Lira?'

'Not-a lire, shit head! Sterlin'. Dollar. Who cares? And I tell you – you give me the right idea, I give you a cut. We'll both be rich, eh?'

'Good morning,' I said three hours later, stamping on the icy doorstep at Radcliffe Hall.

'I got the letter,' said Margaret. 'You haven't a hope. I've taken advice.'

'Me too.'

'Less expensive advice than last time, I hope.'

Unlikely, I thought. The sharks at Coe & Coe, teeth freshly sharpened on dead men's bones, had rubbed their dorsals with delight at the sound of me on the phone again. But what could I do? They were the only ones who would give me credit.

'This once a week business is unreasonable,' I said.

'You agreed to Saturdays only. You agreed.'

'I was over a barrel.'

'Over the limit, more like.'

'Very probably.'

'Seeing you disturbs him as it is. Why don't you think of the child for once, instead of yourself? He's got a home here. What can you offer him?'

'I'm cold. Am I not allowed in any more? Didn't the politburo like it last time?'

'He's ready now. Ben!'

'Oh – still Ben, is it?'

The boy appeared in a donkey-jacket with a pink triangle stitched to the breastplate.

'You're looking fit,' I said, struggling to lift him. 'Getting plenty of protein, are you?'

'Daddy, pot me down.'

'Any crimes to report? Eh? Any pranks?'

'Pinched Gabriel's chocolate!'

'Did you? What next?'

'Ate it! Ha!' He clapped his hands.

'There you are. That's what happens when there's no father figure round the place threatening to castrate you, isn't it? Lose your sense of moral responsibility, don't you, Ben?'

'Yas.'

'Crap,' said Margaret.

'Crap,' said Ben. 'Daddy – Gabriel crapped on the carpet again. Ha!'

'Shall we go now? I thought we might go and see Father Christmas.'

'Don't believe in Father Christmas.'

'Oh dear. Another male icon shattered. What about a bit of consumerism, then, before the revolution starts?'

'Can I have a present?'

'Of course you can. Lots of presents. That's why Daddy lives in a pig-sty, so you can have lots of presents.'

'What about Maggie?'

'Maggie? Oh your mother. Mummy's already got one, sweetie. She's got you. Ah, this is too much. Let's go.'

'Just drop him here if I'm out, will you, then?' said Margaret. 'Six o'clock.'

'I expect I'll be hearing from Smash & Grab?'

'They said they'd reply after Christmas.'

'I suppose that means their fees go up on the first of Jan.'

'I hope so, since you'll be paying. See you later. Happy Yuletide if I don't.'

This was Ben's first Christmas as an autonomous agent. Up to now he'd got sensible wooden toys, non-toxic, indestructible, and been grateful: crude jigsaw puzzles, a rocking-horse, building-bricks – traditional craftsmanship, built to be enjoyed by his grandchildren. I doubted whether much of this year's display would last until the New Year, let alone the twenty-first century. Perhaps I was getting old, but how Zeppo the maths robot could keep the kids quiet beyond Boxing Day was beyond me; and then if a wilful little bugger like Ben did take a shine to him the upscale warble Zeppo emitted when the answer was right and the downscale breaking of wind when it was wrong would surely be enough to merit a severe parental kick in the chip. And even a more long-suffering parent would find Zeppo something of a trial after, say, a day.

Like Margaret, for instance.

'I'll take one of these,' I told an assistant, a neat blonde trying to pretend she wasn't working there. I could have had a weekend in Brighton with her for the price I had to pay.

'Daddy, who's that for?' Ben asked.

I knew this had to be handled with care.

'It's for a friend of mine.'

'Daddy, I wanted one.'

'I'm sorry, Ben, this is for another little boy.'

'Daddy!'

'Oh, all right, Ben. You have this and I'll find something else for him. But make sure you use it, okay?'

'Okay.'

'So,' I said, 'one more present from here, then we'll look in another shop. What about a leather football? Shall we find you a leather football or do you think you might be too small for that sort of thing?'

'I think I might be too small for that sort of thing.'

'I think you could be right. Football's dying, anyway, don't you think?'

'Yas.'

To show how broad-minded I was I whipped him quickly round the doll's houses and was pleased to see that he showed no interest. Most of them would in any case have required a mortgage well beyond my capacity. After that it was board games, which I canvassed hard but without success, and models. I restrained him from testing the foundations of a Lego skyscraper with his toe but couldn't prevent him from sending a do-it-yourself Concorde on its last, unsuccessful flight. They were very good about it once I'd paid.

A tricycle, I thought, might be a good idea. Heading for 'Wheels', we passed through 'War'. For a pacifist, Ben appeared well abreast of the latest developments. (Margaret must have been allowing him to mix with those victims of the class struggle from the council houses down the road again.) Things had come a long way since my day, when we ran round pointing lengths of wood at each other and made a noise in our throats that was held to resemble the sound of a Tommy-gun. Inter-galactic was in this year. Everything in the section was hyphenated: rocket-lasers, astro-helmets, flight-simulators; credit-cards. But these I was determined Ben shouldn't have. Zeppo should provide enough Margaret-agitation for one Christmas.

'Daddy, Daddy!'

'Ben, that's no use at all. You don't want that. I mean, you can't want that rubbish, can you?'

Ten minutes later, as we left the store, he was all smiles again. Zeppo was safely tucked under one of my arms and the Annihilator under the other.

Halfway down Oxford Street we were sucked into one of the big department stores. We played on the lifts for a while and alighted at lingerie. I flicked through some ladies' pyjamas. What else was there to do?

'Hello,' said a girl's voice. 'Do we buy our undies in the same place?'

Hair of pale lemon in the shoplight, eyes of china blue; legs trim and miraculously suntanned; shoulders boxy and draped by a coat of the silkiest cashmere ...

'Hello, Lucy. It looks like we do. I can only sleep if I wear women's underwear.'

'Oh, really? I can only sleep if I don't. Is this one yours?'

'Yes – yes. Lucy – Ben.'

'Sweet.' Ben hid behind my legs.

'Sweet – that means you, Ben, not Daddy. Ben's quite a hit with the girls.'

'I didn't know you were married.'

'The unironed shirts, you mean? Anyway, I'm not, now.'

'Oh ... Christmas shopping?'

'We were just on our way to, er, see Father Christmas, weren't we, Ben?'

'No.'

'He's shy. You?'

'Shy? Not especially,' she said.

'Ha. But I see you've been buying a few things yourself.'

'A few. I gather you had dinner with Daddy the other night.'

'That's a very efficient intelligence service you've got, Lucy.' I

102

looked carefully for her reaction to this reference to Baxter, but she gave nothing away. 'I hope you didn't get all the details.'

'Enough. I hope you enjoyed it more than I would have done.'

'It was, er, very interesting. Ben, stop wriggling, will you?'

'That's what most people say.'

'Stop wriggling?'

'Very interesting. He's a VIP.'

'Very Interesting Person?'

'Very Important Pig.'

'Don't tell me. Tell your analyst.'

'I tell you what,' she said, as if to confirm that this was a different girl from the one in the office. 'No-one ever took me to see Father Christmas. Honestly, never. Why don't we all go?'

'Daddy, I don't want to see Father Christmas. I don't believe in him.'

'We're not going for you, Ben. We're going for Lucy. Lucy believes in Father Christmas, don't you, Lucy?'

'Of course I do,' she said. I was starting to believe in him myself, the way this was going.

'Well I don't.'

'Dry it.'

Santa's grotto was crowded with credulous children and even Ben showed every sign of suspended disbelief, awed by the nylon snow and the gang of animated reindeer running along the wall.

'There he is,' I said as the queue moved forward and we rounded the corner.

'Yes, there's Santa,' an old woman behind us told her charge.

'It's an actor,' said Ben.

Across a snowy mattress, Santa was perched on the back end of his sleigh, ho-ho-hoing and sitting each child in turn on his knee.

'I don't want to sit on his knee, Daddy.'

'You don't have to.'

'I don't want to ... Daddy?'

'Yes?'

'What shall I say?'

'I don't know, Ben. I suppose he'll want to know what you'd like for Christmas.'

'What shall I ask for, Daddy?'

'Ben, I don't know. A word-processor. A country cottage. What does anybody want for Christmas? World peace.'

'Daddy –'

'Ssh, Ben.'

'Is Lucy going to sit on Santa's knee?'

'Santa can hear. It's your turn next.'

Ben clapped his hands and giggled. Lucy smiled in a way that made my knees sag. A blonde Santa-girl with a short red jacket and dancer's legs came over to take Ben's name for the boss. 'Pay on the way out if he has a present,' she said.

'Ben?' Santa boomed. 'Are you next, Ben? Ho-ho-ho! Come and see Santa, Ben.'

'Go on.'

'Don't want to. I don't believe in him.'

'What do you mean, you don't believe in him? I thought you were an empiricist. Look, there he is.'

'Go on, Ben,' said Lucy. She looked at me, her eyes the blue of gentians in the red glow of the grotto, until I had to look away.

Ben submitted and climbed into Santa's lap. I didn't catch the exchange between them but I did catch the look on the old man's face, first of surprise, then of pain and alarm when Ben took hold of his beard with both hands and wrenched it from his face with a velcro-like tear. Santa sent Ben flying through the air on to the mattress and jumped to his feet.

'That's the limit!' he whined. 'I'm an actor, not a comedian!' His face was young-looking now, and the voice androgynous. Flecks of cotton-wool clung to his own horseshoe moustache, and rings shone in his ears. 'I'm nice as pie to 'em, then this little bleeder practically rips my face off. Fuck Father Christmas. I resign!'

'Disgusting! Oh, disgusting!' an old woman whined. 'Call yourself Father Christmas – you should be ashamed of yourself!'

'Piss off, Grandma. I've had enough,' he replied, and disappeared into the Arctic wastes, his bells jingling behind him.

'No mince pies for him this year,' someone said.

Ben got up laughing, clapping his hands, shaking a white rag.

'I gat it! Look, Daddy, I gat it!'

Lucy also laughed, and went on laughing, putting her hand on my arm as she bent forward. My son, my son, I thought: you *are* a genius.

104

CHAPTER TEN

'You're *joking*,' said Kenny Morgan, in the corridor after Parade.

'As true as I stand here.'

How true that was I found hard to say, though. Gravity was suspended since Saturday, and now it was Monday, that fateful Monday, the 23rd of December.

'So what then?'

'So then she says, what about a coffee.'

'You naturally declined.'

'Goes without saying. Two cups of coffee we have. Ben's charming the birds off the trees, and I'm giving her the old chit-chat about being the simple lad from Derbyshire, how you could buy a two-up two-down *and* a Ford Cortina up there for the price of a doll's house down here, and then she looks at her watch and says she's got to go – no, this is the best of it – then she says, what a pity, we'll have to do it again some time. So I think, what have I got to lose? Well, I said, what about Monday?'

'And she said yes.'

'Right.'

'So you're on for the one o'clock spot at the *Mangeur Heureux*.'

'Wrong. I'm on for the *nine* o'clock spot at a very nice little bistro down the New King's Road.'

'And breakfast at Dave's Diner. You jammy sod!'

'I can't imagine that.'

'Not even imagine?'

'I suppose I could imagine. Christ! I think I'd rather not.'

That was how I spent the rest of the day – trying not to imagine; trying additionally not to look at Baxter and trying not to imagine what further miseries he would inflict on me once he discovered that his life assurance policy was putting herself round the town with a gold-digging ne'er-do-well like me. I was also steering clear of Lucy but couldn't help catching sight of her once or twice, looking like a million dollars in a chunky pink sweater with padded shoulders and a pair of those tight slacks that don't quite reach the ankle – the ones I'd always thought were a sign of stupidity but which I now realised were the hallmark of class. But did I say a million dollars? I was forgetting inflation. She looked like a Euroloan, the capitalisation of IBM, the national debt of Mexico.

Two, four, six o'clock came and went. So did nine o'clock. At twenty past I flipped open a new pack of Camel, having decided something snappier than my usual brand was called for, and drank a third Kir, concentrating my thoughts on the world cruise I'd be taking once the good ship ELI came home. At twenty-five past I ordered a fourth drink. At twenty-five to ten I stopped reading the blackboard and turned my attention to thoughts of a suicide note. Every other table in the place was chocked with grinning hearties. They were turning people away. Someone whose face I knew from the City turned up in a white tuxedo. He hadn't got a booking but he had got a girl. I had to stare the waiter out: he was eyeing my table hopefully. I'd eat two dinners if necessary but I wasn't going to move.

Then she arrived. Her coat was off before she got through the door, and handed to the waiter with the ease of one unused to hanging her own. She'd pinned back her hair, and sparklies the size of peardrops drooped from her ears. The pink was gone, except for a touch of pink in the face, and tonight it was brilliant dark blue silk, gathered at the waist and flared at the hips.

'Oh my *God*, I'm *so* sorry!' She kissed the air behind my ears.

'I didn't really think you'd come, anyway. I had a pizza on the way, just in case.' There was a slight pause, an event I was to grow used to, during which she looked at me quizzically before she realised I was joking. Then she smiled. 'Perhaps we should sit down,' I added. 'You look like you've been running.'

'Oh, do I? Oh God. But I have, as a matter of fact. Couldn't find a cab. I was at this dreadful drinks.'

She lit a cigarette and inhaled deeply. I tried to ignore what this did to her bust.

We opened our account with a 1982 Auxey-Duresses, and proceeded via the tooth-shattering wholefood starters to the special of the day (specially unthawed, if you ask me). The first topic of conversation was naturally Rogers & Prickett. I served up one or two sexual titbits of the 'Did you know?' variety, then moved on to the question everybody wanted to ask; or rather, the question everybody wanted to ask after the question they really wanted to ask had been answered in the negative.

'Of course,' I said as casually as I could, 'you'd probably know more about the real office gossip than I would.'

'Me? Why should people tell me things?'

'I was thinking more of what you might tell them, if you chose

106

to.' I waved my butter knife with a circular motion in a show of academic disinterest.

'I'm sorry, I'm not with you.'

'Well – y'know – there are certain –'

'Are people talking about *me*?'

'Constantly.'

'But who?'

'Me, for instance.'

'But saying what?'

'Well – y'know – Baxter.'

'Baxter? Buck Baxter?'

'Oh, come on, Lucy. You're not telling me there's nothing to it, are you? Are you?'

'I've known Buck Baxter for years. Through Reggie. You know Reggie's a friend of Daddy's? I've never thought of Buck at all in *that* way.'

'Fine, then,' I said, repressing an urge to order drinks all round. 'Fine. Well, don't start now, will you?'

'I wasn't proposing to.'

'Good.'

'Good, is it? Pleased about that, are you?'

'Jolly pleased.'

'Don't you like him?'

'Not like him? Me, not like Buck Baxter? A calumny. I worship him. I adore him. Buck – I mean – Buck and I go back a long way. Any friend of Buck's is a friend of mine.'

'Good-looking, I suppose,' said Lucy.

'He wouldn't disagree with that. But why don't we talk about you?'

We talked about her family, her education and her thoughts on fashion. Then we talked about me.

'What happened?' she asked.

'She went,' I replied. 'Christmas Eve last year. Tomorrow's our anniversary.'

'That was nice.'

'Oh, a very sentimental girl, was Margaret. I mean, she could have waited till the next day but she didn't want to spoil my Christmas. More booze?'

'You are funny,' she said.

'It keeps out the darkness.'

'What?'

'Hides the despair.'

'Oh. But you must have loved her.'

107

'She loved me, too. I mean, that's the usual excuse people give for getting married, isn't it? Though I could think of better.'

'Is there a better reason?' This gave me the perfect introduction for a line I'd very much hoped to get in.

'Well – money, for instance.'

'Money, a reason to get married? You must be joking. I'd never do a thing like that.'

'You wouldn't need to.'

'You'll make me angry if you say things like that, London. I pay my own way, thank you very much. Daddy got me somewhere to live but what I want I have to buy for myself, mostly.'

'So do I. I have the privilege of buying what two other people want as well; but I wouldn't boast about it.'

'And do you seriously mean you'd marry someone like – well, I don't know, whoever – just because they had money? I don't believe you. What a rotter. Wouldn't you have asked me out tonight if you hadn't thought I might have money?'

In one tasty eyeful I took in her long bronze neck, her delicate Adam's apple, the glint of spit on her lower lip, her compact biteable ears.

'I wouldn't go quite that far,' I said.

'Oh you wouldn't?'

'Not quite.'

'You're a nice man really, aren't you?'

'My mother always thought so. Margaret thought so at first. Till she got radicalised.'

'What's that?'

'The Women's Movement.'

'Oh God. One of those.'

'It was chiefly a way of visiting the sins of the father on the husband.'

'The what?'

'Sorry,' I said, and explained. Lucy was no Dorothy Parker, granted, but given that she looked like La Belle Dame Sans Merci as well I thought she was managing all right. Beautiful, attentive, easy to make laugh – what more could any man want? And she was there: in a restaurant, in public, with me. And where were all the others? Where were all the sharp thinkers and fast talkers who'd chewed me up and spat me out over the years? Where were they? Married to accountants and doing the knitting – that's where *they* were, chum.

'And then up came Chuck.'

'Who?'

'Chuck. Don't ask me. I never found out who he was.'

'So that's why you're bitter.'

'I'm a spoonful of sugar compared with a year ago. But let's think about something nicer,' I said. For me this was easy enough. I was already thinking about a number of very nice things, like the way Lucy's chin was resting on her hand, her elbow on the table, and the way her eyes made my stomach feel as if the restaurant had hit an air pocket and was falling through a thousand feet of space.

I was also thinking about the way she kept shifting on her seat as girls always do when – no, I told myself; no no no; don't even think of thinking that.

'Pud?' I asked.

'You?'

'You decide.'

Returning from the cork-lined Gents', obscurely labelled 'Paul' (the other door said 'Virginie') I felt a vague pang at the sight of two cups of coffee sitting on the table where I'd hoped a decent slice of *crème brûleé au pêche gratinée* might be. Then followed a more definite douleur: as I flopped back into my chair, smiling warmly, it gave way and the tiled floor rapped me smartly on the coccyx. Even chairs, I thought: they don't make 'em like they used to. Conversations ceased. Lucy jumped up and craned over the table and a waiter with a plate of bouillabaisse in each hand looked round feebly for somewhere to put them. Surveying my options, needing to derive maximum advantage, I considered a remark along the lines of all of us being in the gutter but some of us seeing stars, but decided I wouldn't want to have to explain it to Lucy with the whole restaurant listening. Instead I looked sad, extended my face vertically, arced my hand through the air to scratch the crown of my head and did a Stan Laurel impression. Lucy laughed like the Jolly Sailor and a loud youth on the next table led a round of applause. The manageress made my joy complete with two large vintage Calvadoses on the house.

I paid a bill guaranteed to elicit a Happy New Year card from my bank manager and tried, outside, to find a taxi. There wasn't an orange light to be seen, of course. Normally they'd be kerb-crawling on this stretch, touting you imploringly; but tonight was like Jewish New Year.

'Let's walk,' said Lucy. 'Unless you're too cold?'

I tried to look amazed at the very possibility. After all, whereas she had only an inch-thick greatcoat padded with larksdown between herself and the elements, I was swathed in a Trilon blazer and an open-necked shirt.

109

We walked down the road, not speaking but occasionally bumping into each other. Down in the King's Road proper, a Polar crossing later, our progress was delayed by what felt like a very hard winter of window-shopping. I was afraid I'd never hold a pint pot again. We were nearing Sydney Street when Lucy suggested we go to a club she knew round the corner.

Inside the door she opened a wallet, cut from a deck of Bakelite cards and gained us admission.

'Drink!?' She had to shout to make herself heard.

'Let me!'

'Only members can buy!'

'Do they do Horlicks!?'

'Shaken or stirred!?'

'Whisky and water, please!'

'Grab that table!'

The tables were sited round a dance-floor of coloured squares lit from beneath. All round me, lip-readers in Italian clothes were practising mime. I dipped into a reserve pack of Park Drive and watched Lucy cut her way cleanly to the bar, smiling to melt the opposition.

'On the rocks!' She dropped a long glass in front of me. I couldn't hear the clang as it touched down on the glass table-top.

'Great! Thanks!' Normally I'd have made great show of offloading the ice cubes one by one into the ashtray. 'What's yours!?'

'Margarita!'

'Yum yum!'

We had to try each other's. Hers tasted like a kipper. I smiled, nodded, stylishly exhaled.

After that we sat in silence, apart from the jaws-of-hell roar, and I raised my eyebrows once or twice to show how much I was enjoying it. Hell, I thought: how come the chic theologians baulk at the idea of Hell these days? People like Hell. There's a waiting list.

I didn't mind not talking, though. I'd done enough. The muscles on my face were tired from trying to laugh at my own jokes. In fact there was only one thing we might do here that I wanted to do less than talk ...

'Shall we dance?' she said. Isn't female intuition amazing?

'What?'

She leant forward, giving me a heady whiff of Nuits Passionelles and a fleeting glimpse of the musky golden valley between her breasts.

'Don't you like dancing!?'

'Dancing!? Love it! I could watch it all day!'

'I've heard that one before! Come on, then!'

With the keenness of a soldier going over the top at Mons, I leapt up and bounded on to the dance-floor.

Now under the right circumstances – in total darkness, say – I'm far from the world's worst dancer. True, I often find the experience humiliating, but that would generally be due to the presence of other people rather than to any inherent defect in my style. When it comes to arms, for instance, I can hold my own with the best – waving them, swinging them, spreading them; clapping my hands, punching the air, flapping my wings like a chicken. Stern facial expressions are another thing I'm good at. The feet I find more of a problem. Luckily feet don't matter in the average crowded disco (I've been in two or three). No one can see them, and a gently suggestive movement of the hips is generally sufficient. But when, as now, the floor is empty save for five or six ex-Olympic gymnasts, I start to worry.

At first I was doing well. Lucy stayed close, and by backing her into a corner and interposing myself between her and the rest of the dancers I was able to block her field of vision and prevent any odious comparisons. Then she appeared to acquire a pair of roller-skates from somewhere and slithered away. I carried on with the flat-foot shuffle, pounding my fists miserably on an invisible desk-top just in front of me and wondering why I couldn't have been born in an age when men and women danced together.

I felt I was holding my own until a new record came on and a girl wrapped in swaddling-clothes jumped over the head of a man with a fifties haircut. After that a girl in pink pyjamas did something too fast for my eye which resulted in her being lodged with her legs round a young man's neck, and then I saw Lucy again, skating towards me and intent on something similar. Much as the thought of having her golden thighs clamped round my head might in other circumstances have appealed, it didn't now. I braced myself.

She put her arms round my shoulders. 'Shall we go!?' she shouted.

'Yes!'

'I'm sorry if you didn't like it,' she said outside.

'It was fine,' I said.

'You are sweet, but you hated it.'

'I suppose you're right. I am sweet.'

Lucy laughed. 'You are. But you still hated it. So did I.'

'No you didn't.'

'I did,' she said. 'I hated it because it was making you miserable.'

111

'I'm just a grumpy old bore,' I admitted, trying not to sound too convincing.

'No you're not,' she said, and in one movement stopped and put her hand on my shoulder and swung in on me in such a way that even a simple boy from Wootton, Derbyshire could see that it meant: Kiss me.

'You're – yum yum – trembling,' she said. She tasted like fruit cup.

'Freezing,' I lied. It was terror.

'Come a bit closer, then.'

'I wouldn't – yum yum – have hated it,' I said, 'yum yum – if only they'd played a slow one.'

'You are cold,' she said.

'Deprived childhood – slurp – it left me very reserved.'

'I don't mean that, silly. I mean you're *cold*.'

'Ah.'

'You're not cold at all. You're nice. I live just up here.'

Finding this hard to believe again? So was I: and harder still to believe not ten minutes later that I was locked in her heated embrace on a sofa the size of a Rolls-Royce, in a room the size of an aircraft hangar, nuzzling the flawless ruby of her left nipple and describing with my free hand the perfect half-circle of her rump.

'Do you like my flat?' she asked.

'Your flat what?'

'Ha ha. Bite my back. That's flat.'

Far from being flat, though, her back rolled and reared, like the Shropshire Vold, like the glistening surface of the desert. I sank my teeth into the ridge of muscle between neck and shoulder-blade and the land beneath me shifted, eased further out of its midnight-blue sheath.

'You can't be comfortable,' she said.

'I'm fine. There's no blood getting through to my arm, but –'

'Where's it all going, then?'

'I, er, erm –'

'We'll be more comfortable through here,' she added.

Fate being what it is, London being the place it is, women being what they are, this was the ideal time for me to slip a disc, for a gang of burglars to arrive, for Lucy's mother to ring. But none of these things happened and the way Lucy stepped out of her dress, leaving only a skimpy white triangle of cotton between herself and total nakedness, gave a firm indication, I thought, of where she had in mind. She took me by the tie and led me there.

CHAPTER ELEVEN

I was in Reggie's office again the next morning.

'Good,' he said. 'Very good.'

I'd just given him the latest on ELI. The jobbers had found a chunky seller. I took the stock for the syndicate, a further four hundred thousand shares, at twenty-five pence apiece. The quoted price in the Market was twenty-seven, and I made sure Reggie didn't miss the point that by dint of professional cool I'd managed to negotiate a two pence discount for size. The heartache of thereby saving money for Trender and the gang was eased by the sure and certain hope of a pay-rise in the New Year.

'So that brings us up to – our clients, I should say – up to ...?'

'A short ten per cent of the company.' By now, including a few scraps, we had bought almost a million shares. 'So when you throw in the ten per cent Sir Alfred mentioned the other night –'

'Yes, yes,' Reggie interrupted, exhaling *basso profundo*. 'He shouldn't have. *Most* unfortunate that he did. *Most* unfortunate. Three may keep a secret if two of them be dead, I always say. But as I recall, we said we wouldn't be mentioning that fact again, did we not?'

'I'm sorry, we did, yes.'

'Never mind. At any rate, we seem to be doing rather well.'

'I'm not surprised,' I ventured. 'Perhaps I'm missing something, Reggie, but I really don't see how these ELI are worth twenty-seven pence a share, or anything like that much. I've seen the company, I've visited the sites,' I lied, 'and if I had the stock at this price I'd be rushing for the door. Some of the shareholders must think it's Christmas.'

'It is.'

'Oh, yes. I meant –'

'Christmas, mmm,' said Reggie. 'Mmm.'

He rose, looked east, sat down again. 'A very important occasion,' he added finally.

It comes but once a year, I thought.

'It is indeed,' I said.

'Especially for you.'

I nodded non-committally and assumed an expression intended to suggest that I'd picked up some droll overtone.

'I hope it goes well,' said Reggie.

'I'm sure it will.'

'How are your preparations?'

'Oh, I'm not doing a lot.'

'Oh, are you not? Don't you think you need to?'

I could understand why Reggie should wish all his workers a happy Christmas, but why this sudden interest in mine I couldn't fathom; nor was it obvious why Reggie was sounding so cross.

'I'm planning a fairly low-key approach,' I explained.

'But what about the paper?'

'The wrapping paper?'

'The what?'

'For the presents, you mean?'

'What are you blathering on about, man?' Reggie boomed.

'I thought you were talking about Christmas presents, sir.'

'Christmas presents? I never mentioned Christmas presents. I was talking about your paper. Your presentation. Your talk, man.'

This was a new one on me. I racked my brains for something he might have said.

'I'm not totally sure I've been memoed on that,' I objected.

'Oh, haven't you? I was sure I'd told you. Oh dear. Maybe not, then. There's no fool like an old fool. Right. About the middle of Jan, I think it is. Here we are.' He looked through his diary. 'Yes, the 8th. The 8th of Jan. We're having a seminar to promote the company. ELI. You're down to speak. Big day. Has no one mentioned it?'

'No. Have the others been told?'

'Of course not. We've been keeping it under wraps. It'll be simple enough, though. You know the form. Investment managers. Institutions. The usual bunch of monkeys. All you have to say is, "Buy 'em", with one or two cogent reasons.'

'Erm – what particular reasons should I emphasise?'

'I'm sure you'll think of something.'

'As I was saying, Reggie, ELI doesn't look the cheapest share in the Market.'

'No. But if we knew what was we'd all be a lot richer, wouldn't we? And there *is* this chocolate soldier with his little brown finger in the pie, is there not? That can't be a bad thing. Singh, is it?'

114

'Patel.'

'Patel. Mmm ... Patel ... Ever been to Kenya?'

Reggie pronounced it 'Keenya'.

'I haven't, no.'

'You should. Beautiful country. Anyway, full of 'em. Patels. They're everywhere. Nearly as many Patels as there are genuine darkies. And they love money, these Patel chaps. Love it. Can't have enough of it. You just watch your Mr Patel. He'll get things moving. It's a good story: hungry company, motivated management, keen to make progress. Probably nonsense, of course, but no more so than most of our nonsense. I'm sure you'll cope.'

'I hope so.'

'Good. That's the spirit. Oh, and you'd better let the clients know, too. Go right through the list. Every big client on the books – ring 'em first, then send a written invitation. And while you're at it, you might drop the hint that we're strong buyers. Just to put us in the clear. Then when the things go up they can't say they weren't warned, can they?'

I'd almost reached the door when he said, 'Oh.'

'Yes, sir?'

'Happy Christmas, old chap.'

There was never much happening on Christmas Eve in our workplace. This year followed the same pattern as last. John-boy put a goldfish in Fat Percy's coffee. The goldfish jumped out when Perce took a sip and thrashed around on his desk. Then John-boy picked it up and ate it and we all laughed: only of course it wasn't the fish he ate, it was a piece of carrot cut to look like one. I didn't see what happened to the real fish. After that someone appeared with champagne and paper cups. John-boy, as last year, said 'Nonvintage? Fuck that piss! Let's have the real thing.' He reached into his briefcase to produce the customary bottle of vintage Krug. Opening the oblong carrier-bag with great show, he discovered the frozen rabbit that Perse had switched with the drink.

'Christ!' said John-boy. 'A miracle!'

'You could make a business out of that,' Baxter advised.

'Problem is,' said John-boy, brandishing the rabbit like a baton, 'you could buy half a dozen of these chaps for a decent bottle of fizz! You should know that, Buck – ha ha! Catch!'

He tossed the rabbit to Baxter at the other end of the desk. Baxter picked it cleanly out of the air with one hand and threw it down to Fat Percy, who couldn't hold it. The animal's head banged against

115

the corner of the desk and snapped off crisply at the neck. A tinge
of green shadowed on Perce's features, but when everybody laughed
he laughed too and lobbed the head to someone else; and so it went.
The office closed at twelve. The more assiduous then dispersed to
various bars in search of clients to buy drinks for. The Tuns was
crowded and noisy but happily free of our customers. A mixed
group in party hats were singing 'Silent Night'. By the time I arrived
Ken had made space at the corner of the bar and was standing with
four pints in front of him.

'Thirsty, Ken?'

'I need it, mate.'

'Cheers. Why's that?'

'Compliments of the season. I didn't think you'd have heard the
good news.'

'What good news?'

'About our Len.'

'No?'

'The firm have given him a Christmas present.'

'That's good of them. What?'

'The sack. And a Happy New Year to one and all.'

'Today?'

'The letter came this morning.'

'They can't sack him for being sick.'

'Redundancy. They say they're overmanned.'

'Bollocks.'

'Exactly the part of Reggie Goddard I'd like to be stuffing the
turkey with.'

'It wouldn't do much for the taste. What bastards. But Len'll be
all right. He'll find a job.'

'With his back? And I tell you what else – I'm next.'

'They wouldn't give you the chop, Ken.'

'They won't have the chance. If Len's out, I'm out. You'll see the
print on my nose every Thursday from now on.' Thursday, jobs
day in the *Financial Times*, was the time it was hardest to find an
empty cubicle in the Rogers & Prickett closet.

'Well, here's to Lenny,' I said, raising my second pint.

'Cheers. Plenty more where this came from.'

'I'd better not have too much, though.'

'Why's that? I thought it was Christmas.'

'It is, mate. The Trender's arriving in a minute.'

'Juicy Lucy? What's she – oh Christ, the big date! What happened?'

I took another mouthful of beer.

'Come on, then. How did you get on? Did she show?'

'Oh, she showed.'

'Eh? ... You're joking ... You didn't do the business, did you? ... You dealt?'

'Can't say. Sworn to secrecy, sport.'

'Well, fuck me!'

'I couldn't, mate. I'm worn out.'

'I bet you bloody are. What have you got that I haven't? That's what I want to know.'

'It's not what you do with it, Ken.'

'I know. It's how big it is.'

'Oh – look sharp. So, Ken, what are you and the family doing for Christmas?'

'Eh?'

'Ah, here she is. You know Kenny Morgan, don't you, Lucy? I just bumped into Lucy in the office, Ken, and asked her if she fancied a drink with us.'

'Very nice of you to come,' Ken said. 'What's your poison?'

He leant over the bar wagging a fiver between two fingers.

'Tired?' Lucy whispered.

'Wasted. You?'

'Shattered. What are you doing now?'

'Going to bed, I should think.'

'Right. You are.'

There was plenty of jostling going on, which allowed me to lean against her at right-angles, massaging my tricep between her breasts. I looked up to see that this manoeuvre was being observed by two clerks of eighteen or nineteen. I looked away nonchalantly to demonstrate that this sort of thing often happened to me.

'Unless the Captain's too tired for bed,' Lucy added.

I regretted revealing the name of that intimate part of my anatomy. The dull ache I was still experiencing indicated that the poor soldier in question would in any case prefer to revert to the rank of private for the time being. I also regretted Lucy's decision to slide her hand across my groin and deliver an accurate but unwelcome squeeze, chiefly because this action might be open to misinterpretation by the two clerks who saw it and had to turn away, spluttering into their beer.

'There you go,' said Ken.

Lucy backed off to take her drink. After four gins she got the giggles and Ken, thinking this must be due to his Market wide-boy act, glowed with triumph. What he didn't know was that Lucy's hand had now encroached on the Captain's lines *a tergo* and was

117

trying to prime his artillery. Presently she withdrew for rest and recreation in the Ladies'.

'Incredible,' said Ken, shifting in his collar as if it were too tight. His neck always looked longer when he'd been drinking. 'Completely different. Completely different girl out of the office. None of this, you know, Lady Muck business, is there? I'm a large buyer of that one. A *large* buyer.'

When Lucy returned Ken said he was off to give back some of the beer he had borrowed, and Lucy asked what I was doing for Christmas.

I said I thought I might treat myself to a pizza.

'You can't do that.'

'You can if the alternative is three days with your mother's sister in Harrogate.'

'Oh God. So you're all alone in the garret.'

Lucy hadn't yet seen College Gardens, but the picture of it that I hadn't discouraged her from forming was of bare boards, the feeble light of a bleary sun, the cloak tossed casually on to the floor and the framed print of the dying Chatterton, if she'd ever heard of him, propped against the wall.

'A great improvement on last year.'

'London, you *mustn't* do that. Come to Chum.'

'What?'

'Chumly. Cholmondley, it's spelt. Cholmondley Manor. That's where we live. In Kent.'

'Out of the question.'

'Oh you must. Really you must. How could I enjoy the day with the thought of you at home eating spaghetti?'

'Pizza. And what would your mother say? Three days ago you'd never spoken to me.'

'Mummy would love it. God, last year was so boring. Daddy banging on about biz, Hugo banging on about Northern Ireland. You *must*. I'll be cross if you don't.'

'Don't pout,' I said. 'It makes you irresistible.'

I did resist, though. It was several minutes before I agreed to be picked up from College Gardens at eleven the next morning.

Jean Morgan had agreed to be picked up at two o'clock today outside Sainsbury's in Billericay, a fact which Ken remembered at two minutes past. Lucy and I took a taxi west, to Sydney Street. There, by a triumph of matter over mind, the toiling of the flesh was resumed, and continued until Lucy recalled she was due at someone's drinks.

'What shall I wear?'

'Oh – nothing much. I mean, more than you're wearing now, but casual. Not too casual, though, darling. Mummy likes a man to make a good first impression.'

Only that week, on impulse it seemed, I had treated a bagful of shirts to their annual outing at the Chinese laundry. I blessed the prompting of a kindly Providence and limped up Sloane Street for a quick one at the Turk's Head.

'Okay, soldier – atten*shun!*'

Lucy's footsteps neared the bed.

'Right,' she said in a deeper voice than usual. 'Now we're going in, and we're going in hard.'

Soon, springs awhine, I was pinioned. Passing my hand down the question-mark profile of her bottom and upper thigh, I noticed wrinkles I hadn't remarked before. The hairstyle, too, had changed to my touch: stiff curls had replaced soft waves. Lucy was moaning rhythmically and I thought I'd have a smoke.

'Why?' said Lucy; but it wasn't Lucy, it was Doris.

Then there was a thump at the door. Doris, or Lucy, faded away. Given the Saharan dryness of my mouth, the immobility of my tongue and the guts-in-the-mangle feeling emanating from some-where between pelvis and collar-bone, I assumed the thumping must be in my head and tried to get back to sleep.

'Hey, Mister! Mister!'

I wanted to tell him to stop, but couldn't raise the saliva.

'Mister! Mister! Get up! Someone for you.'

'Don't be ridiculous,' I managed to croak, circumventing my powderpuff tongue. 'It's Christmas D –'

Five seconds later I'd bowled Modigliani out of the way and was in the bathroom searching for my shaving mirror. Close inspection of the sink revealed a few shards of it in there. How it had got broken I couldn't say, any more than I could account for the presence of a saucepan of tagliatelle in the bath. I managed a close enough shave without it, as evidenced by the amount of blood on the towel afterwards, and slicked back my hair with the aid of a handy backscrub.

Checking with finger and thumb to ensure that my tie was centred, I ignored Modigliani's advice to go and see a head-man and swung open the front door expecting to see Lucy leaning on the wing of her GTi. What I saw instead, so far as vision could penetrate a merry Christmas Day rainstorm, was a Daimler the size of the Dorchester and in it a middle-aged driver in a dark suit similar to

119

but of better quality than my own, who was passing the time by tapping out a tune on the steering-wheel. When I pointed first at myself, then at the car he looked hard first at me, then at the general condition of 70 College Gardens before easing himself out and opening the back door. Rushing down the steps, I encountered problems with the gate and we both got wet while I solved them.

'Good morning, Mr London,' he said once I'd made it to the back seat. He twisted round to face me. 'Happy – oh my – ' He looked like he'd seen a ghost; but I felt like one, so that was all right. 'Happy Christmas, sir. Sid's the name. Sid Saddler.'

'Happy Christmas.'

'Not a nice one.'

'No.'

'Worse than last year, in a way.'

'Yes.'

'Better than icy roads, though.'

I didn't reply to that. Better a stand now, I thought, than an hour and a half of meteorology.

'Cholmondley Manor, then, sir.'

'Yes please.'

The glass screen between us slid shut. Before we reached the Bayswater Road I was asleep again, dreaming of summer. I came round intermittently. Every time I did so I saw Sid's satiric gaze fixed on me in the mirror. I was trying to remember what happened when I got home last night. Only recently recovered from the run-in with Baxter, my left eye was hurting inexplicably.

The house was Queen Anne, with a few steps leading up to the front door and one or more of each of everything on either side. The hangover was easing. I opened the door unassisted. Although I tripped over the lip of the doorframe as I alighted this mishap went unobserved by any but Sid, who gave me a discreet hand up and lent me a cloth to wipe my hands on.

'All right, sir?'

'Fine, thanks.'

'Celebrating last night?'

'I think so.'

My suit had escaped the fall unblemished and my tie was still in place. My left eye, true, was continuing to vex: when the throbbing receded from the rest of my head it continued to assert itself there. But these things happen a lot once you're thirty – aches, pains, impotence – you have to ignore them.

When Lucy opened the door, however, I could tell I was about to make the wrong first impression.

120

CHAPTER TWELVE

'London! Are you all right?'

'Happy Christmas,' I said.

'Happy Christmas, darling, but – oh, here's Mummy.'

For the moment all I could see of Lady Trender was a hand extended from behind the door holding, I surmised, a gin and tonic.

'Cluster! Cluster!' Lady Trender shouted. The gin bucked and reared, splashing over Lucy's cream silk flapper dress and trickling down her leg.

'Mummy! Oh, Mummy!'

Lucy flicked the spilt drink off her hip with the back of her hand. Furious growling issued from inside.

'Cluster!' Lucy shrieked. 'Cluster, you little *bastard*!'

Sid's eyes met mine, but the muscles on his face were as rigid as a statue's. What was left of the drink was jerked out of sight and Cluster, a wedge-headed bull terrier, shouldered his way through Lucy's legs towards freedom. At least, freedom was what I thought he was going for. Then I realised his real interest was my ankle. I skipped out of range. Lady Trender clung to the lead. Lucy, cheesewired from below, screamed. She swung back her elbow and her mother screamed. A leather belt whistled through the air, narrowly missed Sid's unflinching nose and landed with a loud report on the dog's rump. At the same time the lead was released and Cluster disappeared across the front lawn.

Lucy's mother now revealed herself fully, instantly composed, dressed in a yellow two-piece and manacled with gold.

'There,' she said. 'Thank you, Alfie. Welcome to Cholmondley.'

Alfie Trender appeared from the other side of the doorframe in slacks and a V-neck with a shirt underneath, and mother and father stood flanking their daughter, as cosy-looking a family group as one could imagine.

'Thank you,' I said.

'I never realised it was *you*,' said Alfie, chewing. 'What's wrong with the other fellers at that place, Luce?'

Lady Trender giggled.

'Mummy, this is London.'

121

'Oh, dear. It does look sore. Very pleased to meet you, London. We've heard so much about you, haven't we? Oh haven't we? Who was that, then?'

'Mummy!'

'Lady Trender.' We shook hands.

'Jill,' she said.

'Jill.'

'You've met Daddy, of course, haven't you?'

'Of course I've met Daddy,' Jill wisecracked.

'So have I,' I said. 'Good morning, Sir Alfred.'

'Afternoon. I 'ope it's better than last night,' Alfie said mysteriously.

'Would you like a drink?' Jill asked.

'Oh, Mummy!'

'Oh, yes – of course. Perhaps you'd like to come in first.'

'Thank you.'

'The book room,' Jill directed as we went through. 'This one, London.'

'Livin' room to you, son,' said Alfie.

The room was high and bright. There were no books in it. The panelling was pink-washed and the furniture chosen by an interior designer as much for its simple up-to-date elegance, I guessed, as for its hard-to-beat old-fashioned comfort. Two wide sofas faced each other across a glass-topped table. A log fire crackled and fizzed. Next to the hearth stood a well-appointed Christmas tree. On the walls I spotted here a Klee, there a Matisse, and facing away from the light a very fine characteristic Girtin.

Alfie caught me looking.

'Like 'em?'

'Very much.'

'Well, don't like 'em too much. They're screwed in. *And* there's an alarm. Mind you, I don't go for 'em much myself.'

'No?'

'Except the Bonington. That ain't bad. I bought 'em 'cos my man told me to. Magic, that man. Got me out of all my Impressionists at the top, then got me into these. Gone up like a skyrocket, these have. Magic. Made me a fortune. Costs me a fortune to insure 'em.'

'Oh, Daddy, don't bang on about that again.'

'See? They can spend it all right, but when it comes to making it, earning it, that's another matter. That's *boring*. See this bit of schmutter?' He pinched the padded shoulder of Lucy's dress.

'Daddy! London wants a drink.'

'Looks like he needs one,' said Jill.

122

'Mummy! London, what would you like?'

'A monkey, that set me back. A monkey!'

'London?'

'Er – dry sherry, please.'

'*Dry sherry*,' Jill repeated.

'Are you sure?' said Lucy.

'Well – anything, really.'

'A monkey! You know how many personnel disposal systems – hand grenades to you – we have to sell to make five hundred quid?'

'I can't say I do, Sir Alfred. Perhaps I'd prefer a gin and tonic.'

Jill looked at me as if I'd gone mad. '*Gin and tonic*. No no, Lucy, I'll do it. *Gin* and *tonic*.'

'Mummy thinks G and T's a lady's drink.'

'What about sherry?'

'Sherry's for queers.'

'I bet you don't,' said Alfie. 'And I s'pose you think I'm about to tell you. Well I ain't. What you think I am, a mug? You could be anybody.'

'It's perfectly obvious he's nobody,' said Jill.

'Mummy!'

'Oh, don't be silly, darling. You know what I meant. Right, London. I'll go and get your drink.'

'Daddy thinks everyone's a spy, don't you, Dad? And where's Hugo? Come and sit down, London.'

I glanced across the room to see what at first I took to be the white-faced, black-eyepatched Trender family pet; then I realised it was my own reflection in a mirror, sporting an aubergine-style shiner round my left eye which only the drowsy numbness of my senses and the unexplained accident of the broken mirror at College Gardens could have prevented me from detecting earlier on.

Alfie, feet apart, looked through the window and I sat down with Lucy.

'I don't know,' I said.

'But you must.'

'I wish I did. I didn't even know I had it.'

'Quite a night, then,' said Alfie.

'I hope so.'

Jill came back with my drink. My arm sagged under the weight of it.

'Where's Hugo?' she asked. 'Cheers. Happy Christmas. I was so glad you could make it. We've so been looking forward to meeting you.'

I tried to stop my face puckering as I took the first sip. Tonic was a rarity down here. Lucy patted my knee and leant against me, her forearm resting along my thigh. I felt a vague unwelcome stirring somewhere near the point of her elbow. Crow's feet cut deeply into the soft tissue round her mother's eyes: at the corners of Lucy's, at this close range, I could see the dainty imprint of a sparrow.

'Cheers,' said Alfie. 'Your very good health. Health, wealth and happiness.'

'*Wealth*,' said Jill.

'Wealth,' said Alfie. 'Don't knock it. You know what they say about life, mate?'

'Oh Daddy!'

'I'm not sure I do, Sir Alfred.'

'Life's a shit sandwich.'

'Daddy!'

'The more bread you got, the less shit you have to eat.'

'Alfie!'

'Oh.'

'See what I mean?'

'Another?'

'Mummy!'

'I haven't really started this one yet, thanks.'

'Please yourself. I certainly will.'

'Would you like to see the garden?' Lucy suggested.

'Christ,' she said outside.

'When do the men in the white coats arrive?'

'What?'

'Your mother seems a bit over-wrought.'

'Mummy? There's nothing wrong with Mummy. It's all Daddy's fault.'

'Oh I see. Of course. Sorry.'

'That's all right, darling. You weren't to know. Like the view?'

From a low rock wall the land fell away for several miles before rising again in the distance. To a lad like myself, born a black pudding's throw from Kinder Scout, raised in the purple shade of the Peak, the Downs were nothing but a bowling-green: but here in the South, where compromise comes easy, one had to make concessions.

'Beautiful,' I said. We crossed to the old walled garden, where now there was a swimming-pool, covered for the winter. It wasn't hard to picture the place on a hot summer's day, all clear skies and

124

open vistas: me in the sun, *Room at the Top* in one hand, a pina colada in the other; Lucy in the pool, a gold flash in the blue water.

'Daddy hates swimming,' she said.

'Can he?'

'Of course he *can*, but he says it's a waste of time. Takes him too far from the telephone, that's the trouble.'

'He could always get a portable. There's a place up the Edgware Road does them cheap.'

'He hates me, too.'

'No he doesn't.'

'He *hates* me.'

'He hates you,' I said. (I've read my transactional analysis.)

'He doesn't really, does he, darling?'

'No. He resents the fact that you've grown up.'

We sat for a while watching the clouds move in.

'He hates Mummy.'

'Does he?

'He really hates Mummy.'

'Does she hate him?'

'No. She should. But he treats her like a dog and she takes it.'

'She must like it, then.'

'Don't be ridiculous, darling. How could she? She can't. He's a pig. He's a great, big, fat, *pig*.' I put my arm round her. 'Not like you, darling. You're not a pig, are you, darling? Tell me you're not a pig. Tell me.'

I reassured her on that point, and a gong rang out from the house. I thought with some satisfaction of the chaos Margaret would be facing at this moment, with the robot Zeppo yodelling and farting and little blond Gabriel screaming like a fallen angel, soundly annihilated by Ben; while I, admittedly in the company of a soak, an hysteric and a mass murderer, was surveying these broad and peaceful acres like the lord of all around.

'Hungry?' said Lucy, jumping up.

'Yes please.'

'That's first gong. Almost ready.'

'Yum yum.'

'We'll have a nice lunch, shall we, darling?'

'Of course we shall.'

'We have nice everything, don't we, darling?'

'We do,' I said. This wasn't the first time it had occurred to me that Lucy's well-cut cloth might be fraying at the edges (she had, after all, made a present of herself to me, not an act generally held

125

consonant with sanity), but I hadn't previously entertained the thought at length.

First gong meant Last Orders for pre-lunch drinks. Sid was doing the serving now, having changed into a white jacket and matching cravat. He looked older, grey and balding, without his driver's cap.

'Sir?'

'Whisky and water?' I tried.

'Before lunch?' said Jill.

'Mummy!'

'A large one, sir?'

'Perhaps a small one this time.'

'A small one, sir.'

'In fact, could you make that a vodka and tonic?'

Alfie was out of the room and Jill now sat on a pouffée and held her knees, rocking gently. Her eyes closed and she assumed an expression somewhere between Santa Teresa in ecstasy and Blanche DuBois in *A Streetcar Named Desire*. Conversation was subdued.

Sid reappeared with the drinks.

'Small vodka-tonic, sir.'

There was appreciably more tonic this time – two per cent, say. I followed him out.

'Still too strong, sir?'

'I think so. Don't you?'

He took the glass from me and drained it.

'Mmm. I think you may be right there, sir. Perhaps you'd prefer a glass of tonic on its own.'

'Terrific. Great idea.'

'I'll bring it through.'

Jill, back in the book room, nodded forward and came to life.

'Oh, my God – I didn't realise you were here, darlings.'

'It's first gong, Mummy.'

'First gong? She rings it earlier and earlier. I know what she wants. She wants us all to get pissed – oops! – she wants us all to get thoroughly sozzled so we won't notice what she's done to the lunch. That's what she wants, isn't it, London?'

'Clever,' I said.

'You have to watch these people, don't you, London?'

'You do,' I said. (I spoke with authority. My grandmother was in service for twenty years. What I don't know about what the butler saw isn't worth knowing.)

'Ah – here's Mr Saddler.'

I surmised from the pleased look on his face that the drink Sid was handing me would be neat vodka, but no, he'd stuck to our

126

bargain. (I should have mentioned above the passing of a small token from my palm to his.) I tasted the tonic water, nodded appreciatively and offered everyone cheers.

'Nice and strong?' Jill asked.

'Nice and weak, actually.'

'Oh, really? I haven't had a weak vodka for years. Can I be naughty?'

'Mummy!'

'He doesn't mind – do you, London?'

'Be my guest. After all, I'm yours!'

Withdrawing my legs to a safe distance, I let go an inch before the glass reached her hand. Happily it didn't break. I could see Sid was watching, and made a note to pass a further token later.

'Oh silly me!' Jill wailed. 'Silly, stupid me! I'm so sorry. I must be a bit pickled. I'm so sorry. Still, there's plenty more.'

'But you'll have to change your dress, Mummy.'

'Oh will I?'

'It's soaked.'

'Oh dear, yes.'

'Shall I help you choose?'

'Would you, darling? Does London want to help too?'

'Of course he doesn't, Mummy!'

'You do, don't you, London? A man often has the best eye for this sort of thing.'

Combining elements of negative and affirmative in my reply, I agreed to express an honest opinion. The women went upstairs and I looked out through the window. It was nearly two. The day was closing in.

'Nice, eh?' said Alfie. I twitched: I hadn't heard him come in.

'The view? Delightful. It's a beautiful house.'

'Queen Anne, they call this style. Could be Old King Cole for all I care but yeah, it's a nice place. Fastest rising property in the country round here, you know. Mind you, with what it's insured for I was thinking of burnin' it down. I hate them insurance bastards. Have a peanut.' He offered me a little silver bowl.

'But surely you're very proud of it?'

'Proud of this? Nah.'

'A lot of people would be.'

'I'm too greedy to be proud. Ain't worth having once you've got it, is it? Never been proud in my life. I tell a lie. Once.'

'When was that?'

'The second of May, 1982. I don't suppose you even remember what day that was.'

'I don't think I do, no.'

'Disgusting. Ought to be ashamed of yourself. Anyhow, I'll tell you. The day the *General Belgrano* went down, that was. Now you *do* know what the *General Belgrano* was, don't you?'

'Oh yes, I remember that. Three hundred and – what was it?'

'Three hundred and sixty-eight of 'em, and every one an Argie. Not a man too many, if you ask me. I mean, don't get me wrong. There's nothing clever about killing people.'

'No?'

'Nothing clever at all. And there's nothin' wrong with Argies, for that matter. Sound people, them Argy generals. Sold 'em a lot of stuff before the bust-up. But war's war, innit? I mean, sink him or he'll sink you. But what you don't know, I bet, is who made the torpedoes.'

'Let me think. Trendix?'

'Don't be daft. Trendix don't make torpedoes. *But* – guess who made the guidance system for the torpedoes.'

'Ah – Trendix.'

'Wrong again, chief. *But* – guess who made the pulsar in the guidance system.'

'Well – obviously not Trendix.'

'Cunt. It *was* Trendix. Give that man a prize. Gotcha there, eh? Eh? Gotcha!'

'You had me fooled for a minute, Sir Alfred.'

'And the point is, there's only one firm in the world, in the *world* that can make this pulsar, and that's us. Without the pulsar, bang goes the guidance system. Instead of which, bang goes the *Belgrano*. The proudest moment of my life, it was, when I heard that – the proudest moment of my life.'

I sipped my tonic water and gazed through the window, pondering the question whether twenty years' enjoyment of a slice of Alfie's fortune in the autumn of my days would be compensation enough for the previous twenty years of earning it.

'An' another thing. No mention of this ELI business, eh? Keep your trap shut and you might make a lot of money. Open it, an' I'll personally ensure you lose your bollocks. Okay?'

'Of course, Sir Alfred.'

'Oh, heads down, here comes trouble,' he said. Jill stood at the door in another new jacket-and-skirt outfit.

'Nice?' she asked.

'Very nice,' I said.

'Lovely, dear,' said Alfie.

'I think Mr Saddler's about to second gong,' said Jill.

'Great,' said Alfie, sliding a handful of peanuts into his mouth. 'I'm starving.'

Second gong sounded. The dining room showed the same instinct for the best of old and new, and Sid wheeled in the openers: drinks.

'Where's Hughie, Lucy?'

'Fuck knows,' Alfie interrupted. 'Seen him, Sid?'

'No, Sir Alfred.'

'I 'xpect he's in his bedroom with a spoon up his nose.'

'Alfie!'

'Anyway, we'll start without him.'

'No. I won't have it, Alfie.'

'*I won't have it, Alfie,*' Alfie mumbled, nodding from side to side.

'It's Christmas, Alfie.'

'Is it?'

'Don't be grumpy, Daddy. Can't we go and find him? And where's Cluster? Maybe he's with Cluster.'

'Oh, taking the dog for a walk, is he? That'll be the day. Seen Cluster, Sid?'

'No, sir.'

'Let's hope he's gone for good.' Alfie swallowed a drink, half-prevented an escape of wind and marched into the hall to shout. He came back in with Hugo. Hugo was tall and fair. He had his mother's features and his father's grace of manner. Dressed in pleated cords with no shoes or socks, hands in pockets, shoulders curled forward, he didn't speak until he saw me. Then he said, 'Christ.'

'Hughie!' said Lucy. 'Hughie, this is London. London, Hugo.'

'What's for lunch?'

'It's Christmas,' answered the paterfamilias. 'What the fuck d'you think's for lunch? Fish and chips?'

Hugo put his finger in his ear and twisted. A clock struck a quarter past two.

'You, er, work for Trendix, do you, Hugo?' I enquired after a long time had passed and the gals had started talking winter clothes.

'You must be jokin',' said Alfie.

'No,' said Hugo, slurping his watercress soup.

'You work at Lloyd's, don't you?' said Jill.

'Speak when you're spoken to.'

'I work at Lloyd's.'

'London works in the City, too,' said Lucy.

'Any red pepper?'

'Don't be ridiculous, darling. You don't want red pepper with watercress soup.'

'I said London works in the City too, Hugo.'

'Does he?'

'At Rogers & Prickett. Where *I* work.'

'Reggie Goddard's firm, isn't it?' Jill asked.

I nodded.

'Nice man, isn't he?' she said.

'Very nice,' Lucy agreed.

'Very,' I said.

'He's a cunt,' said Sir Alfred.

I shaded a second nod to something less definite.

'Alfie! I will not have you using that word at my table. If you want to behave like an animal we can always have your lunch served in the stable.'

'Hear hear,' said Lucy.

'Like Jesus,' said Alfie. 'He was fuckin' born in a stable. Anyway, he is one. Where's Sid?' He pressed the buzzer. 'Sid – get Reggie Goddard on the phone.'

'On the telephone?' Jill objected. 'What on earth for? He'll be having his lunch, poor man.'

'Not for long. You just watch. I'll show you what Reggie Goddard is. Get him, will you, Sid?'

Save for Alfie's grunting, we finished our soup in silence. Mrs Saddler came in and cleared away the plates.

'Shall we have another drink now, or start on the wine?' said Jill.

'London's from Derbyshire,' said Lucy. 'From Derbyshire.'

'Oh,' said Hugo. 'Like the french letters.'

'Sorry?'

'Hughie!'

'The Ffrench Beytaghs. South Derbyshire. Know 'em?'

'No,' I admitted. 'I'm from further north.'

'Oh.'

'Well, we don't all move in the same circles, do we?' Jill observed.

'Mummy!'

'Oh – I didn't mean – I'm sure London didn't think – '

'Of course not.'

Sid came in with a portable telephone (not the cheap sort from up the Edgware Road) and handed it to Alfie.

'Reg?' he barked. 'Yeah – Happy Christmas to you, too. Having your dinner? What you 'aving? ... Enjoying it? ... Bad luck. I've got to talk to you. Now ... No, the phone's no good, Reg. Face to face ... Essential. I wouldn't be ringing Christmas Day otherwise, would I? ... Here. Cholmondley ... It *is* a matter of life and death. Yours ... Half an hour? Fine. See you then.'

130

'Alfie – why?'

'I told you what he was, didn't I? That word I'm not supposed to use. Well there's your proof. Who else but a C.U. Next Tuesday would come rushing here of a Christmas afternoon?'

'All the directors of Trendix, for a start,' said Hugo.

'Yeah. Which just goes to show what they are, don't it? ... Now, when are we pullin' these crackers?'

Mine contained a roll-on moustache to go with the paper hat. Alfie got an eyepatch, which was given to me to wear. Lady Jill pulled three crackers but chose the wrong end each time and burst into tears after the third. Another tumbler of gin calmed her down. Hugo excused himself, saying he'd be back in a minute.

'One for yourself?'

'Not just yet, Shir Alfred,' Sid replied, swaying slightly.

'Lying sod,' said Alfie, when Sid was out of the room. 'Thinks I'm stupid, that bloke. If he's so clever, why am I so rich?'

'Cheers,' said Jill. 'Ha-happy Christmas, everybody. Where's Hughie?'

'I think he went upstairs,' I said. Lucy kicked me. The table went quiet again.

'Hughie's got a bit of a problem,' Lucy said levelly, as if reading from a prompt-card. 'But he'll be all right soon.'

'Exactly,' said Jill. 'He'll be all right soon.'

'Bollocks,' said Sir Alfred.

'He'll be *All. Right. Soon.*'

'The only way he'll be all right soon is if he's locked up, which is where he ought to be, or back in the Army, which is where I put him in the first place.'

'*Where you put him,*' Jill said in her *dry sherry* voice.

'Where I put him.'

'Where he never should have been put.'

'He had to leave.'

'Or be court martialled,' Alfie clarified. 'If selling drugs to your men is still an offence in the Army these days. Where's Sid? Sid! *Sid!*'

Sid leaned through the doorframe.

'Sid – bring the trolley, can you? Come and join us for one. I mean a real one. And the telly.'

'Sir Alfred?'

'The tele*vision*. The Queen's on at three, ain't she? Her Majesty. Wheel it in. And where's that bastard Goddard? When I say jump I mean *fuckin' 'igh.*'

'Oh, London, I am sorry,' Lucy whispered. I touched her hand.

'Lovey-dovey, lovey-dovey! What are you doin' sniffin' round my daughter anyway?'

'Daddy!'

'Can't he speak?'

'Daddy, don't be such a pig. London's my guest. Now leave him alone or *I'll* leave.'

'Mrs Saddler, you darling!' Jill beamed as the old woman wheeled the drinks trolley in. Behind her Sid pushed a castored walnut cabinet, leaning on it heavily.

'What's that, the turkey?' Alfie asked.

'The TV, Sir Alfred.'

'Where's my dinner? I'm famished.'

Mrs Saddler poured more drinks. Lucy was on the point of tears again. Alfie chomped a thickly-buttered bread roll and switched the TV on.

'What'sa time?'

'Ten to three, Sir Alfred.'

'Christ – no wonder I'm starving.'

Sid went away and came back with another trolley, this one bearing a silver dome with a big gold bird beneath.

'Feast your eyes on that,' said Alfie. I could only feast one, though, with the pirate's patch on the other.

'Mrs Saddler, you're a genius. Have a drink.'

'Thank you, sir.'

'Champagne?'

'Thank you, Sir Alfred.'

'Help yourself. What about you, Sid? You look like you need one. Another bloody one. Gin? Bailey's Irish?'

'A drop of whisky would be nice, Sir Alfred.'

'And two drops would be nicer still, eh?'

'It's always like this,' Lucy murmured, one hand on my shoulder, one on my knee. 'Don't worry.'

'Whisper whisper. Don't think I don't notice. Here.' Alfie poured two or three inches of whisky into one of the larger-diameter tumblers and pushed it at Sid. 'Drink this. And one for myself.'

Fixed by Mrs Saddler's glare, Sid hesitated.

'Drink it!'

He threw it back in one. His empty glass and Alfie's hit the table at the same time.

'Good. That's what I like to see – a man enjoyin' himself. Not bad, is it? Single malt, this. Another? . . . Course you will . . . Cheers!'

'Your health, Shir Alfred.'

'Oh – and here's a ton apiece.' Alfie dragged four fifty-pound notes from his back pocket and gave them to Sid's wife.

After due display of gratitude Sid placed the trolley next to the table and carved.

'So nice to have a guest on Christmas Day,' said Jill. 'Even if we don't know who you are.'

'Mummy!'

'I've always depended on the kindness of strangers,' I said.

'You've what?' asked Lucy.

'But where's Hugo?'

'He'll be down in a minute, Mummy.'

'But he should be here *now*, Lucy!' Jill brought her glass down hard on the table. A bright slice flopped slowly from its side.

'Oh, fuck!'

'Never mind, Mummy!'

'I've broken the glass, now.'

'Here's another.'

'But I've broken it, I've broken it,' Jill sobbed. 'A present from my mother. Oh *God!*'

'Oh dry it,' said Alfie. Using remote control he turned up the volume on the TV. They were showing a cartoon.

'What I don't understand,' he complained, waving his knife at the screen, 'is why this *stupid* bleedin' cat never catches the mouse. I mean look – look! – he's got him there and he still gets away.'

As Sid passed out the plates the door flew open and Hugo lurched backwards into the room.

'My God,' I said.

'What is it?' asked Lucy.

'Hughie – where have you been, darling?'

'My eye. I've just remembered.'

'Here it is! Here she comes,' said Alfie, rising from his chair.

'That bloody Eyetie threw an icecream at me.'

'London!'

'Hughie!'

Hugo had turned to face us, mouth open, eyes dull, pink face gone white.

'Something wrong, something wrong,' I thought I heard him mumble. Then he fainted on to the table, imparting just enough impetus to the gravy-boat to send it coasting to the far end, where it poured itself neatly into Jill's lap. Ignoring it, she rushed past me screaming and cradled Hugo's head in her arms, smearing gravy across his face. Lucy howled like a cat – I thought: but no, it was one of the local moggies, which, hotly if hopelessly pursued by the baying Cluster, entered the room in a great hurry, leapt along the table in two bounds and made its exit through a closed window, leaving my life forever.

'Alfie! Alfie! Hughie! Hughie!'

Cluster scrambled on to the table.

'Nothin' like a family Christmas, is there?' said Alfie.

'Alfie! Hughie!'

'*Fark* 'im,' said Alfie. 'Look!'

On the screen the royal banner, quartered or and azure, fluttered gaily in the wind machine. Drums rolled down to a whisper.

'Now sing, you buggers! You – conduct!' Alfie thrust a turkey leg my way. 'Go on – wave the fucker!'

The Saddlers knew what was expected. They arranged themselves on either side of their patron, Mrs Saddler erect, Sid on sea-legs, and as I beat time with the drumstick the three of them sang the National Anthem. Jill wailed in counterpoint, slapping Hugo's face, and Lucy, her head on the table, thumped her fists and howled like a baby. Cluster, deprived of his first prey, slavered over the turkey.

We sent her victorious, happy and glorious. 'Ahem!' I heard: in the doorway, a holly-wreath in one hand and a bottle of scotch in the other, stood Reggie Goddard.

CHAPTER THIRTEEN

Kenny Morgan laughed like a punchball. His feet didn't budge but the rest of him was spring-loaded and he rocked from the ankles. Pink face glowing brightly, he was demonstrating this technique in the bar of the Tuns on the Friday lunchtime, the first working day after Christmas.

'And the best of it is,' I continued, 'Trender completely ignores Reggie, carries on to the end of God Save the Queen, then says, "Get an ambulance, will you, Reg? We're all too pissed."' (For this part of the story I squashed my nose with my forefinger and twisted an ear.) 'So Reggie rings 999 and when he's done that Alfie tells him to push off home. Reggie says, "But I thought we had something to talk about," and Alfie says, "What do you mean, something to talk about? Can't you see we've got problems? Fuck off, you silly old cunt."'

'So what did Reggie do?'

'What could he do? He went home. Then the ambulance turns up. By that time Hugo's come round, so Alfie slips the lads a tenner apiece and off *they* go.'

'And did you ever get your dinner?'

'Oh, yes. After that everything goes quiet, the dog gets a kick in the jacksie and we all sit down at the table again, Hugo included, and then – oh yes – and then Alfie gets Sid to say *grace*.'

'Get away.'

'No kidding. Did it beautifully. For what we're about to re-shieve –'

'Magic.'

'So finally we eat. Cold turkey and hard-boiled Christmas pud.'

'Make mine a large one.'

'No stinting on the wine, though.'

'Good stuff?'

'Oh, Jesus, yes. But what about your Christmas, Ken?'

'Oh, very jolly, ours, as you can imagine. Len on his back, Gayle cutting his food up for him, mother-in-law's face cracking the mirrors. Best thing since the Two Ronnies. See the lad?'

'I get him tomorrow. I was round at Lucy's most of the time.'

135

'Oh, yes? Heavy turnover?'

'A few quick deals. I find I'm not so good at taking the long-term positions these days.'

'I know what you mean. Sustained performance, that's the problem.'

'Time to go,' I said, and we drank up and left.

'What's the Market like?' I asked on the way back.

'Like Southend Pier in the winter. ELI are the only feature. Thirty-four, give or take the turn.'

'So now it's the big squeeze, is it, Ken?'

'I tell you what else it is. It's embarrassing. The jobber's as short as a Chinaman's winkle and there I am forcin' 'em up.'

The market-maker had sold shares he didn't have, in other words, in the hope of buying them back at a lower price later and thereby making a profit. But no one was selling, so every time Goddard gave Ken the order to buy a few more the price was forced up further. The loss on the market-maker's book was looking horrific and the man himself was no doubt reserving his place in the dole queue.

'Don't blame me, mate,' I said. 'I'm only obeying orders. So's Reggie, by the look of things.'

'Not that I should mind,' said Ken. 'If they keep going up like this I won't be needin' another job. I'm making a fortune.'

'How many have you got?'

'A ton,' said Ken. He meant a hundred thousand. 'You?'

'Likewise.'

'How are you paying?'

'Cash-and-new. Praise God for the system.' Using the cash-and-new, a practice unacceptable at most firms but normal behaviour for my man at Stag & Co., I could sell Ben's shares before I had to pay for them, then repurchase them for another two-week run. By this means I could hold the stock for months without ever stumping up. The gutters and wine-bars of London Wall were littered with the corpses of those who cash-and-newed.

Back at the office, Baxter had erected a shaving-mirror and was trimming his nasal hair.

'Ah,' he said, flexing his nostrils, not looking up. 'An unexpected pleasure.'

'I was feeling the need for some witty repartee, so I thought I'd better drop by.'

'Good – good,' said Baxter. Folding his scissors, he took out his toothpick and grinned at the mirror. 'Know the Latin for sheath, old chap?' he asked.

'I can't say I do,' I replied – though I did.

'Vagina. Odd, eh?'

'Very odd.'

'Funnily enough that very fact came to mind when you walked into the room just now.'

'I didn't know you were up on philology, Bax. Couldn't apply your tool to *my* teeth when you're finished, could you? I could do with a scour and scale.'

''fraid not, old chap. Never know what you might catch, these days. They say you can get it from spit.'

This, I thought, was a cheek, considering what Baxter spent much of the time doing with his tongue, but I didn't say so.

'Oh, but that reminds me, London. I forgot to ask you how your Christmas went. Out to lunch, weren't we?'

'Your agents are everywhere, Bax.'

'I've been following this little saga for some time now.'

'I hope you're enjoying it. I also hope I haven't disrupted the riding lessons.'

'Ah – pretty well-informed yourself, I see. But that's to be expected.'

'I don't suppose you'd care to reveal which little birdy has been tweeting in your ear.'

'You're right. I wouldn't.'

I gave him my hooded eyes look and went to see whether Lucy had come. She hadn't been decided, that morning, whether to clock in at Rogers & Prickett or to go straight down to Hampshire, where she and her mother were spending a few days with an aunt.

Doris, alone in the office, jumped up. She'd got another new hairstyle, apparently selected at random from the pages of *Sixteen Plus* or *The First Time*. She turned away, but I'd already seen that the loose skin round her eyes was wet and reddened.

'Doris, what's the matter?'

'Nothing's the matter.'

'You've been crying.'

'I'm *all right*. What can I do for you?'

'The still small voice of calm hasn't been raised again, has it?'

'Oh – I don't know. I really don't. After all these years I still don't understand him. The season of goodwill, it's supposed to be. All I do is tell him to be careful, and –'

I was going to ask her what she wanted him to be careful about, but she started crying again.

137

'He must have had a bad Christmas,' I said. 'It's nothing personal, Doris, I'm sure it's not.'

'What kind of Christmas does he think *I've* had?'

'Better than mine, D.'

'I doubt it.'

'Here, a pound says it was. Tell you what, D – give us a ring at Lord Dismiss Us and I'll take you down the Tuns for a port and lemon.'

'Port and lemon? What do you think I am?'

'Sorry, D. I always say the wrong thing.'

'A whisky and dry might tempt me, though.'

'You've dealt.'

Baxter folded his 'Kleerpore' patent pimple-remover into its ebony frog and slightly furrowed his wheatear brows. On past performance this could well mean a thought was edging its way towards utterance.

'Not there?' he asked loudly.

'Doris? Yes, she's there.'

'Ha ha. She rang in to say she wasn't coming.'

'Who did she speak to? I knew she wasn't.'

'Well, you're the expert on when she's coming and when she's not, these days.'

I answered my telephone.

'Mr London?'

'Mr Patel! Yes, London speaking.'

'I see from the *F.T.* that our shares were up again on Christmas Eve. Twenty-nine pence!' This pretence of following the share price only in the papers, at a day's remove, rather than minute-to-minute via his mole on the hotline from the Market, was Patel's way of showing contempt for the quick profit.

'They're twenty-five today,' I said.

'What? But my – but –'

'Oh, sorry – thirty-five, I meant. Slip of the tongue.'

'Thirty-five, ah yes, right,' he said. Then he remembered to sound surprised. 'Thirty-five? Up another six, then!'

'And how many have you got, Mr Patel? Thirty per cent of the company?'

'Twenty-nine point nine.'

'Three million shares. Congratulations. You're a paper millionaire.'

'Exactly, Mr London. But only on paper. That's the problem, is it not?'

'From what you say I take it you'd prefer the kind of paper with the Queen's head on it.'

'Now Mr London! You're teasing. You are leading me up the garden path. I never said such a thing.'

'Of course not; what I meant to say was that for a company with the management and prospects of East London Industries thirty-five pence a share is on the cheap side, did I not?'

'I think you probably did, Mr London.'

'But even so –'

'But even so, I feel in the interest of prudence it might be right to release a part of my holding.'

'You mean all of it.'

'I didn't say that, Mr London.'

'*Mister* Patel,' I said, 'when the stock was fifteen, you wanted to sell. And what did I advise you?'

'Er – hold.'

'And when the stock was twenty, what did you want to do then?'

'Well –'

'You wanted to sell. And what did I advise?'

'Hold.'

'Hold. And when the stock was twenty-five?'

'I may perhaps have considered releasing a few.'

'And now they're thirty-five. Hold 'em, Mr Patel. Hold 'em.'

'Very well, Mr London. I shall do as you say.'

'You're not going to sneak off to another broker and chip a few out?'

'Mr London, I give you my word of honour.'

'And you know how highly I value that,' I said. 'Oh, but since we're on the question of promises –'

'Yes?'

'That case of Glenlivet.'

'Oh?'

'The one you were sending me for Christmas.'

'Oh, that one. Has it not arrived?'

'It must have got held up in the traffic.'

'I'll send another.'

He never did, though. A few minutes later, the Rogers & Prickett PABX awash with inactivity, I opened the bulky package which had arrived this morning in the familiar doom-laden envelope of Coe & Coe, solicitors to the desperate.

Just when I thought my life was moving into new and uncharted

139

territory, on a pathway paved with gold, C & C had been working night and day to make sure I kept to the tried and tested pathways of penury. The envelope contained photostats of a lengthy series of billet-douxs exchanged between themselves and my ex-wife's retainers. (My retainers, I ought to say, since I was the one who'd been keeping them in business for the last twelve months.) Most of the letters were short, presumably because letters were costed per unit rather than per helpful, humane or original idea, and all of them were chargeable to me. Coe & Coe's dispatches in particular appeared brief and off the point. They were evidently doing a good trade at the moment, though: I had only the feeble light of common sense to guide me but it was still clear that their side of the exchange could not have been penned by anyone above the rank of janitor. It was also apparent, even to me, that the oppo had them tied up in knots.

A covering letter explained 'in layman's terms' that the position was as follows: given the voluntary nature of my previous under-takings and the straitened circumstances in which I was living it was extremely unlikely that the Courts would reverse the previous custody order on young Benjamin. Appeal to the High Court would be risky and costly and in the event of my deciding to persevere with such a course of action Coe & Coe would regrettably be unable to continue my existing credit arrangements. It might, however, be possible to extend visiting rights by applying for an order from a judge in chambers, which would be relatively inexpensive though not *per se* more likely to succeed.

Not, i.e., I submit, chum, a hope.

Be positive, I thought. With great care I removed the staples and paper-clips that held the letters together. Rising to my feet, I wiped the seat of my trousers with each sheet – not an unknown sight in the Rogers & Prickett office, though generally reserved for briefing-notes from the economist – after which I piled them on the floor and did the Twist on them. Then I blew my nose on the more recent ones, reflecting too late that it might have been wiser to do this first, and having done that I fed the whole lot into the shredder. This'll show 'em, I thought.

After that I felt much worse. I rang Coe & Coe. My man was at a funeral, they said. I rang Margaret. She was at her Know Your Own Body class, they said. I asked to speak to Ben. He was with his mother, I was told – peering down a periscope trying to find his clitoris, I suggested, but the line went dead then. I rang Lucy and there was no reply. Even the Ansafone refused to talk to me. Finally I rang Harbottle. 'He can't speak now,' they said. Very likely, I

140

thought: he's been having lunch again. I took a P. G. Wodehouse from my drawer and read it morosely until five.

Doris didn't like the look of the Tuns, so we went to the Great Eastern, where I brought her up to date over a pint of bitter and a whisky and Canada dry.

'Well you never can tell,' she said. 'People have all these problems and you'd never guess from looking at them, would you? Not for a minute.'

'Enough of my problems. What about yours?'

There was only one problem in Doris's life: Reggie Goddard. The same problem that she had had for thirty years; Reggie who loved her and left her but never quite got rid of her; who expected a wife's devotion but wouldn't favour her with a wife's rewards. Doris didn't say that, though.

'He's getting so moody lately,' she said.

'Stress?'

'Stress, is it? I don't know. There's something going on, isn't there? Something to do with this Alfie Trender. I don't like that man. I don't like the look of him.'

'Nasty, British and short. I know what you mean.'

'There's some sort of monkey-business going on. I know there is.'

'It may not be for long,' I said. 'Don't let it worry you.'

It didn't stop worrying her for the next two hours, though. It worried her through five rounds of drinks and was still worrying her when I said I thought we shouldn't get drunk. By that time I felt I knew why no one else had married her either.

At half past seven she decided it was time to head for suburbia. My feeble protest delayed us another half-an-hour.

'Out celebrating tonight?' she asked as we parted.

'Not tonight. I'm on for the early bath.'

I almost made it. I managed to catch the last cottage pie and two at the Feedwell in Portobello Road and I very nearly managed to walk past the Warwick Arms without walking in.

At ten o'clock the next morning I knocked as cheerily as possible, the electric bell having been vandalised, on the door of the Rainbow Co-operative. The day was sluggish and cloudy, suffering sympathetically. The door was answered by pale, flame-haired, emerald-eyed Jan.

141

'You've come for Ben,' she said.

'Yes please. How's things?' I asked brightly.

'I'll fetch him,' she replied.

'Thanks. Can I have a word with, er, Maggie, first? If that's possible.'

'I'm not sure it is.'

'Oh – why's that?'

'I'm not sure it's possible.' This was the one who had only been here a few weeks, wasn't it? The one who was so nice last time. Liberation was working wonders.

'Is she here?'

'Yes.'

'Perhaps you'd like to tell her the father of her child is shivering on the doorstep.'

'Just a second.'

She came back presently and said, 'This way.'

I followed her up the stairs to the back of the house past a series of posters of 'Prisoners of Conscience' (all detained by right-wing governments, surprisingly enough).

'In here,' she said, pushing a bright yellow door. Apart from two fixtures the room on the other side of it was bare. Floorboards were scrubbed, walls stripped down to the brickwork. One of the features was a gas-fire, the other a trestle-table on which my ex-wife lay, face-down, naked and inert.

'Good morning,' I said.

'Uuh,' Margaret replied. Her face was towards me, resting on the backs of her hands, but her eyes were closed.

'Sunbathing?' I asked. Then I saw we were not alone. Far from it: previously obscured by the door, clad only in a saffron loin-cloth, was a very large woman indeed. (Admittedly the second such to adorn these pages within a few short chapters: but so it was. I bear no malice towards Nature's more fulsome expression. On the contrary – leanness I hate. I've never liked thin women. Midland man though I am, I can't stand whippets.)

'Oh, good morning,' I said again.

She didn't reply.

'I said good morning.'

'Ng ng ng,' Margaret interjected.

'You'll find it easier if you open your mouth. What's going on here?'

'I said,' Margaret explained, this time lifting her head a weary inch but not yet opening her eyes, 'this is Daffodil. She doesn't speak to men. She's a separatist.'

'Pleased to meet you anyway, Daff,' I countered. 'You must be looking forward to Spring, eh? You'll be able to come out.'

'Ha ha,' said Margaret.

'Thinks he's funny, does he?' Daffodil asked.

'Think, Daff – if only your name were Tulip and you came from Amsterdam, there'd be a song about you.'

'Are you here just to waste your own time or were you intending to waste ours too?' Margaret enquired. 'Shall we carry on, Daff?'

'Carry on what?' I said.

Moaning something, conceivably a tune on a twelve-note scale, Daffodil moved, possibly danced, round the table. Whether it was this that had brought the plaster off the walls I didn't like to ask. At each of the more striking discords she would pinch the nearest outstanding muscle, generally one or other of Margaret's buttocks, between her finger and thumb. This couldn't have hurt much, but I did flinch when the periodic low growls arose. These were the sign for Daffodil – head cropped, sweaty-necked, massive-bicepped – to bring a meaty palm down on the same broad target with a force that drew my breath: and also increased my attentiveness, for what I knew, and Daffodil conceivably didn't, was that in moments of ecstasy my ex-wife was not averse to encouraging such treatment as an act of stimulation.

'Mmm – uh – mmm,' said Margaret as I sidled round to a better viewpoint.

'What exactly is this?' I asked.

Daffodil whacked more assertively. '*Keep still!*' she chortled.

'I *said*, what exactly is this?'

'Oh, London – ooh! – dry up, will you?'

'Forgive my importunity, but I really would like to know what kind of household my son is growing up in.'

'Hang on, Daff.'

'But –'

'Sorry, love. Can you jus' do the kneadin' so I can talk a sec?' said Margaret, modifying her speech to express solidarity. (Quite a different thing, I felt, from my own parodic use of Market jargon when I went down the drinker with Ken.)

'Well, if you like, love. But you know it's best if we do it in the right order.'

'So what is it?' I insisted. 'What's all this terrible groaning for?'

'The chant is part of this therapy,' said Margaret.

'Therapy – ah – therapy. What therapy?'

'This therapy.'

'I know it's this therapy. What other fucking therapy could it be? What therapy? What's it called?'

'It's. Called. This. Therapy. It doesn't have any other name. A name just objectifies it. It's not an object, it's an experience. Get it? As a matter of fact there was a television programme about it last week.'

'I must have been watching the snooker.'

'Can you do my legs, Daff?'

'You can do mine while you're at it, Daff.'

'Daffodil doesn't touch men.'

'That's a blow.'

'I'm warning you, London.'

'You can't in all seriousness tell me you feel better after this,' I said, as Daffodil warbled and pinched anew.

'*Bor-ing.* Aren't they predictable? You're not supposed just to *feel* better. It's the long-term effect that counts. Anyway, I thought you wanted to talk.'

'I do.'

'Good . . . uuh . . . Go on, then. Talk, for God's sake. I'm all ears.'

'Here? I can't talk like this, with –'

'London,' said Margaret, assuming her world-weary tone, 'I *don't* have to listen. If you want to talk, talk. If you don't, don't. Quite frankly I think we'd all be greatly relieved if you'd just piss off. I should think Ben's getting bored waiting.'

'You don't have to talk tough because Mister Sister's here. But fine, I'm a reasonable man, I'll talk. You know what it's about.'

'What is it about?'

'What is it *about?*'

'You know, London, one of the things that always irritated me about you was the way you had to always repeat what I'd just said.'

I sighed dramatically. 'What it's about is that gang of thugs at Blood & Guts.'

'Where?'

'Your lawyers.'

'Oh, them. Well don't ask me. Ask them. Ask – ngh, that's great, Daff. Mmm. Just there again. By the tendon. Great. That's what they're there for. They're supposed to take care of these things.'

'These things?' I repeated after her. 'These things?' Margaret's bodywork, I noticed, was showing signs of wear and tear. Moth and rust were beginning to bite. But her ability to rev me up, crashing through the gearbox with aplomb, sweet contentment to raging despair in seven point two, was not by the years diminished. 'These things?' I said again. 'That's my son you're talking about!'

'Now calm down, calm down,' she said in the patronising tone she always used when she wanted to provoke me. 'All that's going to happen if you come round here ranting and raving is that – Christ, Daff, that's *really* good – '

I grabbed at her hair.

'Ow!'

'Look, you bitch! Get rid of this gorilla or *I'll* massage your neck for you!'

All of a sudden I noticed that the floor was further away from my eyes than the length of my legs would justify. The table too, and Margaret on it, were receding. Daffodil, approaching from behind, one hand on my jacket-collar and the other on the seat of my trousers, was removing me from the scene of temptation. I felt like Elijah.

'Hey!' I protested. 'Now come on. I'm a man. It's true. I really am. You're not allowed to do this, flower. Margaret – tell her, will you?'

Before very long I was hoist on Daffodil's shoulders. This was very unpleasant, given my already delicate condition. There didn't seem much chance that I was going to enjoy her next trick, either, so I took the initiative. Reaching down past her chin, avoiding an attempted bite, I grasped what might have been the half-inflated bladder of a football and squeezed very hard. Daffodil cried out, wobbled and fell – backwards, on to the table from which Margaret, forseeing disaster, had only partly removed herself. We met on the floor as the table folded beneath us. Margaret, yelping, threw as perfect a right cross as I'd seen from her in three years of marriage. It landed, crisp as an apple, in the tender spot just below Daffodil's cheekbone.

'Daff! Daff, I'm sorry, I'm sorry! It was meant for –'

'I know who it was bleeding meant for.'

Crushed between them, feeling like the last dreg of the toothpaste, I decided this might be the moment to squeeze myself clear. I had almost done so, reluctantly using Margaret's face as the only available hand-hold, when the earth moved again and I found my own face immovably lodged in the furry familiar zone between Margaret's thighs.

Could be worse, I thought.

Very soon it was, as Daffodil's knee bore down on my back with the force of a bag of cement.

I tried to negotiate.

'Guh –' I managed.

'Kill the fucker,' said the voice of one with whom I had once

145

watched *Brief Encounter* four times in a week.

'Little bastard!' Daffodil enthused.

There was only one target available to me and only one means of attack. I clenched my teeth and tugged. Resulting convulsions seemed to break most of my ribs.

'Wanker,' Daffodil grunted, discouraging me from further vice by dislocating my thumbs.

My position worsened. A hand restricted my breathing. Another hand menaced my groin. My whole life flashed before my eyes. A voice said, 'Daddy!'

So there is, I thought, a God. The hand was withdrawn from my mouth.

'Morning, son,' I said.

We all sat up. Daffodil wiped her forehead.

'Are you having sax?' Ben asked.

'No, son, we're not having sax. Just a little altercation. Let's get out of this shit hole, shall we?'

'Daddy said shit! Ha!'

Ben clapped his hands.

CHAPTER FOURTEEN

Back on the home front I was keeping clear of flying objects. Projected by its proprietor, Modigliani's Supa-Kreem was not as soft as it looked. My eye was now a glowing shade of yellow.

Coming in after the day with Ben, I trod as softly as I could. Modigliani, poor sod, had taken seriously my suggestion about tobacco-flavoured ice-cream and was sweating round the clock in his laboratory to produce this monstrous hybrid. Well-intentioned comments on his first effort, the Marlboro Melba, had resulted in my injury and I was trying to keep out of his way until after the competition deadline, the last day of December. Moreover, I was exhausted. These days out with Ben were getting harder. In the last three months I'd taken him to the waxworks, the toy museum, the War Museum, the Tower of London, Buckingham Palace, Big Ben (twice: he liked that), Hyde Park, Green Park, Regent's Park, St. James's Park, Battersea Park, Victoria Park, Trafalgar Square and the Zoo. I was running out of tourist traps. What I needed was a place of my own, with clean carpets and a built-in cooker; a house; a garden; a dog.

I lit up a high-tar special, poured a cup of whisky and lay on my couch in the darkness feeling the steam rise off my socks. This wouldn't be such a bad place to live in, I reflected, if only I didn't have so many senses. Without one's organ of smell, for instance, the house would be much improved. Deafness would certainly help. Blindness would be a major advantage. Greatly taken with this idea, I redesigned the room for a life of total sensory deprivation. When the first cigarette was finished I stubbed it out on the head-board and lit another, feeling drowsy and relaxed. The whisky was finished now and I felt the approach of a light and pleasant sleep.

Not for long: bursting through the silence – I didn't really notice the traffic any more – came a wail that might have been the sound of a cat with its tail on fire but was in fact Modigliani tripping up the stairs, singing 'Quando le sere'.

My door rattled in its frame.

'Hey – Mister!'

'Mm?'

'Mister!'

'Mm?'

'Mister! This time I got it!'

'Eat it, then. I'm asleep.'

'You talk in your sleep?'

'I'm tired, Ricardo.'

'Hey, Mister, you know me. You don't answer the door, I knock and-a knock till you do. Why we have to have this argument every time?'

I opened the door. Modigliani, in trousers and vest, was carrying two cones of mustard-coloured ice-cream.

'Here!'

We bit together. I awaited the revolt of my taste-buds.

The first bite was awful. I didn't enjoy it at all. But for some reason I took another. I suppose it gave me something to do with my hands. The second bite was better. It gave me a lift. It made me more confident in social situations. By the time I took the third bite I was hooked.

'What do you call it?' I asked.

'You like it, eh? You like it.'

'But what do you call it?'

'You like it!'

'Okay, I like it. But what's it called? You've got to have a good name for it.'

'Knicker Licker,' he proudly announced.

'Knicker Licker. I'm not sure that gives quite the right impression, *Duce mio*. Oh wait a minute – you mean Nic Lick?'

'*Si*. Nicotine Lick. Nic-a Lick-a for short.'

'You'll have to do better than that.'

'Forget-a the name. It's sensational, eh? *A dio!* Ten thousand to start with, then the royalties. Wow! And I even thought of a slogan for the TV.'

'Oh, yes?'

'"Lick the habit". Like it? "Lick the habit". Just imagine. All over the country. *Dio*, I'm gonna be rich!'

'Er – hang on, Maestro. Don't you mean *we're* gonna be rich?'

'We? Ah si – *we*. Me, my wife, my family. We're all-a gonna be so bloody rich!'

Swallowing another mouthful, he retreated down the stairs.

For the shareholders of East London Industries the last days of the year were a time of high excitement. One or two newspapers picked up the story and contacted Patel. Patel refused to comment. Then, diverging from my instructions, he commented that he thought the shares would be going 'much higher'. On Monday morning, the 30th of December, they went from thirty-seven to forty-five. That afternoon they hit fifty. Businesslike calm, and the fact that I had a hundred thousand of the little winners tucked away for myself, tempered my remonstrations when I rang Patel to suggest he might have spoken out of turn.

'Mr Patel,' I said, 'your company is making losses. Its total assets are eight hundred thousand pounds. That's eight pence a share of net worth; plus, of course, the inestimable value of your own services as chief executive. Is there anything you're not telling me about this company? Is there something I ought to know which might make the shares worth more than eight pence apiece? Please be frank, Mr Patel.'

'Frankly, Mr London – no, there's not.'

'And again being frank, Mr Patel, is there any reason why the shares might in fact be worth considerably less than eight pence apiece?'

'Now Mr London – I'm trying to play fair, but be a sport. There are limits to one's frankness.'

'I understand.'

'Which is why I'm feeling at this juncture that I should perhaps be selling one or two.'

'One or two million, you mean.'

'Indeed.'

'Your entire holding, in fact.'

'Precisely.'

'Mr Patel, I understand your position. But will you do one thing for me?'

'Anything within my power, Mr London.'

'Will you give me an hour to make a few further enquiries? Then I'll come straight back to you, and we can make a decision and take it from there.'

Fast thinking, like hard work and hard playing, was one of the things that made me hate the City so much. Everyone else seemed so good at it. The state of my thoughts at that moment may serve as a welcome recapitulation.

Patel's game was obvious enough. Here was a two-bit entrepreneur who had made a fast rupee in the multi-let business, a field of human endeavour in which an excess of humanity was never much of a help, and who was now trying his luck with the Stock Market, buying cheap into a bankrupt company and hoping to sell

149

out dear on the back of a ramp. As luck would have it, someone else was doing the ramping for him. The company had no earnings, no management, no prospects and practically no assets. The price of the shares in the Market was now fifty pence because it had been driven there by heavy buying from Trender and the boys and now by the timely intervention of the City editor of a certain Sunday paper, whose crusading zeal had doubtless been well rewarded. Patel, knowing what ELI was really worth, was naturally anxious to sell.

What the triumvirate were up to was equally clear. Hiding behind their nominee in Zurich they had bought twenty per cent of the company, two million shares, at about twenty pence a share. This was out of order: the Rules and Regulations required them to announce anything over five per cent, a measure designed to restrain philanthropists like Alfie Trender from gaining control of public companies on the sly. At the moment, with the shares at fifty, the profit was two million thirty pences -- a nice turn but hardly enough for Alfie to risk his good name for. The syndicate wanted to see the shares higher, and further brown envelopes would no doubt be finding their way to Fleet Street to facilitate this process. It wouldn't be long before every punter in the Market had a few under his belt. Once the enthusiasm reached the point of frenzy, aided by my bullish presentation on the 8th, they would start releasing the stock at, say, a pound a share, and after that the price would fall back into the shrubbery.

My own first principle was the same as everyone else's – maximum personal enrichment. (No one could accuse me of being an angry young man. That lot saw the light *years* ago.) Immediate gratification lay the way of leaking the whole scheme to the Press. That, however, would lead to a sharp reversal of my own long-awaited financial recovery and also eliminate my prospects with Lucy. Alternatively I could sell my shares now, taking my own profit, and allow Patel to let it be known that he too wanted out. This wouldn't do Patel any good, because once the Market knew that the Chairman was a seller someone was bound to ask why, and there wouldn't be a buyer in sight. But it would leave Trender and the boys locked into a hopeless position and I couldn't be blamed as I roared off to Paris for the weekend in a customised Porsche: an agreeable prospect in itself, but not yet called for. With Trender, Reggie and Baxter competing for stock against the usual Market operators, and now against the lucky readers of the Sunday papers, the shares looked set for a further rise and I looked set for a tasteful little third-floor *pied-à-terre* in Pimlico. As long as Patel didn't sell, things were going well for me; and about time too.

'Ah Mr London,' he chirped when I rang him back. 'Is everything sorted out now?'

'It is indeed, Mr Patel – and very satisfactorily.'

'Oh?'

'Yes – and the news is good. I think you should be able to sell without any trouble. I've traced the source of the buying.'

'And?'

'And you wouldn't expect me to betray a professional confidence, would you, Mr Patel?'

'Oh – of course not.'

'The point is, this is good quality buying. I think they'll take your stock. The shares are going higher, of course, so in that sense you won't be getting the top price if you sell now, but you know what they say: sell while they're still going up.'

'But if they are going up, why should I sell at all?'

'Oh I'm not *advising* you to sell, Mr Patel. On the contrary. I think you'll lose a lot of money by doing so. But this is a keen buyer, and if your mind is made up I would naturally be delighted to do the business for you.'

'I'm sure you would, Mr London.'

'A profit's a profit, Mr Patel. Shall we proceed?'

'Now wait a minute, Mr London. Perhaps we should hang on a few more days. If he's this keen, perhaps there's something even I don't know about.'

'Could be, Mr Patel. It's your decision.'

'And perhaps I ought to take some independent advice. Perhaps my bankers might be willing.'

This was disturbing. The button-down shirt brigade would be sure to think up something too clever for me; and whatever they thought up would almost certainly require me to read, or even write, a long and tedious document.

'Good idea,' I said. 'Of course, if it leaked that you thought your shares were over-valued, and you the chairman of the company . . .'

'I see what you mean, Mr London. Better keep mum.'

'On reflection, I agree.'

'And hold off selling,' Patel concluded.

'Perhaps you're right,' I confirmed. I spent the afternoon working on the text of my talk. As there was so little to say about Patel's company I concentrated on the prime mover. Banishing from my thoughts any encumbrance of fact, I used as a starting-point a biography of John D. Rockefeller which I happened to be keeping in the top drawer of my desk.

151

Lucy came back to London on the Tuesday. I'd failed to get in on a New Year's Eve lunch and was hoping to make up with a six-course Chinese in Soho, but the dear girl rang me at the office to say she'd popped into Safeways on the way home. She'd made up her mind to cook for me.

'It's about time I did.'

'You don't have to,' I assured her, trying to hide my dismay. 'We can always go out to save trouble.'

'But I want to, darling. It's nice to cook for someone. It's a sign of affection.'

'I know it is, sweetie. Shall I bee a bee?'

'What?'

'Bring a bottle.'

'It's not a dinner party, darling.'

'What are you making?'

'It's a surprise,' she said. I had a nasty feeling she might be right. Reason suggested they must have taught her something at finishing school, but it didn't have to be cooking. Instinct counselled caution. On the way to the flat I dropped into the Potter to line my stomach with a quick quart and a steak and kidney pie.

'Oh dear,' she said. 'I think the soup's a bit on the thin side.'

'Not at all,' I replied, scouring my bowl for nourishment.

The main course was quite different: a brittle wafer covered by a dark green crust.

'Oh dear. I don't think the spinach quiche is up to much either.'

'It's fine,' I said, crunching, 'fine. I think you might have given the salad dressing a shake before you put it on, though.'

'Oh.'

'I think so. Just a little – you know – a little shake, just to get the oil and the vinegar mixed up a bit.'

'Oh.'

'It does help sometimes.'

'You are enjoying it, though, aren't you?'

'Oh God, yes. Loving it. Nothing like home cooking, is there?'

The wine was all right. The brie, straight from the fridge, was firm but sound. While Lucy powdered her nose I rounded the meal off with a stealthy glass of bubbly. I drank it while it still fizzed, as instructed on the side of the packet.

She was having to sort out her makeup because she had been invited to a party down the road in Flood Street. We got there shortly after eleven. There were two large rooms in the flat, which belonged to someone with a long name, and we went first to the one without the music. As we arrived a champagne cork bounced

152

down off the ceiling and rapped me on the crown. Concussed, I shrugged my shoulders and assured the culprit I was fine. Lucy rubbed my head painfully, dabbed my shirt with a cloth and disappeared into the crowd.

'Well, ours has nearly doubled in two years,' someone said.

'I know,' said another. 'Where *we* are....'

'Unless you're a gay black one-legged lesbian, of course. I think she's right.'

'I know. It's got to stop ...'

Most of the crew were in suits and dresses, but I also saw kilts, blazers and a pantomime horse. The vernacular was catching. Oh *God*, I caught myself thinking, what am I doing *here* when I could be at *home* with my feet on the *pouffée* reading Ronald *Fir*bank?

The chat was suspended for a few minutes while we all sang *Auld Lang Syne*. One or two of the Scots, of the type that only go hame to kill, knew the words in full. Then we did the conga. Lucy reappeared with a brunette.

'This is London,' she said. Too right, I thought.

'And what do you do?' said the brunette. 'Oh, the City. In that case ...' But no, I didn't know him.

As soon as the brunette had turned her back on me I asked Lucy who these awful people were.

'Darling! They're my friends. Oh, look, there's –'

While Lucy was only being a second I fell into discourse with a tall youth in a white tuxedo and a whirling bow-tie.

'Usually go away,' he said.

'Oh, yah?'

'Yah. Home.'

'Best place.'

'You?' he asked, looking round the room.

'Stay in London. Where's home?'

'Derbyshire.'

'Oh. Same here.'

'Really?'

'Derbyshire born, Derbyshire bred,' I said.

'Strong i' the arm, weak i' the 'ead,' he replied in what I supposed was meant as a Derbyshire accent.

'Yes,' I said. 'In Buxton we tend to apply that one to south county folk.'

'Really? I'm south county myself.'

'Oh,' I said. 'French letter country.'

'What?' he scowled.

153

'The Ffrench Beytaghs. Thought you might know 'em. The F.B.s, as they're known locally.'

'You seem to think that's funny.'

'I do, quite.'

'Know 'em yourself?'

'Not well.'

'*Jamie!*' cried a familiar voice. Lucy, interposing, put her arms round his neck and kissed him. There followed a long debate, one I'd heard several times in the past half-hour, about whose it was at that they had last met. Ignoring my suggestion (Kevin's), they decided it must have been Tiggy's.

'Oh, but Jamie, I see you've found London.'

'Not hard. Straight down the M1 and there it was.'

'We weren't properly introduced,' I said.

'Oh, right. Jamie – this is London London.'

'Who?'

'London London.'

'Christ. Jamie Ffrench Beytagh,' said the youth.

'An old friend of Hughie's.'

'And of yours, Luce.'

'Oh, and of mine, of course.'

'Excuse me,' I said. 'All this booze is dehydrating me. I need a drink.'

Swiftly adding another two glasses to the washing-up requirement, I took myself to the music-room. There I stood on the sidelines with a further measure of mulled wine watching the young things dance. It took me back to the old days. In those days it was different, though. I was young myself then. In those days I'd have had a can of Newkie Brown Ale in my hand as I stood on the sidelines watching the young things dance.

Once my eyes had adjusted to the lower light I noticed I wasn't alone. There was another watcher on the shore. This one, paunch straining the buttons of his DJ, did have a can of brown ale in his hand. He was growing a beard to compensate for hair-loss. I recognised a soul-mate.

'All these vile bodies,' I said.

'Eh?'

'All these vile bodies.'

'Christ,' he said. 'Artificial stimulants I can't do without, but literary allusions I can.'

'I wish I'd said that,' I countered.

I hadn't noticed until now how very big he was. His punching did him credit. Granted, my expertise in this area is limited by

154

thoroughgoing cowardice; but even so, as I picked myself up I knew I'd been put down by a good 'un.

I offered my hand.

'You're not a fuckin' karate expert, are you?' he asked.

'Do I look like one?'

'Not a lot.'

'Enjoying the party?'

'Not a lot. You?'

'No,' I admitted. 'What brings you here?'

'Social climbing. Nice of 'em to ask me, I thought. Now I'm not so sure. Sorry about the eye. Can't stand a smart-arse, and I thought for a minute you might be one. You better put some ice on it. There's plenty round. Take it easy.'

Despite the ice I soon started feeling what a good 'un the good 'un had been. We had to leave.

'But why did he do it?' Lucy asked.

'Perhaps he'd been in the City too long.'

'You didn't hit him back, did you?'

'Not hard.'

'Oh London – why do you keep getting involved in these things? You're not very – *steady*, are you?'

'Compared with who?'

'That's not the point, London. Oh, London.'

Braving stares and avoiding mirrors I left Lucy snoozing the next morning and made it to the Vat and Vulture for a chicken curry and something to wash it down. As soon as I got back to the flat I was summoned under the duvet, despite my injury, for the afternoon event. As I pointed out, if Lucy had really wanted evidence that I was thirty and not twenty she could have looked at my birth certificate; but she insisted on practical proof.

We were woken by the 'phone shortly after six. Lucy answered it. I pretended to be asleep and listened hopefully for the rustling sound of her bottom hitting the wickerwork chair, which would presage at least half an hour of peace. In this I was disappointed.

'London – London! That was Suzy.'

'Ng?'

'Come on, you old bore. That was Suzy. Suzy Draycott. You know. Of course you do. Anyway, we're going out. Come on. Up.'

Knowing that nothing, not even a further demonstration of my sexual decline, could keep her from a friend, I felt it safe to pretend that I wanted her to come back to bed.

'No, darling, we can't. We're going round to drinks.'

'What's the rush?' I asked. This was a bit of a risk: if I'd misread her tone the result could be painful and possibly embarrassing. For a terrible moment she hesitated.

'The thing is, I said we'd go straight round,' she said. 'They're going out.'

'Oh, all right,' I conceded, reluctantly springing out of bed.

'Anyway,' Lucy added, 'it's exciting really. She's got a new man, but she won't tell me who it is. I wonder who it could be. Hope it's not Julian.'

Haling as I do from the dark satanic North, I've never seen the point of wearing sunglasses indoors. Suzy Draycott had compromised, this stygian winter's evening, by putting hers on the top of her head.

Braving the five-minute trek to Oakley Street, location of Suzy's delightful s/c garden flat; stunning drawing rm, 1 bed, bath, kit/bfast rm, full gas c.h., we were greeted like Arctic explorers home against the odds.

'I've heard *so* much about you,' Suzy enthused.

'All of it bad, I hope.' I was on sparkling form.

'Most of it. Come through.'

'Where is he, then?'

'In the loo. He's doing a spot.'

'Of what?' I inquired.

'Of *what*! Of *what*! Luce didn't tell me you were funny too. No – he's *got* a spot. You know – a zit. He's terribly worried about it. God, he's vain. And the thing about it is, it's on his back. He'd never have noticed it, but –'

'You did!'

'But I did!'

Once the hysteria had died down we sat on twin sofas facing each other across a glass-topped table.

'Fizz?'

'Brill.'

'Yes please,' I said, ashamed to ask for Milk of Magnesia. My head was throbbing in familiar fashion, especially in the once-again prominent environs of my left eye.

'Happy New.'

'Hey you!' Suzie shouted. 'Stud! Get a move on! ... He's such a fuss. But I must ask you, London – London, is that how you like to be known? – I must ask you what happened to your eye, poor thing? She hasn't been beating you up, has she?'

'London's in disgrace.'

'Oh dear. Was it a matter of honour?'

'I was trying to prove I was a man.'

'Some hope,' said Lucy.

A door opened and closed and I heard the sound of a voice I knew.

'Right then, where's the shampoo?'

Buck Baxter bounded into the room. 'Hi! Happy New Year!'

Guessed already, had you? Well I hadn't.

'Suzy! Suzy, you *devil* for not telling me! Oh *God*!'

'Hi,' Baxter snapped, striding past me in his peerless cords.

'Good evening,' said I. 'What a pleasant surprise.'

Lucy and Baxter kissed the air behind one another's ears and then what Baxter referred to as some serious whistle-wetting commenced; though on the basis of his unusually high colour I inferred that this process had already begun, possibly in earnest, before our arrival.

An hour or so later Baxter's cheeks were flushed to a deep vermilion and he was keeping the party entertained with an account of his career so far and his views on the future of the Stock Exchange.

'Could move, you see. Could move. No shortage of offers these days, is there?'

I nodded judiciously to imply agreement in principle; no doubt there were lots of offers, but I didn't want to be asked for details of any that had come my way of late.

'Could go to a bigger firm,' Baxter elaborated. 'Work for the Americans. They're always looking. Even the Japs. Not that I would. Little yellow bastards. Remember Burma, that's what I say.'

'Do you, Buck?' I asked.

'Course not. Not personally. But I would if I could. Anyway, what was – ? Oh yes, yes. Could move. Triple the loot overnight. Over bloody night. And let's face it, do the business and you're worth your crust. Aren't you, London? Ha ha. But then, working for the Yanks, or the Japs, you've got no say, have you? You get the cash but what you've also got is these buggers telling you what to do. That I *don't* need. Whereas at Rogers & Prickett I'm king, er – '

'Rat?'

'Pin. King pin. King rat – right, very funny. Very funny, this man, Luce. Not as funny as he thinks he is, though. Not as clever either. Not nearly as clever as he thinks he is. Involved in a bit of biz together, aren't we. Thinks he understands what's going on.

157

Doesn't, though. Doesn't. Anyway – yes – king pin, old Buck Baxter at Rogers & Prickett. Big man. And getting bigger. All going to change, you see. Year of change. Big bang. Getting bought out, aren't we?'

'Are we?'

'Of course. God knows who by. Try reading the papers. Anyway, get taken over, get fresh capital, get rid of the dead wood, Fat Perce and the rest, John-boy, that bunch, then I'm, top, er – '

'Dog?'

'Man. Top man, you snide fucker.'

'This *is* jolly,' I said.

'Another glass, Buck?'

'What?'

'Buck! Will you have another glass?'

'Just pour it, will you? But no, look, don't want to make things unpleasant but this bugger's always the same. Sarcastic. Lowest form of wit, I call it. Sorry, Luce, but I tell you. F–, fass–'

'Facetious?' I suggested.

'Facetious. And I tell you something else. He's really pleased, I mean really pleased, about, about, you know, getting in the saddle with you, Luce. Really pleased. Big man's daughter and all that. Aren't you? Eh?'

'Buck!'

'And now here he comes to, er, er – '

'The name's Suzy.'

'Sorry, old thing. He comes here to Suzy's and starts taking the piss. Taking the piss out of me. Or trying to. Wha's he come for, tha's what I want to know, wha's he come for if he just comes and takes the piss?'

Carried away by his rhetoric, Baxter slipped forward off the sofa and knelt in front of the low glass-topped table.

'Pity he hasn't the balls to say it in the office.'

'Buck!'

'Balls is something you'd know a lot more about than I would, Bax.'

'London!'

'Too damn right I would,' said Baxter. 'And not only balls – '

Still kneeling, Baxter looked at the two girls in turn and then at me before executing his famed slow smile. A boyish frown touched his brow as he struggled with his flies. Then with a flip and a slap, he deposited on the table-top, among the dry-roasted peanuts and the empties, the weapon which had conquered so many dizzy débutantes.

158

'Cock too!' he said.

It wasn't the grossness of this gesture that bothered me. It wasn't the tastelessness or the arrogance. It was the innocence. It was the simple stupid pride. It was – ah, well, let's be honest – it was the sheer *size* of it.

Lucy followed me out, and after her came the hoot and whine of Baxter's devilish laughter.

CHAPTER FIFTEEN

'*Bonjour.*'

Baxter checked his cufflinks and tucked away his bi-monthly copy of *Look Good, Feel Good.* This was the third morning of the year and the first Friday.

I slung my jacket and unwrapped an apple doughnut.

'I'm pleased to say we managed to stagger through yesterday without you,' he added. 'Down at Toad Hall, were we?'

'I was out with the lad.'

Inexplicably, Margaret had offered to lend me my son for a day while she and some of the other gals were off on an acupuncture course. Ben and I divided our time between travelling on the underground and getting wet in the streets.

'Good,' said Baxter. 'Hope you enjoyed it. Now – we're having lunch today.'

'Sorry, Bax. I'm out with a client.'

'I'm afraid you'll have to cancel. Lunch with Alfie, Reggie and yours truly instead. All right?'

'I can't wait.'

'You'll have to – till one o'clock.'

'Where?'

'One of Alfie's favourites, you'll be pleased to hear. The Shit and Shave.'

For one of Alfie's favourites it might have been worse. The Ship and Slave, though ghastly in every other respect, had a name for reasonable food.

'Oh, er, one other thing.' Baxter rolled his eyes to call me closer. 'About, er, Wednesday. New Year's Day.'

'I think I know what you're referring to.'

'I'd had a bit to drink, of course. Rather a lot, in fact. That's no excuse, I realise. But nothing personal intended. Only old Suzy seems to think I might have overstepped the mark. The point is, no offence, eh? Nor to Luce, obviously. Great girl.'

'That almost sounds like an apology, Bax.'

'Well, no hard feelings, I hope. Let's leave it at that, shall we? ... You, er, you don't ride, do you?'

160

'Occasionally.'

'Got a bit of experience, though?'

'A bit.'

'Only I thought – well, it was Suzy's idea, actually – I thought you might like to come out in the Park tomorrow, since I'm in Town this weekend.'

'I've got my son tomorrow.'

'Christ, bring him along. They love it. Do him the world of good. We'll get him a pony. Luce too, of course.'

'I'm not sure if she'd want to.'

'There you're wrong. I've asked her already. Likes the idea a lot.'

'It seems to be settled, then.' Resuming my place, I opened the newspaper.

'Ahem!'

Baxter had cocked an eyebrow.

'You must admit, though,' he said.

'What?'

'Not a bad bit of tackle, is it? They don't call me the Python for nothing.'

At twenty to one that afternoon, leaning on the bar of the Straddle, an establishment favoured by options dealers and only a hundred yards from the Ship and Slave, Kenny Morgan poured another glass and looked troubled. He closed one half of his mouth and through the other half said: 'I don't like it.'

'We should have had the Liebfraumilch,' I suggested.

'Not this, cunt. This! This ELI business. They only have to rumble it and we all get a one-way ticket to the twenty-third floor.'

The twenty-third floor of the Stock Exchange building in Throgmorton Street was where, in Kremlin-style secrecy, inquisitions took place on the matter of insider dealing.

'What do *we* know?' I asked. 'A nosey Swiss client buys the stock in large numbers, so we have a few for ourselves in case something interesting turns up.'

'But we deal through another broker.'

'Admittedly.'

'And we don't tell our employers.'

'Granted.'

'And when they turn the heat on Reggie, he tells 'em we knew what was happening all along.'

'But that only happens if they get rumbled.'

'Maybe. May be. *Or* – ' He was using an even smaller segment of his mouth now. 'Or somehow they turn the whole thing on us. Or rather, mate, since you was the one doin' the dealing –'

'On me.'

'On you, mate.'

'That wouldn't be very nice.'

'So what you need, just in case, is proof.'

'Proof,' I echoed.

'And that, me old darling, is where this little chap comes in.'

I looked over Ken's shoulder, where one little chap was dropping a cigar into another little chap's half-full bottle of bubbly.

'Who?'

'Here,' said Ken, producing a black box the size of a cigarette packet. 'The latest thing, mate. Perfect quality, perfect reliability, latest technology, and look at the size of it. Brilliant.'

'What is it, Ken?'

'What is it? It's a bunch of grapes – what do you think it is? You intelligent people. It's a cassette-recorder. This to stop – this to record – this to rewind – this to play back. Standard cassette. Genius.'

'Answer me a question, will you, Ken?'

'Anything you like. You won't get better than this.'

'How many have you got?'

'Twenty. *Very* cheap.'

'How much?'

He whispered in my ear. 'That's cheap, mate,' he added. 'State of the art, this.'

'Where's it from?'

'Japan.'

'I mean, where's it from more recently?'

'Oh I couldn't say.'

'Not Rambo again?'

'Yeah. I dunno why he can't get videos like an ordinary fence. That kind of thing I could place. It'll be artificial legs next. Mind you, it's a good make, this one. But they hadn't got round to putting the logo on when we, er – '

'Half the price and I'll think about it.'

'Start thinking.'

'Quarter the price and I'm firm.'

'You've dealt.'

'I'll take it now. Has it got a tape? Right. Settlement tomorrow. I've got to go.'

Next to us a youngster with a moustache ordered another bottle of the one with the gold label.

'You know, London,' said Ken, 'they used to get a really nice type of person in this place.'

My forehead pitted by hailstones, I arrived at the Ship and Slave two minutes early. Obscurely sited in one of the alleys south of Cannon Street, the Ship had survived the Blitz but had fallen in recent years to a public-spirited company promoter who failed to obtain a casino licence for the site, despite the crying need for such an amenity, and compromised by turning this spacious Victorian public house into a theme restaurant. Barmen became crew, jolly middle-aged barmaids became scowling young slave-girls and the bar became the Long John Silver room, where sterling deposit traders sat back-to-back with gold arbitrageurs. The air was thick with well-informed whispers, market gossip and buttered buns.

'Ah, yes, sir, Sir Alfred Trender's party. A private room, sir: the Captain Bligh suite,' said the pirate at the door. We walked through the main dining room, as calm and congenial as the Battle of Jutland, and up some stairs.

'First time here, sir?'

'Unfortunately not.'

Our room, rendered nautical by fibre-glass beams and ship's lanterns, looked down on the main fray through a thick glass screen. Reggie and Baxter were already there, sipping pinkies.

'A drink, sir?' This enquiry came from a blonde slave-girl in a low-cut bodice.

'Alfie's just nipped to the Sailors',' said Baxter.

'Tomato juice, please. Worcester, no ice.'

'Had too much already?' said Baxter.

The door creaked open. Sir Alfred Trender took a step forward, looked perplexed, paused, and seemed to think for a second. Cocking his hand to his ear, he farted loudly.

'Whoops! Sorry,' he said to the slave-girl, who smiled. 'Thought I'd left that one behind. Better out than in, though. Whisky and coke for me, love.'

'Good afternoon, Sir Alfred,' I said.

'Eye-eye,' he quipped. 'Look who's 'ere. How's my daughter? Better than you, I hope, from the look of you. What's on the menu, then? Christ, is it hot in 'ere or is it me?'

We all agreed it was hot. Sitting down, we were steered through the menu by our boatswain, who wore a spotted scarf round his head. I followed his advice and went for the Pieces of Eight. The others had the Pirate's Platter. Conversation charted a predictable course through cricket and the latest sexually-transmitted disease (for which Sir Alfred's cure was eugenically feasible but perhaps not politically acceptable), and on to the choppier waters of making money. The boatswain and the slave-girl looked on attentively. Alfie winked for more grog.

'Enjoying the meal?' the girl asked as she leant over to pour.

'I am now,' he said, resting his hand on the small of her back.

'Naughty naughty,' she said. 'Any bad behaviour and you know what happens. I'll have to report you to the Captain, sir.'

'Oh yes please,' said Alfie. 'What do I get, forty strokes? Your place or mine?'

Punishment was the main draw at the Ship and Slave. Working in the City wasn't enough for some of them. Down in the ratings' mess first offences earned three lashes of the cat-o'-nine-tails administered by the ship's matron, who would then turn nurse again and rub the affected part better. Persistent offenders rolled up their trousers and walked the plank.

'So,' Alfie continued. 'Biz. ELI. What are they today?'

I tried to say they were fifty-five but Reggie interjected.

'Perhaps this part of the luncheon should be in camera.'

'Camera? Christ, where?' Alfie hid his face behind his arm.

'In private, Alfie.'

'You're right. Sorry, love. An' you, mate.'

I asked them to excuse me, too.

'No, you can stay.'

'I've got to go to –'

'Can't it wait?' asked Reggie.

'I'm not sure it can,' I said, assuming a pained expression.

Safely locked in a cubicle, I pressed the 'record' button on my mini-cassette and slipped the gadget into my breast-pocket, flushing the lavatory for effect in case anyone was listening. When I returned to the Captain Bligh suite the room was quiet, as though they had been saying something I wasn't meant to hear.

'Christ, it's 'ot,' Alfie reaffirmed. 'What do you two think?'

'Like a scrum-half's jockstrap,' said Baxter.

'Could do with a bit of fresh air,' Reggie suggested.

'Jackets off,' Alfie ordered.

'I'll keep mine on,' I said.

'Take it off. It makes me sweat to look at you. I think we must've sailed into the Tropics.'

No matter, I thought: my little friend could still hear every word.

'What are they, then?' Alfie asked. 'ELI.'

'Fifty-five-six.'

164

'Good. And how many have we got now?'

'About a million.'

'What d'you mean, about?'

'One mill fifty,' I hazarded.

'Plus a mill already.'

'Makes a long two million,' I computed.

'A mathematical genius,' Alfie declared. 'Promote the man at once.'

The boatswain pushed the door open.

'Sir?'

'Eh? Who asked you to come in?'

'Did you not ring, sir?'

'Did I?'

'Oh,' said Reggie. 'I think I must have pressed this button.'

'Cunt. Mistake, mate. Anyway, bring us another bottle. Oh, and while you're at it, get rid of these jackets, will you?'

'I'll keep mine,' I said.

'What for? You can wipe your mouth on your serviette. Go on, chief, take 'em.'

I watched in despair as the jackets were carried away.

'Now,' said Alfie. 'Let's get on with it, shall we?'

I thought of giving up, but Ken's warning rattled through my head: They only have to rumble it and we all get a one-way ticket to the twenty-third floor. Nor would it stop there. The next special excursion would be the six-month return trip to Wormwood Scrubs. Inside information wasn't what it used to be. They were coming down hard on the old days these days.

'Oh dear,' I said. 'I'm terribly sorry. I do seem to have a bit of a problem. I hope you don't mind.'

The slave-girl was taking the top off the next bottle of Burgundy outside the door and retrieved my garment with reluctance. I slyly removed the cassette and retreated to the Sailors'. The next problem was where on my jacketless person to secrete it. In my front pocket it might be visible. In my back pocket the quality of sound-recording might be impaired. I tried it in my shoe, but there it made me walk very oddly. No, the only place for it, I finally conceded, was next to Nature's own hardware package, down the front of my underpants. It so happened that the Y-fronts had run out this morning and I'd been obliged to wear a pair of almost-clean low-cut knickers in which there remained, however, sufficient space for the gadget. I switched off 'record', rewound, and positioned it snugly. Better not mention this to Ken, I thought.

'All right now?' said Alfie a minute later.

165

'Sorry, Sir Alfred. Much better, thanks.'

'Touch of nerves?' said Baxter.

'It must be something I've eaten,' I said. 'Not here, I mean.'

'So,' said Alfie. 'Fifty-six this morning, and we're just over twenty per cent. That right?'

'Yes,' I said.

Oh *no*, I thought. I'd forgotten to switch back on. Thank God the thing was easy to operate. Summarising the position in the Market – jobbers short, buyers keen, price rising, a classic bear squeeze underway – I felt for the right button through my flies and pressed.

'So unless a large holder is shaken out, we can safely assume that the Market will be absorbing any loose stock to square its book.'

As I was saying this I became aware of a low hiss coming from under my side of the table. It was not unlike the sound a mini-recorder makes when about to play back. I raised my voice and tried to ignore it. This became more difficult when the hissing was followed by the roar, well-reproduced but fortunately muffled, of a lavatory cistern. Then a cubicle-door opened and closed.

Lowing, I clutched my abdomen and hastened from the room.

The slave-girl, awaiting a summons, extinguished her cigarette.

'You all right, sir?'

'*Christ it's 'ot,*' my crotch replied. '*What do you two think?*'

'*Like a scrum half's jockstrap,*' said a second voice.

'*Could do with a bit of fresh air,*' said a third.

'Don't be alarmed,' I explained. 'It's just that there's a tape-recorder down my trousers.'

I ran into the Gents', where panic turned my hands into boxing-gloves and I couldn't undo my zip. Ignoring the tearing sounds I heaved my trousers down with both hands and grasped the contents of my briefs. The boatswain came in.

'Having trouble, sir?'

'No!'

'Only you seemed to be, er – '

'Everything's fine,' I said, trying to be calm, trousers at my ankles, hands clamped on my genitals.

'Very well, sir. I'll be off, then.'

'*Now,*' my groin insisted, '*let's get on with it, shall we?*'

'I'll leave you to it, then, sir.'

Before I could stop him he was gone.

My return was greeted with a battery of understanding looks.

'Plain sailing from now on,' I assured them.

'ELI,' said Alfie.

'ELI,' said Reggie. 'The question of ethics.'

'Ethics? Eff the ethics!'

In the next twenty minutes the little black box recorded enough evidence of the syndicate's below-the-belt activities to qualify them for permanent resident status in Paraguay. After that we all relaxed. Regrettably I felt obliged to decline pudding on the grounds of my indisposition. The boatswain and the slave-girl got friendlier as the meal drew to an end. The waif let Alfie's hand stray downwards from the small of her back and the boatswain laughed. Reggie stared at his lap and Baxter tried to talk about horses.

'That was great, love.' Alfie patted his belly with his free hand.

'Very nice,' was the consensus.

'Bill to my account, please.'

'Thank you, sir.'

The girl simpered. Alfie unfurled a twenty from his pocket and slowly rolled it up.

'Now, if you'll kindly allow me to put this where I think it might fit ...'

'That depends on where you had in mind, sir.'

'Hear that, lads!? I should have made it a fifty!'

The twenty and the greater part of Alfie's right hand disappeared into the girl's cleavage.

'There.'

'Thank you, sir. Very generous.'

'They certainly are!'

As we stood to leave Alfie wagged his finger at the boatswain, who had gone very quiet, and said, 'Oh. Nearly forgot you, mate. S'pose you wouldn't mind a tip yourself?'

'That's very kind of you, sir.'

'Here's a tip for you, then. A good tip. Buy yourself some East London Industries. You won't regret it.'

CHAPTER SIXTEEN

The reason I'd steered clear of booze at the Ship, save for a token four or five glasses of Corton Grancey, was not the shadow of the previous evening falling across my palate (though memory suggests that I had, in fact, had to nurse Modigliani through half a case of Barolo) but the three o'clock appointment I had lined up with Coe & Coe, my West End solicitors. Up to now all such contests between their open-hearted willingness to redistribute my wealth and my own reluctance to let go of it had resulted in victory for the forces of law and order. Experience informed me, however, that some degree of sobriety at this stage of a Friday afternoon might easily give me the edge.

The office was three flights of stairs, no lift, above a kebab takeaway in Tottenham Court Road. They had started professional life above a beigal shop in Brick Lane but went West when they went legit: or so I was told by the man who introduced me. (A tidy percentage *he* must have been on.) The waiting room was just large enough to accommodate clients one at a time, at which disadvantage they could easily be seen off by Sandra, the fearsome receptionist.

'Er – Mr London, for Mr Coe.'

'Which Mr Coe?'

'Is there more than one?'

'Coe,' she said, and paused, 'and Coe.'

'Of course. The elder,' I tried.

'Are you sure?'

'Er – yes.'

'Possible,' she said. 'He did leave a few things outstanding.'

She looked through the list and shook her head.

'I spoke to him last week,' I said.

'No you didn't.'

'Yes I did.'

'No. You. Didn't, Mr London.'

'Yes. I. Did. What is this, a pantomime?'

'*Where* did you speak to him, then? At a séance?'

'Oh, I'm sorry. It must have been the younger Mr Coe.'

'That's what I was thinking ... Mmm ... Yes, here we are ...

Well I'm afraid you're rather late for your appointment.'

'I was at a meeting.'

'I'll see if he can fit you in.'

While she was out I looked at the diary. There were no further entries that day.

'Please take a seat,' she said when she came back, as if there were more than one to choose from.

The telephone rang.

'I can put you through,' she told the caller. ' ... Oh, if you wish. Yes, I have got a pen.'

She wrote down a message and handed it to the younger Coe when she showed me in. He stared at it for a moment, laid it on the palm of his hand and slapped it face-down on the desk.

'I heard the news,' I said. 'I was sorry to hear it.'

'Unbelievable, unbelievable,' Coe replied, head bowed.

'These things often are,' I sympathised. 'Was it – sudden?'

'The bastard,' Coe replied; unhinged, it seemed, by grief.

'You feel angry with him,' I said. 'It's a common reaction.'

'Eh?' said Coe, looking up. His office was untidy, needing a clean; and his sallow face went well with it. Directed there from just above the ear, hair lay in lank strips across an otherwise bald scalp.

'Angry. You feel angry with him.'

'How do you know?' said Coe. He looked again at the message Sandra had given him and picked up the phone. 'Get him for me, will you, Sandra? ... Right. So. Down to business. Now – the charge is – ?'

'I don't think we've discussed the fee yet.'

'What fee?'

'The charge.'

'Oh, the *charge*.' A near-smile passed across Coe's features. 'I'm afraid you misunderstand.'

'I was hoping I might have.'

'Quite so. What I mean is – what exactly have you been charged *with*, Mr Linden?'

'London.'

'Mr London. London? Are you sure? I suppose you must be.'

'I haven't been charged with anything.'

'Oh, haven't you? Well there's a start. With any luck they won't press charges at all.'

'Who won't? Mr Coe, I am here to discuss my divorce.'

'Ah, yes – *now* I remember. Well I'm sorry to hear it's come to this, but of course we'll be pleased to help in any way we can.'

'Just to refresh your mind of the minutiae of the case, Mr Coe:

169

my divorce took place a year ago. It was your Mr Brooks who dealt with it. Now I gather he's left the firm.'

'Quite so. He has. A very sad case, Mr Brooks. But I'm sure he'll find some outlet for his abilities once he's, er, paid his debt.'

'Debt?'

'To society. But that's another matter. Shall I get your file?' He rummaged round in a cabinet. 'Dead, dead, dead,' he said. 'I don't seem to be able ... Now what was it? L-i-n-'

'London. L-o-n-d-o-n.'

'Quite so. Got it ... Stupid little fucker,' he muttered.

I was on the point of remonstrating when I noticed his attention had strayed once more to the scrap of paper on his desk.

'So, Mr London,' he continued, 'would you mind just bringing me up to date? And then we can take it from there.'

This I did. Coe's habit of looking back at the written message and mumbling 'Damn!' or 'Hell!' or '*I'll* bloody *goose* him!' suggested that he found the details less than engrossing.

'I've finished now, Mr Coe,' I said some seconds after doing so. 'Mr Coe?'

'Eh?'

'That's about it.'

'Ah. Fine. Quite so. Well, as we said in our letter of the – er, the other day, the solution is undoubtedly to forget the barristers, forget the High Court and go straight to a judge in chambers. Very simple, very economical – and with your permission I will of course be able to represent you in person. Always best to have someone you can trust, isn't it?'

The telephone saved me from having to answer.

'You've got him have you?' he whispered excitedly. 'Right. Hold him. I'll take it next door ... Will you excuse me a moment, Mr London?'

He left the slip of paper face down on his desk. Wondering what subtle point of tort might thus be exerting him, I couldn't resist a peep. It read thus:

Doncaster 3.00
    1. Cossack Dancer
    2. Goose Bay
Going too soft – apologies – Arthur

Apologies weren't enough for Coe. The framed diplomas on the wall shook with his wounded bellowing. After a quarter of an hour he pushed open the door and said: 'Sometimes one has to be firm.'

'I know. I should have been, with Margaret.'

'Your daughter?'

'My wife.'

'Quite so. But you will be. *We* will be. So, next Tuesday it is.'

'What is?'

'The hearing. Didn't you know? Didn't I say? Oh, yes – easy to arrange, a judge in chambers. Any fool could do it. Here it is – on the file. Must be right. Tuesday the 7th. Three-thirty.'

'Oh my God.'

'I assure you there's nothing to worry about, Mr Linden. Half a day a week is not standard at all. You ought to get the lad for the whole weekend at least. I can't imagine who ever could have advised you to settle for half a day.'

'That was Mr Brooks,' I said.

'Was it?'

'I daresay he had his hands full at the time.'

'Almost certainly. He was found in a public lavatory.'

'Is that an offence?'

'It is when you're doing what he was doing. Anyway, chin up. The judge is a reasonable chap. Justice Jefferies. He won't want to keep a lad from his dad. Look desperate and we'll be all right.'

Now I knew that my son's future was in safe hands, I was inclined once I'd made it through the slush to Baker Street to take the westbound line and lose myself in a late afternoon half-gallon of Egginton's Old Disarmer, a case of which, to be drunk in extremis, was gathering dust at the bottom of my wardobe. Then I recalled I was due at the Man for the weekly debriefing with Ken.

On the train I ran through some possible hiding-places for the tape. Down my trousers was definitely out. Taking it home was out because I didn't know when I might need it. My desk was possible but risky: it was not unknown for Baxter, in prefectorial fashion, to rifle through other people's drawers in search of contraband tuck. Lucy could be relied on to play the tape as background music to a drinks party. What familiar friend could I trust?

I looked around and the answer came back – Doris; Doris to whom I was a helping hand, a kindly arm, a listening ear; Doris who would ask nothing and say nothing; of legendary discretion and unimpeachable loyalty. Doris wouldn't let me down.

By close of business I was back in the office. The cassette was safely stowed in Doris's desk, no questions asked, and Ken was talking on the railway line.

'Forget the Green Man,' he said.

'This is the end of an era,' I objected.
'We're going to Bubbles. Be there.'

When I first arrived in the City, those seven long years ago, these premises were let to a firm of gentlemen's outfitters. Middle age had gone out of fashion in the Square Mile since then, and Bubbles, conveniently situated behind the Royal Exchange, was now the place where the boys and girls from the futures market met to reflect on the day's speculations. The markets were up today; the bar was full and there was only one drink on the list.

'What'll it be?' Ken asked. 'One bottle or two?'

'What are you smiling about? Don't tell me you've come into some videos? Cheers.'

'This is between the two of us, right?'

'My word is my bond.'

'Had an interview, didn't I? Last night. I didn't want to tell you in case it came to nothing.'

'An interview where?'

Ken named an American house.

'Not a bad shop,' I said with measured calm, hoping to hide a surge of envy.

'That went all right. Then this morning I get the call: come round lunchtime and see the chief trader. I go round, bit of a chat, get the offer there and then.'

'Your health. No wonder you're smiling.'

'If I told you the figure, you'd see why I'm smiling.'

'Large?'

'Large.'

'How large?'

He told me.

'*How* much? We'll have the vintage next time.'

'Right you are. Now you can tell me 'ow this business with the tape went.'

Later that evening, duly emboldened, I took a bus to Sydney Street. Letting myself in with my own key ('I want you to feel at home, darling,' Lucy had said. 'After all, this isn't just a casual thing, is it, darling?'), I surprised Lucy reading a novel. I was surprised too, though less so when I saw what it was.

Curled up on the sofa, She didn't move when I arrived. I angled in to kiss her.

172

'Hold on,' she said. 'I'm on a good bit. Wine's over there.' She waved a hand but didn't look up. I sipped a couple of glasses of tasteless Soave, by which time the pace of the narrative had swept her irresistibly to the end of the chapter, and she was ready to be kissed.

'London,' she said after that had been done.

'Yes, sweetie?'

'Why do you always look shattered after work?'

'What a lovely thing to say, sweetie. Do I?'

'Mostly.'

'Well, I suppose being worn out must have something to do with it.'

'But why don't the others look like that?'

'Who were you thinking of?'

'No one in particular. Aren't you going to kiss me again?' she asked.

'London?' she said again shortly afterwards.

'Mm?'

'Tell me something.'

'Mmm.'

'London, why don't we ever go to *your* flat?'

'Because – first you tell me something.'

'What?'

'Who's been stirring it?'

'Stirring what?'

'It,' I said. But I knew anyway. 'The reason is that my flat is horrible. That's why.'

'It can't be *so* horrible.'

'Oh, it can,' I said.

'You're ashamed of it, then.'

'Of course I'm ashamed of it. You would be ashamed of it. Anybody would be ashamed of it. It isn't fit to house a pig. If you don't believe me, come and see it. I tell you what, let's go there now.'

Outside, in the darkness, a balmy January sleet was tinkling on the roofs of frostbitten cars. The weather man, in optimistic mood, had promised us five degrees below. If I knew Lucy at all (and in all honesty she was a nice little thing but there wasn't much to know) there was one thing about her I knew for certain: all the king's horses couldn't drag her from the King's Road on a night like this.

When we got to College Gardens all the lights in the house were out save one in the basement. The sound of Gigli mingled with the smell of sugar on the stairs.

'The poor bugger thinks he's going to win a competition for his ice-cream,' I told Lucy.

'It is a bit dirty,' she said.

'This is the clean bit.' We reached the landing. 'But now – dadaa! – the London suite.'

I generally used a side-lamp these days, but this time opted for the main fluorescent light for maximum effect. The ring took some seconds before bursting into full flicker.

'Oh my God.'

My stately pleasure-dome, I observed with some satisfaction, was at its bohemian best, raffish charm accentuated by the contents of my laundry-bag, which I'd strewn about it this morning in the fruitless search for Y-fronts.

'London. Oh, London. You live here? It's horrible. I mean, it's really horrible. The carpet. Look at the walls. Oh my God – how can you bear to *sleep* in it?'

I'd left the window open for a change of fumes. The room was fearfully cold. A convoy of bulldozers, it seemed, trundled by.

'Now you see why I come to your place,' I said.

'Yes, now I do see.'

'How does it compare with Baxter's pad?'

'I wouldn't know. Oh, London, let's go, shall we?'

To make up for this trauma I took her to dinner in a restaurant in Tite Street, drinking perhaps a few sambucas too many to brace myself for the bill and thereby rendering myself unfit for further duties, a fact which aroused complaints lasting until the onset of unconsciousness. I slept the sleep of the humble poor and woke with a throbbing head. This agony was as nothing, however, compared with the sickness arising in my stomach when I remembered what I had agreed to do later on.

Perhaps it had been a mistake to tell Baxter I 'occasionally' went riding. I'd been right to add that I hadn't done it for some time, but I should have gone further. Given Baxter's determined approach to leisure, it might have been wise to admit that I hadn't done it for really rather a long time. Indeed the evolution of the equine species might have advanced considerably since the occasion I had in mind. Furthermore, a donkey-ride on Scarborough front at the age of six was hardly 'experience', I now reflected. I croaked, I sighed, I moped around the flat – in vain. Last night's refusal had put me in a weak position and Lucy was raring to go. You know what they say about women and horses.

A complicating factor was what to do about Ben. The planned riding-lesson was unlikely to show his father to best advantage. The opposite was a more probable outcome. I pondered the matter over a couple of Alka Seltzers and rang Margaret.

'I'm in Manchester,' I said.

'No you're not.'

'Yes I am.'

'You sound like you're next door.'

'That's privatisation for you. And why would I lie?'

'Okay, so you're in Manchester. Why are you in Manchester?'

'Ong *ong*-ong, ong ong-ong, ong ong *ong*-ong-ong.'

'What?'

'That was the tannoy. I'm at the railway station. Manchester Piccadilly. I was here on business yesterday. I missed the last train.'

'What business?'

'Ong ong ong, ong *ong*-ong-ong,' I added.

'That was you.'

'Look – my train goes in two minutes. I'll be round about two – all right?'

'By two? It's eleven now. Has that train got wings or something? Where the hell are you? Surely – but surely not – don't tell me you're with a woman. Don't tell me you've gone and got yourself *laid*.'

I held the receiver next to Lucy's digital clock and released the alarm-button.

'There's the pips,' I said. 'Sorry – no more change. About two, then. Cheerio!'

I don't know much about horses but I do know a lot about vertigo. The only thing that could get me up top on a London bus is the thought of no smoking downstairs. Trees I could never climb, even as a boy, despite my natural athleticism. Thank God I'm not tall. So although I can't tell the difference between a fetlock and a forelock I can tell you that when, an hour or so later, I found myself perched on the back of a horse, the distance between my feet and the ground made me writhe. Observed from below, my mount had apppeared markedly smaller than those selected for Lucy and Baxter; but this optical illusion was rapidly dispelled once I made it into the saddle.

'Now you're sure this is the slow one, aren't you?' I asked the girl. We were outside the mews stables just off Hyde Park Corner.

'Oh, yes. No trouble. Very placid, aren't you, Lady?'

The horse growled evilly.

'What's she called again?'

'Hurricane,' said Baxter.

Lucy giggled.

'Lady,' said the girl. 'Magic Lady.'

'*Allons-y*,' said Baxter. In a silk blouson and a pair of funnel-shaped trousers he did perhaps look a shade more the part than I did, hurriedly kitted out in jeans and a sweater after turning up in my work suit.

'Won't you be cold?' I asked, hoping to postpone the dread hour.

'Oh God, no. The faster you go, the warmer you get.'

'How do we get to the Park? I mean, do we put the horses in a box, or something?'

'What d'you think they're for?' Baxter retorted. 'We ride 'em there, funnily enough.'

Surely they didn't expect a novice to ride round Hyde Park Corner? I looked to Lucy for support, and Lucy looked away.

The next few minutes were the worst of the year so far. Although my nag was pretending to have trouble picking its feet from the tarmac I could sense there was mischief in its mind. I didn't like the way it kept looking round, as if for a bus to throw me under. I didn't like its deceptive calmness, either, or the way it constantly dribbled. Despite these problems, I managed by use of my thighs to steer a successful course through the very thick of it. I couldn't use the reins, because they were being held by the stable-girl walking in front of me.

Baxter and Lucy cantered away while the girl led me round in a circle on the end of a rope. During this humiliation I mulled over the mystery of why Suzy hadn't turned up. 'Just didn't fancy it,' Baxter had explained. 'Said she'd done enough riding lately.' Why had she suggested it, then? Perhaps she hadn't. It couldn't be that he'd kept her out of the way so he could demonstrate his dressage while I was kept tethered on an old dobbin scarcely fit for the dog food, could it? The girl groom, meanwhile, was giving me hints on where to put my feet and which way to look, plus a few other obvious tips not worth paying much attention to. After a while I felt I'd got the hang of it and thought we might try a little show-jumping, but the girl counselled caution.

'Now,' she said. She unhooked the rope.

'Now,' she repeated, retreating. 'Do this!' She made a movement of the hips which in other circumstances might have had very agreeable results. 'And walk her over to me.'

I gave a little thrust and the horse moved slowly towards her, a distance of some yards.

'Good. Now again.'

She walked away, I gave a shake, and the horse responded as planned.

'Good,' said the girl. 'Very good. You're a fast learner.'

I shrugged my shoulders modestly. This was a major turning-point. The horse took my gesture for something it wasn't intended to be and careered forward at great speed, pursued by the girl.

'Whoa!' I called. It stops them in the movies, but it didn't stop this one. 'Whoooa, boy!' I tried.

All of a sudden the saddle slipped and the world moved round by ninety degrees. I didn't know much about horses, but I knew that shouldn't have happened.

Who put this saddle on? I thought. Baxter, I thought; but the lights went out all over London before I had time to curse him.

CHAPTER SEVENTEEN

Furtively sucking a fistful of Amplex to hide the smell of beer, I limped up the stairs at Coe & Coe and found the waiting-room empty. I put my ear to the door of Coe's office.

'Great!' I heard him pant.

'Faster!' Sandra's voice replied.

'Yes.'

'Yes!'

'Come on, baby,' my lawyer urged.

'Push! Push!' his secretary howled.

'What about the whip?'

'Yes!'

'Faster!'

'Faster!'

'Go on!'

'Yes!' Sandra whined. 'Oh yes! Fan-*tas*-tic!'

'Brilliant – brilliant,' Coe sighed, his voice now subsiding. 'Marvellous!'

I tapped smartly on the door and marched in. Aglow with satisfaction, Coe and Sandra were watching a re-run of the 2.30 from Haydock Park on a portable black-and-white television set. Coe's fancy, Ayatollah, had obliged at nine to two.

'Since we've a little time to spare,' Coe said some minutes later, 'perhaps we should take this opportunity to discuss the fee.'

'You don't want to wait till after the hearing?'

'What difference, Mr Linden? Even if we win – I mean, even if we lose – the amount of work has been the same. So just by way of guidance, perhaps I should present the preliminary account now.'

He handed me the bill. 'Open to revision,' he said. What he meant was he'd added his usual margin for a generous discount later.

'You *have* got the decimal point in the right place?'

'Er – ha ha – I think if you look through the individual items you'll see more clearly how the final figure was reached.'

I scanned the list: telephone calls at a tenner a time; letters at Samuel Beckett-style cost per word; consultation fees to make a headhunter blanch.

'. . . But perhaps you're right, Mr Linden. Perhaps it would be better dealt with afterwards. Quite so indeed. And I think we ought to be going.'

'Knowing these Lefties, of course, they're bound to have your wife with her hair in a bun and a tweed skirt on,' Coe told me in the taxi on the way over. 'You come across it all the time in this business.'

'Her hair's too short for a bun.'

'Oh. Quite so. But you know what I mean. The judge will soon see through them. Very astute, Justice Jefferies.'

We passed from New Oxford Street and High Holborn into a region of narrow canyons and quiet.

'You wouldn't mind, would you? Or shall I put it on the bill?'

I paid the cab fare. We walked up steep white steps and through a large hall into an intimate series of corridors. Coe played the old pro, bustling along with confidence and leading us down several wrong turnings. We knocked on a numbered door and a servant let us in.

Margaret's was the first face I saw. She was wearing a turquoise jump-suit, and over that a combat jacket and badges. My lawyer shook hands with hers, a well-dressed youth with a shiny khaki face. I asked after Ben. Margaret said he'd been disappointed not to see me on Saturday. I said it was unavoidable – I'd slipped on the ice at the station and banged my head – why hadn't she let me see him on Sunday? That had been impossible, she said. Most things seemed to be impossible when it came to doing me a favour, I said – and so it went. Ten minutes were passed in this playful badinage before the servant made a loud noise and the judge walked in.

'Good afternoon.'

After a mumbled general response we placed ourselves in a semicircle round the front of a wide mahogany desk.

'So. Shall we begin? London versus London.'

The pleasure of hearing Margaret thus addressed was at once effaced when I realised that despite being powerfully set with a healthy Zapata moustache, Justice Jefferies was a woman. Don't get me wrong, though: my disappointment was only temporary. I'm all in favour of the working woman. God, am I in favour. I'd merely hoped that my solicitor might be well enough in with the judge to know her sex.

'That's me, your honour,' I said when she read out my name – as things transpired the only statement I made all afternoon which was not challenged as to relevance, honesty or procedure. Not that

179

the rules of combat were at all clear to me; or, it seemed, to the younger Coe. The informal style of the occasion appealed to my notion of justice-as-common-sense only until the opposing party began to harry and disrupt every time I spoke; while my own advocate eschewed such tactics, and in a gesture of contempt spent much of the time flicking through his notes, for all the world as if not fully apprised of the facts of the case.

As always when it's most important, I found it hard to concentrate. Images of Saturday morning clamoured for attention: my hands slipping from the reins; the fast approach of the turf, soft in aspect but hard on impact; the face of the stable-girl easing gently into focus. After that it took a long time for Lucy and Baxter to arrive and the pain in my right wrist got bad as the numbness wore off. Lucy's face, to which I looked for sympathy, wore its 'Oh London' expression and Baxter tested the wrist for a break. (But no, it was only a sprain.) Then he drove me to hospital; the next image was the well-appointed interior of his car.

Lucy must finish her ride, I'd insisted. (She didn't take much persuading.) I'd be fine, fine on my own, I said, and Baxter went back to the Park. For three hours at the hospital, jumped in the queue by the bleeding and dying, and then for the rest of the weekend also I was fine, fine on my own, dialling Lucy's number with my left hand and each time getting the answering machine; tipping back with the same left hand a lake of surplus Italian red, for soothe-a the pain, while Modigliani soliloquised on the virtues of fag-flavoured cassata and the prospect of being the emperor of ice-cream.

'Mr London? ... Mr London, please pay attention,' said the judge.

'Forgive me. I'm not feeling well. It must be nerves.'

'You were asked for your comments.'

Look desperate, I remembered.

'Would you mind going over that again?' the judge asked.

Margaret's lawyer replied: 'The question as my client sees it is whether Mr London really does wish to increase his access to the child, or whether this is in fact part of a long-running battle which he has been conducting against my client, the rights and wrongs of which are of course not necessarily under discussion at the moment. I was saying that only last Thursday my client allowed Mr London to see the boy – '

I tried to qualify this, but he didn't stop.

'– so that in our view the question of her being unreasonable does not arise. Furthermore, as recently as this past Saturday Mr London failed to arrive to collect his son at the time agreed, and rang with an excuse which quite frankly my client considered unsatisfactory, if not downright misleading.'

'In what way?' the judge asked.

'Mr London claimed he had been in Manchester on business the previous evening and had somehow contrived to miss the last train back.'

'And *was* Mr London in Manchester?'

'Yes indeed.' This was Coe, finally bursting into life. 'In fact my client resents the suggestion that he should have invented an excuse for not seeing his son at the very time when he is going to considerable trouble and expense – ' he emphasised this last word ' – to have his visiting times extended to a more reasonable level.'

'So, Mr London, you were indeed in Manchester?'

'Yes,' I said. Then I thought about the horse-ride; falling off; shaking the shock out of my head. I recalled the floating stomach I'd had, standing at the public 'phone in the bar at the Warwick with everyone's eyes on me and Lucy's Ansafone playing in the earpiece again. This was followed by a more familiar gastric churning, the consequence of the emollients I'd needed to drink after making each call. After that I thought about all the questions there would be if I insisted I'd been in Manchester. Where in Manchester? Doing what? Who was *in* the film, then, buddy?

Ah, sod it, I thought.

'Well – no,' I said.

Coe turned towards me, his mouth opening slowly.

'Where were you, then?' asked the judge.

'In Chelsea.'

'You lied?'

'Yes.'

'Deliberately?'

'Yes.'

'Could you say why?'

'I was with my girlfriend. I was going riding.'

'Riding.'

'I fell off and hit my head.'

Margaret laughed.

'Could we adjourn for ten minutes?' said Coe. 'My client does not feel well.'

'Do you wish for an adjournment, Mr London?'

'Yes ... No. I want to withdraw,' I heard myself say.

'I really think a brief adjournment – ' Coe began.

'I wish to withdraw,' I said. 'I'm sorry if I've wasted everyone's time.'

'This was, perhaps, the opinion I was beginning to form,' said the judge. 'I think we can end the proceedings here, then. Costs against Mr London.'

'There was one other matter,' said Margaret's man.

'Yes?'

'The question of the maintainance order, which we agreed at a time when my client's expenses, particularly those on the child, were at a rather lower level than they are now.'

'What's this?' I whispered to Coe.

'God knows. Have they mentioned this before?' He fumbled through his papers. 'Oh, yes – so they have.'

'A pity, that,' Coe said as we ducked into a cab twenty minutes later, pursued by Margaret's cry of 'Wanker!' echoing down Chancery Lane. 'I felt we were having the better of it till then. Tell you what – since things haven't really gone our way I'll treat you to the cab this time. We're seen as a rather rapacious profession, I know, but all we're trying to do is make a living, like anybody else. Performing a service ... Which I fear brings me to the matter of the fee. I don't suppose you can, er, afford it, can you?'

'What do you think?'

'Instalments? Not to worry. I'll send you a scheme of proposal.'

Outside his office we shook hands.

'At least we didn't go to the High Court,' he said. 'Now that really would have cost money.'

'You're right. It wouldn't have been worth the risk.'

'No. We'd still have lost. But, er – you're not, er, a gambling man, are you?'

'With my luck?'

'Since you can't pay the bill anyway, and since it's only a matter of instalments, it just occurred to me that, well, you might as well be paying for two years as one. You wouldn't be interested in double or quits, would you?'

I should toss, we decided, and Coe call.

'Don't mind if I use the double-headed penny, do you?' I said.

I tossed a pound coin.

'Tails,' he called. Tails it was.

The clouds waited patiently while I wrote the IOU, then obliged my storm-wracked soul by breaking. This time I didn't hesitate to take the homebound train.

As soon as I opened the front door diminutive, black-haired Gina Modigliani was on me. Something was amiss. She tried to tell me what, but the only Italian I spoke was what I'd picked up from her husband's records. Perhaps she was scolding me for the state of my clothes. How to explain?

'*La tempesta è vicina! Più scura fia la notte,*' I tried from the storm scene in *Rigoletto*. She responded by pushing me into the kitchen.

There a pathetic sight awaited me. Modigliani himself, hunched up, face on the table, was weeping like one of the lost, like an old man robbed of his daughter. His hair, in this dim light, was silver rather than grey. His shoulders heaved at the straps of his vest. Two bottles of Safeway Chianti Classico lay empty and toppled on the table.

I put my arm round Gina. Outside, the rain beat down and the thunder crashed. I approached the broken old man and laid my hand on his shoulder.

A giant sigh shook his frame.

'*Amigo mio,*' I said, hoping this was the Italian for 'my friend'. 'Ricardo. *Duce.* Speak to me.'

He only shook his head.

'No unnerstan',' said Gina, her brown eyes brimming with love.

'*Io capisco,*' I said. 'Ricardo.'

His face lifted slowly from the table.

'Ricardo – is it – ?' Here I paused dramatically. 'Is it the competition?'

It was, he seemed to say.

Another great sigh shook him, his sticky breath redolent of cheap wine and tobacco-flavoured ice-cream.

'My friend – I'm sorry.'

I thought I heard a whisper.

'Ricardo. *Duce.*'

I leaned closer.

'Bastard,' he groaned.

I pulled away sharply.

'Ricardo, I'm sorry. Truly I am. I only suggested it because I thought they might go for the outsider. It's a great British tradition, favouring the underdog. Except in my case, of course.'

He shook his head.

'You'd never have made it with the cornflake crunch, Ricardo. Or the prawn cocktail choc-ice. It was a brave try, Ricardo. Bear up.'

Now there was another heave, and he hauled himself on to his elbows.

'You don't understand,' he said.

'I do understand, Ricardo,' I assured him, looking into his red and puffy eyes. 'I do understand. Life's a shit sandwich. I know how much this meant to you. The honour – '

'The money.'

'The fame.'

'The money.'

'The sense of achievement.'

'The money,' he repeated more emphatically. 'The *money*! *Porco dio*, the *money*! I won, you son of a bitch, I *won*!'

A splash of water almost restored me to consciousness. I reached for my razor. God, these mornings were dark. Why couldn't the day start later? And why did I feel so ill? I lathered my face, ignoring these conundrums, remembering only the time: eight o'clock on Wednesday, the 8th January – London London's big day; the day of the ELI seminar. I might have lost my son, but at least I still had Lucy; I might not have a share of Modigliani's winnings, but I did have something more – a hundred thousand shares in ELI, bought below twenty pence, now standing at sixty and looking like being a pound or more before the day was over. Eighty thousand profit, maybe ninety, that would mean. A car would follow, and a nice deposit on a place of my own, a place with Poles by invitation only; with ice-cream confined to the fridge; with Lucy tucked into the bed.

Eight-thirteen. I should be on the train. Baxter would be getting his second wind by now. Why did my alarm clock never ring? You'd think I had a cheap one, the way it kept letting me down. And yet it was one of the best: Kenny Morgan had told me so, pointing to the blank space on the side where the logo ought to be. Perhaps I'd forgotten to set it. Baxter was right. They were all right. I was a slacker.

Questions accumulated. Why so little stubble this morning? It was hardly worth the bother of shaving. And why, for that matter, was I wearing my suit? I didn't recall putting it on.

I looked out through the plastic curtains to watch the eastbound traffic jam on the Westway. This was one of the high points of the morning. It made me glad not to have a car. Only today the eastbound track was empty, and the westbound was in full swing.

Yes, you beat me to it again. It was eight o'clock at *night*, and

184

still the 7th of January. I'd merely taken a nap after joining in Modigliani's celebrations, giving him a hand with the Chianti, smoking the cigars, spending the royalties and helping him up the stairs.

Yes, yes; now it came back. He'd got the phone call that morning. There hadn't been very many entrants. The lab boys tested the formula, the marketing boys raved, the sales department loved it and the boys on the board made the final decision, all a month ahead of plan. Trial runs were planned for the spring, production for early summer. Royalties would flow in the autumn. By next winter Modigliani would be somewhere in the sun. And the house, by the way, was up for sale. I had a week to find somewhere to live.

I wiped the lather off my face and wondered what to do next.

Lucy, I thought. Where was she, anyway? I walked down the street and rang her, so wrapped in my own concerns, I now realise, that I failed to remark the miracle of a functioning public callbox.

'Hello. Is that Mr Trender?' I asked in a strangulated voice.

'*Miss* Trender. Who's speaking?'

'Ah, this is-ah, Brian Glass of Opaque Double Glazing,' I said. 'I was-ah wondering if you might be interested in-ah saving on your heating bills.'

'I don't know where you got my number,' she said, 'but I'm not in the least interested.'

Good. Back at number seventy I opened the laundry-bag and eased myself, not without effort, into a pair of flannels. My face was red and crapulent, my eyes reduced to slits, my entrails staging a putsch; but overall I didn't feel too bad.

In Ladbroke Grove I hailed a cab, which responded with a stinging broadside of water and sent me scuttling back to College Gardens to change. This time I chose jeans. The casual look was in any case more appropriate, I reasoned; that cabbie did me a favour. At the second attempt no taxi appeared, so I went to the Warwick and rang for a mini-cab, warming up with a couple of bloodies while I waited. After those, and one or two more to keep the barman company on this slack and rainy night, the car came and I asked for Sydney Street.

About to ring the bell, I backtracked instead to the late-night florist and picked up some blooms to get the evening off to a good start. I decided to ignore the doorbell and use my own key instead, going for the element of surprise. I tiptoed up the stairs and crept in.

There was music coming from the sitting room – the latest release from a popular artiste I'd associated with feebleness of intellect

185

until I met Lucy – but the room was dark and empty.

The little darling was having an early night.

I pushed open the bedroom door, preceded by my outstretched arm bearing white carnations.

The room, a careful selection of pinks, was lit by low-set lamps. The curtains were closed and to one side of the bed, on a glass-topped table, stood a two-thirds empty bottle of rosé champagne. To the other side of the bed, on a second glass-topped table, where the old photo of me on the top of Snowdon had previously been, was a pale green jug with roses in it. Between the wine and the roses lay Lucy herself, stark naked, facing down but propped up on her elbows as if reading a book, though reading was not at all what she was doing.

'Good God,' said Baxter, who was sitting upright against the headboard. 'That's jolly decent of you, old chap. Couldn't put them in a vase, could you?'

He took a mouthful of wine, swilled it round his teeth, swallowed, and rested the glass on Lucy's head, which was very close to his lap, straddled by his thighs.

'Glass of fizz before you go?'

'Thanks, I will.'

'Here – take this,' said Baxter.

'Guh,' said Lucy.

Baxter was more modestly attired. Though trouserless, he had retained the protection of a red hunting-jacket, a yellow waistcoat, a hard peaked cap and a gleaming pair of black boots. What he'd been doing with a chic little riding-crop it was possible to surmise from the tangle of welts on Lucy's gently deflating buttocks.

'Bottoms up!' I said.

I downed it in one.

'*Santé*,' said Baxter. 'Couldn't make yourself scarce now, could you, old chap? Big day tomorrow. Cheer-ho!'

CHAPTER EIGHTEEN

'Good morning,' said Baxter.

I put my coffee down, managing to retain half of it in the plastic beaker. Carefully unwrapping a sticky bun so the icing wouldn't stick to the bag, I opened the newspaper and simulated a lively interest.

'Get home all right?' he enquired.

'Ready for the off?' he asked.

I flicked through the paper, staring hard at the pink columns. Some minutes later I was aware of Baxter looking over my shoulder.

'Not that bad, is it?' he said.

Pulling my eyes into focus, I found myself reading a feature on the Finnish machine tool industry.

'I was thinking we might have a little man-to-man after Parade,' Baxter continued. 'I mean, better that than ill-feeling. Specially on a day like today.'

'At your service,' I said, but as I chewed my bun I couldn't help noticing a tear slip down the side of my nose. Enough's enough, I thought. Being easy-going was getting expensive. Thus far, no further. Revenge; revenge. The plan came quickly, easy and complete.

After a dark and sleepless night the morning meeting made even less sense than usual, the analysts' tales of profits, overheads and price-earnings ratios enlivened by waking dreams of Baxter riding, galloping, whipping.

Ken was there to represent the dealers. I collared him at the end.

'You look terrible,' he said.

'Ring Brian Puffer for me, will you, Ken? Sell the ELI. Yours and mine. Forget the price: sell.'

'You sure?'

'I'll tell you why later.'

'When's the seminar?'

'Twelve.'

'And what's – ? Watch out, here's trouble. I'll ring you, then,' Ken said as Baxter descended.

'Sorry to break up the party, chaps. Shall we, er – ?'

Once the room was cleared Baxter closed the double doors and locked them.

'I must say,' he told me, 'you took last night's development very well. Congratulations. A real player, if I may say so.'

'You may indeed, Bax. Am I finally in the club?'

'I hope things can continue that way.'

'Is a real player allowed to ask for a few details? Or would that be letting the side down?'

'I think if Lucy wants to tell you anything she can tell you herself – don't you?'

'I'm sure she'll be most helpful. May I presume last night's event was not the preliminary trial?'

'You may.'

'Well, I hope you found the filly up to scratch.'

'You'd know as much about that as I would.'

'Why are you such a shit, Baxter?'

'I like the girl. I intend doing right by her.'

'Christ, Bax – not the honourable thing. Is there no end to what people will do for money?'

'I don't want to be impolite, London. I know what's happened won't exactly endear me to you. But these things happen. I like her.'

'And what does she think?'

'I should have thought that was apparent from what you unfortunately saw last night. What I'm concerned about is that there should be no hard feelings. I know Lucy shares that view. I said a minute ago I thought you were taking it like a player. I also said I thought we'd all be better off if things continued that way. I'm sure when you think about it you'll agree.'

Sitting across the table, Baxter adjusted his cuffs to the correct degree of exposure.

'I'll be leaving the firm, of course,' I told him.

'That's up to you. I don't suppose Lucy will be staying long. As far as I'm concerned I'm happy for you to go on working with us, if "working" is the right word for what you do here from nine to five. Don't act in haste, that's my feeling. Look before you leap. And where else can you go?'

'Thank you for that.'

'Just being realistic, old chap. You may not be the king of the castle here but for some reason you're tolerated. Possibly because we can't find anyone else ... Anyway, that's all in the future. What we've got to worry about for the present is the seminar this morning. You know the form. We want to see these shares higher. A good performance today won't do you any harm, whatever you decide to do. Come on, man – think positive. This could be your finest hour.'

Could be? *Could be?* Would be! My mind flipped through a full deck of past insults to go with those of the moment. Revenge; revenge.

Ten minutes later Ken rang through on the railway line to say we were out of our ELI. We'd sold them all at seventy. So I'd made fifty thousand: not as much as I'd been hoping but better than a poke in the eye and more would follow after Stage B. I got through to Harbottle at the third attempt and advised him to sell at market. He came back to me shortly after ten o'clock to say he'd sold at seventy-two.

'Seventy-*two*,' Ken reflected. 'Somebody must be buying large. There's nothing gone through us this morning. Who can it be?'

'Your guess is as good as mine.'

'Your guess is the *same* as mine.'

At half past ten he came through again; the stock was up to eighty.

'What's all this whispering?' Baxter asked, putting down his nail-buff. 'Not trying to pull something, are you?'

'Pull something? That's not the sort of thing a real player would do, is it, Bax?'

'Certainly not. Have you got your script there?'

I showed him my notes, in which Patel emerged from his East End sweatshop as a businessman of the highest integrity who nevertheless combined the vision of Abraham Lincoln with the drive of Citizen Kane.

'Seems on the right lines,' said Baxter. 'You've been working hard. Well done.'

He marched towards the Gents', *Management Monthly* under his arm, and I went straight to Doris's room.

'No Lady T today, D?'

'Not today,' said Doris. 'She must have had a hard night again.'

'I expect she did, poor dear. I wanted that tape, D.'

She brought it out of her desk. 'Is it a present? Oh – Reggie was asking after you this morning. Asked if you were all right. I told him you seemed your usual self.'

'Well said. Must rush, though, D – see you later.'

'Good luck with the talk. You won't need luck, though, will you?'

I waited until Baxter got back, then took his place in the lockup. Snapping the cassette into the mini-recorder, I plugged in the ear-piece and ran through the tape until I found one of Alfie's more statesmanlike moments. *'Ethics? Eff the ethics,'* he was saying. As the tape wound on I considered the problem of how to spend the fifty thousand I'd made on my sale of ELI. Fifty was a difficult sum. A hundred would be much less of a problem. I rustled a few sheets of Saniroll and flushed.

'Having trouble?' Baxter asked on my return.

'A touch of Lucy's Revenge.'

'All ready for the off?'

'Ready as can be,' I said.

Several more items remained to be seen to before revenge would be mine. Shortly before eleven, almost as if to make it easier for me, Baxter went in to see Reggie, leaving me free to ring Patel.

'Now's the moment,' I said.

'But I don't understand this. I thought we were waiting till after this talk you were giving.'

'Change of plan, Mr Patel. No questions.'

'But what is the price?'

'Eighty. How many have you got, exactly?'

'Two million, nine hundred and ninety-five thousand.'

'Two mill, nine ninety-five to sell at best, then?'

'Mr London, I can't deny that this change of plan worries me.'

'Mr Patel,' I said, 'so far you have followed my advice. In that time your personal wealth has increased by two million pounds or more. Now I'm telling you to sell.'

'I need to think about it. I need to think. Just give me five minutes, will you, Mr London?'

Five minutes later he was back on the line. 'I have decided to trust you,' he said. 'Sell.'

'I think that's a very shrewd decision. Of course, this could take an hour or two. I'll come back to you before lunch.'

Not for the first time, I reflected that given Patel's overall level of greed it was surprising he knew so little of how the Stock Exchange worked. ELI might be flying in a thin and frothy market, with no stock for sale and buyers forming long and disorderly queues at the jobber's pitch; but once the boys on the floor knew that three million shares had suddenly been made available, not to mention where they were coming from, the price would head for earth like a ham sandwich off the Empire State building. Additional downward impetus would be imparted by the tape. Come lunchtime, Patel would be a million pounds poorer, I would be leaving the office smiling from shoulder to shoulder and Alfie and the gang would be heading for the Costa Brava.

Next I went to Dixon's in Cheapside. The mini-cassette was good for casual listening, but a room full of people demanded something better. For sentimental reasons I chose a British make of ghetto blaster – the components were all Japanese, thank God – and paid by Permit card.

Baxter was away from his chair still. Slipping past the desk, I deposited the noisebox, discreetly wrapped in brown paper, in a cupboard in Doris's room, first clipping the cassette into place ready to play back.

'Another secret?' said Doris. 'No, of course I won't tell anybody. I don't know. This is a very funny place these days. All these secrets. People acting very strange; very strange.'

I was just asking her what she meant by that when Baxter rushed in, rubbing his hands and saying, 'Bejaysus, it's cold out there.' I winked at Doris and departed.

Two requirements had yet to be fulfilled. The first of these I managed to squeeze in at the desk before Baxter reappeared. I rang Brian Puffer at Stag & Co. and told him I wanted to sell a hundred thousand ELI.

'Too late,' he said. 'You already 'ave. Kenny Morgan rang through with the order.'

'This is another hundred.'

'I thought you'd only bought a hundred.'

'I'm going short.'

'Going short? Christ – turned a bit bearish on this one all of a sudden, haven't we? I thought today was the great leap forward.'

'It is. Short me a ton, will you, Brian?'

'Anything you say, me old darlin'. But I 'ope you're not asking me to deal on inside information.'

'Brian – the thought of it!'

'Take it as done. They feel like they're goin' up to me, though.'

'Good. Always the best time to sell, eh?'

Three minutes later I was short of a ton at eighty-five: which being interpreted is, I had sold a hundred thousand ELI shares that I didn't have, at eighty-five coppers apiece. Once London's Revenge struck the syndicate and the can of worms was opened the price would collapse and I could buy them back at the lower level and pocket the difference. Assuming the price fell by, say, forty pence a share, that would make another hundred thousand forty pences, a round forty K, to add to the fifty I had already. Things were going right again. The shining hour approached.

The final item of preparation had to take place on licensed premises. At twenty-five past eleven Kenny Morgan strode grinning through the office on his way to hand in his notice. At half past he strode out, jerking his thumb in the direction of the Three Tuns.

I met him in the bar.

'You told him, then?'

'"My brother goes, I go," I said. Wanna know what he said then?'

'Go on.'

'"Where's your loyalty?" he said. Where's your fuckin' loyalty. Can you believe it? After what they did to our Len. And then, to cap it all, he offers me another lousy five a year – to which I told him exactly, and I mean exactly, where he could stick it.'

'Good lad. Let's hope it gives him a warm glow. Your health. Here's to the future.'

'The future. When does it start?'

'Twelve.'

'High noon,' said Ken in his Gary Cooper voice. 'But – Christ, I almost forgot – what's with all this sellin' ELI? I mean, not that I'm complaining. Not with what I've made out of 'em. I'm fifty gorillas better off. But I thought today was the big jump.'

'It is – the high jump for Baxter and the boyos. That little black box you sold me – gave me, I mean – is going to come in very useful at this meeting.'

'That was a cunning little stunt.'

'I think this exhibit may also prove incriminating.' I handed Ken the dealing slip on which I'd written Patel's order to sell.

'Jesus H. That should liven things up.'

'Will you be there?'

'Wouldn't miss it for the world. But what I want to know is what's brought all this on. I thought we was going to pump 'em up at this seminar, then knock the stock out after.'

'Bearish developments. I went round Lucy's last night.'

'Oh, yeah?'

'Baxter was there.'

'Baxter? What was Baxter ... *No ... No!*'

192

'Yes.'

'Not givin' her a portion?'

'Large.'

'Well, fuck my old boots. You never can trust 'em, can you?'

'Talking of boots,' I said, 'the best of it is this . . .'

'Ready?' said Baxter.

'Aye, ready,' said I. It was now a minute to twelve.

'I'll fetch Reggie and Alfie.'

'Alfie? What's he doing here? He's not down to come.'

I brandished my copy of the guest list, which featured chums of Reggie's, analysts from a range of financial institutions, and one or two friendly Press boys.

'Reggie thought Alf might be interested in what you've got to say.'

'I think he will.'

'Good. You were out of the room again when he arrived. Not up to mischief, were you?'

'Trap three,' I said. 'Bum trouble again.'

'Only I could have sworn I saw you going into Dixon's earlier on.'

'Must have been my brother. Where were you?'

'I was there too.'

'You should have been close enough to see it wasn't me, then.'

'My mistake. Guts all right now? No rushing off in the middle, eh?'

'I know the form, Bax. Dinnae fash thasen.'

We went to collect the Senior Partner. Doris looked flushed.

'What's up, D?' I asked while Baxter was in with Reggie.

'Oh, London!'

'Has he been at you again?'

'London, just be careful, will you?'

'Careful? No fear. I'll soon be telling Reggie Goddard exactly what I think of him, D. I suggest you do the same.'

'Good,' said Reggie, emerging from his den. 'They should all be here by now.'

Alfie appeared behind him in a shimmering mohair three-piece.

'London! Pleased to see you, mate. How are we? Stopped any good punches lately? Ha ha!'

'Good morning, Sir Alfred.'

'Afternoon. 'aven't seen you down our way lately.'

'I'm afraid not.'

'Lucky you, boy, I tell you: lucky you.'

The long oval table had been removed from the conference room. In its place were thirty or forty moulded grey chairs arranged in rows of seven or eight and, at one end of the room, the end opposite the doors, a standard-size desk behind which two chairs had been placed to face the audience. Reggie took one of these and pointed me to the other. Alfie and Baxter sat on the front row of the audience.

Seven or eight places remained to be filled. In those that were occupied sat a gathering far more illustrious than would normally be expected to hear about a company of ELI's size at a broking house like Rogers & Prickett. I might have guessed Reggie and Baxter would go behind my back with the invitations. Every old school tie in the City had been pulled to get this lot together. The saturnine features of Ron Rackett glowered at me as I flicked through my notes.

'We'll just wait for the stragglers,' said Reggie. Then he treated us to a few jokes.

'You're supposed to put that hair-restorer on your head, Biffo, not on the roses,' he said to one of his chums.

'Oh *that's* the secret,' Biffo replied. 'But, I say, you must tell me where you get that other stuff.'

'What other stuff?'

'That *dye*. The wife could do with a touch of that,' Biffo cackled.

'Oh for the *wife*,' Reggie retorted. 'I was going to say: it's not dye you need for yours – it's *paint!*'

Baxter joined in the laughter.

This seemed the moment for action. First employing the repressed-smile method to suggest restrained though profound amusement, I then allowed a sudden worry to shadow my features over. 'Actually – ' I said. I nursed my belly in two hands and made my eyes bulge. My face grew grim.

'I'm sorry – I really must – the old gip again – I'll only be a second,' I stammered.

Scooting down the flank of the chairs, escaping Baxter, colliding indecorously with an incoming client, I made at once for Doris's room. I wanted to ask her what she'd been so nervous about, but she wasn't there.

My parcel was, though, all its parts in place, including the tape, and as my finest hour drew nigh I raised the box with both hands and did a little jig. Sliding the player back into its carrier-bag, I took it through to the conference-room.

'What on earth's that?' Reggie exclaimed. 'A parcel bomb?'

'Just something I might need later on.' To my surprise, that satisfied Reggie's curiosity.

The last of the guests arrived at five past twelve, followed closely by Kenny Morgan, who slipped in at the back and gave me a V for Victory sign as Reggie began his preamble.

'Well, I think we're all present and correct. So: it gives me great pleasure to welcome you to Rogers & Prickett this morning, gentlemen – er, lady and gentlemen – and particularly because it gives us the chance to introduce to a wider audience a young company, or rather an old company in young hands, which we believe is going to be one of the great Stock Market performers of the late eighties. A stock in which we believe all our serious clients should be involved. Indeed to use the modern parlance it would be no exaggeration to say that in our view this share is the hottest little thing in the Market – ha ha. I am speaking, of course, about East London Industries – ELI, as it's more commonly known, though there *are* those of us here who remember it better as Cairo Jute. My God, those were the days ... '

This went on for several minutes; the odd cough started up; eyelids began to droop; but I was wide awake, my hands leaking chilled sweat and my heart knocking like a metronome.

'So now,' said Reggie, 'I want to introduce you to our specialist on the stock, who some of you may know already – London London. London?'

As I stood up Ken made a gesture from the back row urging me to commit an unnatural act on the Senior Partner.

'Good morning, gentlemen,' I said. 'Good afternoon, rather: as you know, at Rogers & Prickett we like to be up with the times!'

'Rath*er*!' said Biffo.

'Hear hear,' said Reggie.

'They say there are three things that matter about a company: management, management and management. In the case of East London Industries the latter two considerations can be dismissed. ELI, as now constituted, is unashamedly a one man band, and that one man, Mr Swraj "Call me Tony", otherwise "Mind your Eye" Patel, is the beginning and, some would say, probably the end of the ELI story. Thus any account of ELI must begin with a eulogy. I come to praise Patel, not to bury him.'

This was not tripping quite so daintily off my tongue as it had when I'd rehearsed it last night after four bottles of Old Disarmer, but I was pleased to see I'd already caused a slightly uneasy polishing of trouser-bottoms.

'Tony Patel is a man of toughness and dedication. He operates

195

from the East End of London, and like many of the East End's most famous sons he has a reputation for being hard but fair. Ask his workers. They won't understand, unless you speak Gujurati, any more than they understand some of the more profit-inhibiting provisions of the Factories Act; but ask all the same. You'll find them a diligent and contented group of workers, and every one of them, like their patron, bottom-line oriented: orient being the operative subset, since it is from the Orient that many of them have recently arrived, in most cases without the connivance of Her Majesty's immigration control. Ask: and when they reply, their faces wreathed in woe, their language incomprehensible, what they will be saying is: These tears of gratitude are for Mr Patel – a hard man, but fair.

'Now let us turn to the company, East London Industries – a company whose profits have declined in each of the last six years but for which our hopes are nonetheless high. Ask Mr Patel: he'll tell you. The future is bright, he'll tell you; the world is his oyster, the sky his limit.

'What he won't tell you, gentlemen, but what in the interests of fair play I feel I have to reveal, is that a short while ago Tony Patel spoke to me on the telephone. Confident as he is in the future of his company, a confidence which he very much wishes me to convey to you this afternoon, he has regrettably asked me to sell his entire holding in the company's stock ... Gentlemen, do not allow this fact to cloud your judgment. As I say, Mr Patel wants me to emphasise what a golden future the rag trade has. And in any case, who cares what the chairman does, as long as the stock is going up?'

I'd calculated that the syndicate would be getting restive by now, but on the contrary, all three were keeping remarkably cool. I paused for a glass of water and removed the music-machine from its bag, landing it heavily on the table.

'Excuse this object, gentlemen,' I said, 'only I thought we might have an interlude in a minute.

'What I want to try and explain now is why the share price of this company – which some people would call the hottest little thing in the Market and others would call a load of old rubbish – why this load of old rubbish should have gone from ten pence a share a month ago to eighty-five this morning. It can't be the company's record: the only consistency about that is the steady diminution of profits. It can't be the company's assets: if you'd seen them you'd know what I mean. It can't be the company's management – now Patel's heading for the life-raft there's no-one else left to sail.

'The answer to this question, gentlemen, the question of why this load of old rubbish should have outperformed the Market by seven hundred and forty-six per cent in the last month, must clearly lie elsewhere. Is ELI a recovery stock? Well, the chairman doesn't seem to think so. Is it a growth stock? Hmm – its debts are certainly growing. Is it a concept stock? A concept stock – perhaps that's the answer. The company's projected profits are still at the conceptual stage, that's for sure.'

'Is he drunk?' someone asked.

'Sounds it,' someone replied, despite my denial.

'Who is this clown, Reggie? Get him off!'

'One minute, gentlemen,' I said. 'One minute. Lick your pencils, lads, I want you to get every word of this. I'll tell you why ELI have gone from ten pence to ninety. Or rather, I won't tell you myself, I'll let somebody else tell you in his own words. If you want to know how it was done, gentlemen; if you want to know how three skilled Market operators, not without a little help from their friends in the Press, have engineered in the past month a ramping operation to rival the South Sea Babble – er, Bubble – listen to this. No, sit down, Sir Alfred. If you want to know, gentlemen, why the shares in this tenth-rate knocker-up of street-market T-shirts has suddenly become the hottest thing since the Great Fire of London, listen to this.'

Savouring the moment, already picturing the headlines, I let my finger hover in the air like the executioner's axe before it fell, swift and deadly, on to the button marked 'play'.

The sound of familiar voices filled the air.

Ken's broad smile began to droop. Baxter's face, however, curled into a grin. A door opened and a smartly-dressed figure stepped from behind it: Patel, also grinning. A camera flashgun popped in my face. Someone started to laugh.

It wasn't Alfie's voice that filled the air. It wasn't Reggie's, or Baxter's. It was the Walker Brothers, singing 'The sun ain't gonna shine any more'.

CHAPTER NINETEEN

'Doris, how could you? How could you?' I said. 'I thought we were allies – friends.'

'We are friends,' she said, but in the voice of someone booking an airline ticket.

'I asked you to keep that tape a secret.'

'Well, you shouldn't have asked, London. What could I to say to Reggie? What was I to say when he came in demanding to know what was going on, saying he was sure you were up to something? What was I to do? I didn't know what was on your tape, did I?'

'You said you didn't want to know.'

'I didn't. I wish I hadn't found out, either.'

'But don't you care what's been going on? Don't you care that these crooks have rigged the market, bribed the newspapers, broken the law?'

'I don't know what's been happening and I don't want to know.'

'Oh Doris. Don't you know that pompous old bore doesn't give a damn about you?' Once I'd said it I wished I hadn't.

'That's a matter for him and me.'

'But in the pub the other night – '

'In the pub the other night I'd had too much to drink.'

'Closing ranks, eh?'

'I value my job,' she said. 'If I didn't have that I'd have nothing. And, more to the point I'd never see him again.'

'Dead right you wouldn't. And that would be the best thing for you.'

'Maybe it would. We're not all so strong. Oh, London, for goodness' sake, do you think I'm pleased about what's happened? Why don't you just go? Go. Go and find a place where you'll be happy. Don't hang around here like me, just because you haven't got the strength to leave. Oh, go *on*!'

As I left I found Ken outside the door.

'Thought you might be in there. Switched the tape on you, did they?'

'Doris cracked. Told 'em.'

'Bastards. I suppose they put the pressure on.'

'What now?' I wondered. 'What's the honourable thing?'

'I wouldn't go long of your future here.'

'No. And it's all over with La Trender, of course. The home front's not looking too bright, either. Modigliani won that bloody ice-cream competition. He won it! And by some extraordinary coincidence he seems to have overlooked the percentage he said was in it for me. He's selling up.'

'You can always stay with us,' Ken said. 'You'll find something to do.'

'Not in the City. Not after this.'

'You're better off without. You never liked it much, did you? Maybe you could go back North.'

'There's no hurry. I suppose it'll take me a while to get through the fifty.'

'Fifty?'

'Less tax. From my ELI.'

'There is that.' Ken looked away, to where the gilts boys were throwing paper aeroplanes at the equity desk.

'Ken – is there something I should know?'

'There is, a bit. Something Reggie said after you left the meeting. These ELI – apparently they could be worth a tenner a share.'

'*How* much?'

'Apparently they've worked out ELI have got this secret option on some land, prime acreage in the Docklands. It's worth a fortune.'

'Oh, shit! I am sorry. But in that case there's something you might as well know, Ken. I went short of these ELI.'

'Short?'

'I went short of a hundred this morning.'

'You're joking.'

'It is a bit of a joke. I'm a minus millionaire.'

'So,' said Baxter. 'The first thing, of course – '

'The first thing is, I resign.'

'Very decent of you, old chap, but that won't be necessary. You're fired. As you can imagine, I've been looking forward to saying that for some time.'

The twenty minutes between leaving Ken and being pulled up by Baxter on my way out had been among the most satisfying of my City career. Keenly observed by the other salesmen, ignoring their winks and innuendoes, smiling at the glee with which they greeted the news of my fall, I crammed the contents of my files into two metal waste-paper bins. Cheered on by Fat Percy, I tipped into

199

them all the research notes, the dealing slips, the contracts, the *Welcome to Rogers & Prickett* bumf, the pension plan, the leaflets on tax-efficiency, the payslips, the business cards, the membership cards, the Christmas cards, the newspaper cuttings, the Daily Official Lists, the holiday brochures for Bali and a dozen or so Sewell's bags from my early morning buns; all these things and more, the documentary evidence of my career as a stockbroker, a salesman, an investment adviser, a cost-efficient, market-determined channeller of the nation's savings, I trampled on, squashed up, pounded tidily into place.

Then I went to Fat Percy's end of the desk. He shied away, but all I wanted was the quarter bottle of brandy he kept in his desk, which I removed unchallenged. I poured the brandy over the papers in the two bins, lit a cigarette, took one deep drag and dropped the match into one bin and the cigarette into the other.

'Anything else?' I asked Baxter.

'I thought you might like to know what's been going on. You haven't got the tape-recorder in your pocket this time, have you?'

'Not this time. Tape-recorders don't seem to have done me much good lately.'

'No. So where do I start?'

'Perhaps by telling me whether Reggie's greed has got the better of his sanity. Saying these ELI are worth a tenner a share. Has he lost his marbles altogether?'

'Oh no, he hasn't at all. Far from it. If you cast your mind back you may remember doing some research on the company ... You may also recall that just after the War the site the old Jute Wharf had stood on, which the Germans had flattened completely, was sold to the London County Council ... Yes? ... Happily, as we thought you would, you stopped there. Didn't do your job. Didn't look at the fine print on the contract, did you?'

'I didn't know there was any.'

'Luckily we did. The dear old L.C.C. in its wisdom gave ELI, or Cairo Jute as it then was, an option to buy the land back if it wasn't built on within fifteen years – i.e., by 1962 – at cost plus ten per cent, which as even you can probably work out is a hell of a lot less than it's worth now. Prime commercial land, now. Biggest thing in Europe.'

'And how come you know this? How come nobody else knows?'

'Just one of those things. Reggie got a sudden attack of memory one day and thought there might be some sort of buy-back clause. He'd only ever heard it second hand. Things were so chaotic at the end of the War, everyone else clean forgot. As did Reggie, till a few months ago. Of course, there was that one character – he must have known. What was his name? The property man. The Jew.'

'Epstein.'

'David Epstein, that's the one. Well remembered. He must have known. But he went to the great prime letting in the sky without telling anybody.'

'And how did you confirm all this?'

'Went and had a look at the contract. This was before you were ever involved, of course. Just went to County Hall and asked to see it. If there's one thing these Reds are good at, it's filing-systems.'

'So how did Alfie get involved?'

'Capital. Reggie and I didn't have the ready cash, so Alfie provided the money and got himself cut in for a quarter.'

'A quarter? Not a third?' I thought for a second. 'Oh, shit – Patel.'

'You're quick enough now,' said Baxter. 'A pity it's too late. You could have gone long instead of short.'

'How do you know I did that?'

'Inside information – there's no substitute. But, oh yes, old Gandhi was in from the start. We went straight to him as soon as we found out what we'd got. Didn't tell him straight off, of course – we tied him up with a call option first, then let him in on the act.'

'I'm lost again. The little bugger was constantly pestering me to sell.'

'That was to convince you there was nothing in the company. We didn't want you thinking it might be worth something. You might have found out – unlikely, but possible. So part of the arrangement with Patel was for him to play stupid and throw you off the scent.'

To what I next said Baxter replied, 'Never mind what colour he is. Or his parentage, for that matter. He's a sharp lad. We knew that. That's why we didn't simply offer to buy his stake. He'd have smelt a rat. We couldn't risk that – so Patel had to be in.'

'Tell me, Bax, how much are you going to make out of this?'

'Between the four of us? Not hard to work out: five million shares at ten pounds apiece – no, let's say eight to be conservative – forty million, less tax leaves twenty-eight. Seven mill apiece.'

'Jesus.'

'It's a help.'

'One last thing, Bax – '

'I know what you're going to say. You're going to ask why we brought you in. Am I right?'

'As always, Bax. Why *did* you bring me in? Why couldn't you just get on with it and leave me with my own problems?'

'Good. I'll tell you. You see, what we could have done between the four of us is to settle for the thirty per cent, the three million shares Patel had, and leave it at that. Very nice, thank you very much. But we wanted more, and what we realised was that you could help us get them. Well, I say we – it was Reggie's idea, actually.'

'I don't follow.'

'Don't you? The idea arose after the Boxing Dinner. We were on the point of firing you, as you can imagine after your performance that night, when Reggie had a brainwave. You see, London, I think it's fair to say that you do have a certain reputation in the City. A niche, one might call it. Yes – a niche operator, that's what you are. To be precise I think it's no exaggeration to say that from a long list of candidates for the honour you are almost certainly the most clownish, irresponsible, unproductive incompetent in the whole of the City.

'This has its advantages – or it did from our point of view. It means, for instance, that when you go round the houses, as you did, as we asked you to, inviting people to a big seminar and telling them they should be buying a certain stock, what do they do? ... Well, first they laugh: not in your face, but behind your back. That's business. You're either a winner or a loser. Then when they've finished laughing they go and do exactly the opposite of what you've been suggesting. If you say buy, they sell. They sell in thousands; in hundreds of thousands. And so it happened – exactly as Reggie had predicted. No fool, Reggie Goddard. And who was there to buy them when the others sold? Who was there? We were.'

'But why this farce today? Why didn't you stop me? You've got your shares – why put me deeper in the shit?'

'Just one of those things, old chap. Work hard and play hard, that's my approach. Today was what I call playing hard. You really thought you'd get one over me, didn't you? Really thought you'd get the last laugh? Well you didn't. *C'est la vie, mon vieux.* Now look who's laughing!'

Opening his mouth, displaying to the full his thirty-two perfect pearlies, Baxter roared with laughter, and was still laughing when I pushed back my chair and left.

Ken was waiting at the Green Man.

'Cheers,' I said for the last time in this autobiography.

'*Hasta la vista,*' said Ken.

'Tierra del Fuego. I suppose after this all I have to do is go home and wait for the bailiffs.'

'Here,' said Ken, passing me a small packet from his inside pocket. 'Don't open it now.'

'You know, Ken, in seven years in the City this is the first brown envelope I've ever been offered. No thanks. I couldn't.'

'It's not from me, mate. It's from our Len. I rang him after the meeting to tell him what had happened. He nearly fainted. These ELI, you see. I know we said we wouldn't tell anybody, but I did. Just mentioned it, you know. So apparently he went and bought some. Quite a few, as a matter of fact. Never told me. Still got 'em. He's made a fuckin' fortune. Take it – he'll be insulted if you don't.'

'Very good of him. Thank him from me, will you?'

'I will. Seven years, is it? Well, they say you need a change every seven.' He finished his pint. 'Another?'

An old pal of Ken's from the floor joined us. I left the two of them to speculate on life after Big Bang and took a cab to Sydney Street.

'But why Baxter?' I asked, some way into the argument. 'All right, so you don't want me. Maybe I'm too much of a maverick, in my way. Maybe I'm too intelligent for you. Too good in bed. But why a smug, self-satisfied, vainglorious prick like Baxter? Why not a human being?'

'I'm sorry, London. Would you like a glass of wine?'

'No. Nor should you be drinking in the middle of the day.'

'Hah!'

'Do as I say, not as I do. I'll have a cigarette, though. Just tell me one thing, Lucy. How long has this been going on? . . . Ah – no reply. Longer than I thought, evidently.'

'It's none of your business.'

'Oh, isn't it? You'll be telling me to keep my chin up next.'

'You should.'

'And take it like a man.'

'You should do that, too.'

'Like Baxter.'

'Like Baxter,' she said. 'And if you really want to know I'll tell you why Baxter. It's tell you exactly. He's *solid*. He's reliable. He's dependable.'

'Like a pair of old boots.'

'Things don't go wrong when he's around.'

'He pays for them to go right.'

'What's wrong with that? And he doesn't fall off his chair.'

203

'It broke. You loved it at the time.'

'Nor does he fall off his horse.'

'No. He doctors other people's saddles instead.'

'That's a ridiculous suggestion.'

'Jesus Christ, I've had enough of this! You know what's wrong with you, Lucy?'

'Buck doesn't think there's anything wrong with me.'

'You're really bloody stupid, that's what's wrong with you. I always thought you might be. In fact I always thought you were. But for a while I thought you might have certain qualities that could make up for it – tenderness, you know, sensitivity – that sort of thing. Human warmth. The rare talent to see beyond the main chance: not a talent I possess, admittedly, but one I thought you had. I was wrong.'

'I think it's time you left.'

'Oh, do you? Well I don't. On the contrary, I think I've every right to a long and tiresome grumble ... Baxter ... Baxter – my worst enemy.'

'He's not your worst enemy, London. You are.'

'I can do without the *Cosmopolitan* psychoanalysis, thank you. God, you make me sick, the whole greedy, bloated, self-congratulatory fucking crowd of you.'

'That's a nasty thing to say.'

'Nasty? Nasty? Far from it. If you really want me to say something nasty I'll say it. In fact the nastiest thing I can think of to say is I hope it all works out. You deserve him.'

I took a last draw on the cigarette and tossed it into the fireplace.

'So long,' I said.

Lucy's eyes opened wide with alarm. I didn't budge. I could see she didn't want this to happen.

I waited for her to make the first move.

She did – very suddenly. Not towards me, however, but towards the fireplace. I'd forgotten that was where she kept her cuddly toys. A teddy bear was already on fire, his head a burning bush, and the plump cheek of a doll sagged as if diseased. In a few seconds the whole gang, Bunny and Panda and Flopsy and Topsy, were all crackling merrily.

'You fool! You fool!' Lucy screamed. 'Put it out! *Do* something!'

What would Baxter have done?

'Sorry,' I said. 'I never could pee in public.'

'Ladbroke Grove,' I told the cabbie. As we drove up Sloane Street I opened the envelope Ken had given me. I had to, to pay the fare.

The envelope contained fifty twenty-pound notes. Putting it back in my inside pocket, my fingers bumped against something stiff: my passport. (Why was it there? I don't know. These things *happen* in books.)

I flicked through the stamps: France, Poland (why?); Italy, Yugoslavia (of happy honeymoon memory), Egypt, Morocco. Towards the back, inserted between two pages, I found a photograph of Margaret and Ben taken when the boy was about a year old. He was more like me then, I thought: rounder, less pensive-looking, not so dark. Now he would get more and more like her. He'd be better off without me, I thought. Better, surely, the myth of the bad dad who did a runner than the constant strife of weekly reunions and yearly trips to the Lake District.

Ah, sod it, I thought. As we broke clear of the lights at Knightsbridge I opened the glass partition between myself and the driver.

'Change of mind,' I said. 'Heathrow.'

'Sure you know where you're goin', mate?'

'I'm sure I don't,' I said, handing him a twenty.

'Fair enough, guv.'

On the M4 I looked again at the picture of Margaret and Ben. I gave it a kiss, carefully avoiding Margaret's side, then tore it into little pieces and threw them out of the window.

At Terminal One I made my way to the British Airways desk.

'When's your next flight?' I asked.

'Where to, sir?'

'Anywhere.'

'You've no idea where you want to go, sir?'

'Abroad.'

'Well our next flight – '

'First class, I want. Where's it going?'

She flicked up the details on a screen.

'That'll do,' I said. 'One way. Smoking. Window seat. Free drinks. All the trimmings.'

She punched my details into a machine. The only anxious moment was when I gave her my credit card, provoking a call to HQ. Someone at Permit House must have thought I looked a good bet, being a stockbroker. They'd put my limit up again.

Takeoff was smooth; the day was clear and brilliant. Soon, as we headed east, they were all below me: Margaret, Lucy, Baxter; Goddard and Trender; the trading floor of the Stock Exchange, the Rainbow Co-operative, Ben. What would they think? Why should I care? The present was past. I called for more drink and thought about the future.

EPILOGOS

London London, have no fear.

Ten years from now, or less perhaps, or more, you will be sitting on the roof-terrace in the cool of the evening, as you do at this hour every day, or almost every day, reading the London Times. *Nothing, it seems, will greatly have changed. Governments – monarchs, perhaps – will have come and gone; storms arisen and abated. England will be failing gallantly in the Test Match. The Market will be up, or down; sterling will be down, or up; the old will be dying, the young getting married, the unions going on strike – or not. Doctors, you will read, are greatly alarmed: but it was ever thus. This time it's obesity: cigarette-flavoured ice-cream, it seems, is going to Europe's waistline. Even this is not new. Sipping a can of chilled yellow beer, that thin and gassy parody of the real thing, you will stretch your arms, scratch your beard and yawn.*

A child young enough to be your grandchild will appear from the stairwell and run to you.

'Daddy, Daddy, I don't want to go to bed yet,' she will say in a language you do not now understand, but will then.

'Now now, Thumper,' you will say, also in that language, or possibly in your own, 'think of what we can do in the morning if you go to bed early. The nights are boring, Thumper. They're all talk.' The child's real name is Mina, but when she is cross she stamps her foot.

Now you will put down the newspaper, pick the child up, dandle her, tickle her perhaps, and when she struggles kiss her forehead and sit her on your lap. You will tell her a story, and when the story is finished, which may be true or untrue, you will send her to bed; and as she toddles off you will think of another three-year-old. He, however, is no longer three, but thirteen, or a little more, or less, and an orphan. His father went away long ago. His mother was killed in a fire. The fire was in all the English papers but none of them mentioned that Ben himself started it – not only that, but poured a can of kerosene up and down the stairs to make sure it didn't stop.

Soon, when the child is asleep, her mother will come to the roof. She is young enough to be your daughter also, and when you first arrived in this island – as white and lovely as the White Peak itself;

206

hot for most of the day but now, in the evening, cool and holy – when you came here and took the room above the bar, and ended by helping the old man who owned it, who died, leaving the girl alone; then, at first, you treated her as your daughter, and it was strange for both of you when she ceased to be your daughter.

If things are as they usually are, she will sit next to you on the roof and watch the lights grow bright on the boats in the bay; and you will watch her. After that you will go down to eat, perhaps with a few of the regulars, perhaps with a German or an American; but never with the English.

Just for the moment, things are as they usually are. Saying nothing, as she often says nothing, she will sit next to you, putting perhaps a hand on your knee, and you will smoke a cigarette or two as the light fades, and finish the beer.

The bar will be quiet, as it often is until later on, but Manos or Panos or one of the other boys will be there behind the counter and you will tell him what you want to eat and sit in the corner, the two of you, on your own, and wait. While you are eating, friends will come in and you will ask them to join you, and they will, for they knew if they came you would ask. You won't charge them for the food – you never do – but what they spend on drink will make up for that.

And then, perhaps, to make this evening different from others, the door will open and you will hear the sound you like to hear less, though sometimes more, than any other sound in the world: the sound of English voices; of London.

You will reach at once for the pair of dark glasses you keep in your top pocket.

'I don't like the look of this at all,' the woman will say.

'We'll just have a quick one, then we can go down and find some-where decent to eat,' the man will reply.

'Daddy, I'm hungry,*' a child will complain. By then all four of them will have come in. They will sit at the table furthest from your customers, and the man – tall, fair, sun-tanned – will wave his hand at Manos, or Panos, and call for attention.*

'God, I'm tired,' the woman will say. The woman is still beautiful, but already the lines run down from the corners of her mouth and her eyes, and her hand shakes as she lights a cigarette. 'Sit down, will you, darling?' she will say, and the boy will repeat, 'I'm hungry.'

'Ssh,' she will say. 'We can't eat here. Lemonade?'

'Oh, all right,' the boy will say, blond and pretty, six or seven.

'Lemonade for Nicholas,' the man will say. 'What about Pansy?'

The fourth member of the group is a girl two or three years younger than her brother; also fair, perhaps having long, wavy hair.

'Pansy?'

'Nothing.'

'Have something, darling. Lemonade?'

'She'll have lemonade,' the man will say. 'Beer for you?'

'I suppose so,' the woman will say with a sigh.

'Christ.'

'Well, I suppose I will. I don't see why we couldn't just go straight down to the harbour.'

'Because you said you wanted to see some local colour, that's why.'

'I wouldn't call this colourful.'

'Oh do shut up. They all speak English.'

'Nicolas, will you keep still?'

'Two li-mo-na-da,' the man will say slowly to Manos or Panos, raising two fingers, 'and two bee-ra.'

The waiter will bring the drinks and they will drink them in silence which is finally fractured when Nicholas pinches Pansy, Pansy cries, the woman slaps Nicholas, Nicholas cries, the man shouts at the woman, the woman cries, and the man says, 'Oh Jesus wept! Let's go and get some food, shall we?'

'I can't stand another week of this,' the woman will say as they leave. 'At this rate I wish we'd stayed in London.'

But you, London London, will be happy that they came.